READINGS FROM THE PERSPECTIVE OF EARTH

The Earth Bible, 1

READINGS FROM THE PERSPECTIVE OF EARTH

edited by
Norman C. Habel

Academic Press

THE PILGRIM PRESS

Copyright © 2000 Sheffield Academic Press

Published by
Sheffield Academic Press Ltd
Mansion House
19 Kingfield Road
Sheffield S11 9AS
England

ISBN 1-84127-084-9

Published in the USA and Canada (only) by
The Pilgrim Press
700 Prospect Avenue East
Cleveland, Ohio 44115-1100
USA

USA and Canada only
ISBN 0-8298-1406-X

Typeset by Sheffield Academic Press
and
Printed on acid-free paper in Great Britain
by Bell & Bain Ltd, Glasgow

British Library Cataloguing-in-Publication Data

A catalogue record for this book is available
from the British Library

Library of Congress Cataloging-in-Publication Data

A catalog record for this book is available
from the Library of Congress

Contents

Foreword

Archbishop Desmond Tutu

Planet Earth is in crisis. More and more life systems are being threatened. Scientists estimate that at least half, and perhaps as many as 80 per cent of the world's animal and plant species, are found in the rainforests. The rainforests are the lungs of the planet producing much of the oxygen that humans and other oxygen-dependent creatures need to survive. The rainforests, alas, are still being destroyed at an alarming rate.

Resolving the ecological crisis of our planet, however, is no longer a problem we can leave to the scientists. Just as we are all part of the problem, we are also part of the solution. We all need to come to terms with the forces that have created this crisis and the resources within our traditions that can motivate us to resolve the crisis. One of those traditions is our biblical heritage.

It is significant, therefore, that the Earth Bible project has chosen to take the Earth crisis seriously and to re-read our biblical heritage in the light of this crisis. The Earth Bible team has listened closely to ecologists and developed a set of principles to re-read the biblical text from an ecojustice perspective. The concern of Earth Bible writers is not to defend the biblical text blindly, but to identify those passages which may have contributed to the crisis and to uncover those traditions which have valued Earth but been suppressed.

I commend the Earth Bible team for including representative writers from around the globe, including the Southern hemisphere. I commend the team for confronting the biblical tradition honestly and openly in dialogue with ecologists. And, in particular, I commend the writers for daring to read the biblical text afresh from the perspective of Earth. Feminists have forced us to confront the patriarchal orientation of much of the biblical text. Earth Bible writers are now confronting us with the anthropocentric nature of much of the biblical text. We now ask: does the text de-value Earth by making the self-interest of humans its dominant concern?

I recommend you read the Earth Bible series with a critical but empathetic eye. As a critical reader you will want to assess whether writers make their case for or against their interpretation of the text in terms of the principles employed. As an empathetic reader, however, you will need to identify with Earth and the suffering Earth community as you read the text.

I hope that the promise of 'peace on Earth' will be advanced by this laudable project as scholars probe our heritage to understand and assist in resolving the crisis of our planet.

Editorial Preface

Norman Habel

I am proud to be associated with the Earth Bible series. This project, I hope, will make an important contribution to the public debate about how humans should relate to Earth and the Earth community in future years. The ecojustice approach and principles enunciated in the first volume signal a fresh discussion about how the Bible has played, and may continue to play, a role in the current ecological crisis faced by our planet.

I am also proud of those who have chosen to write articles in this series, and through their writing and conversations with the Earth Bible Team have come to appreciate the intent of the project. It needs to be stated at the outset that the writers in the first two volumes of this series represent a wide range of social contexts, religious backgrounds and hermeneutical perspectives. They have one concern in common: justice for Earth. That concern is translated into a serious search to locate Earth in the biblical text and understand whether its presence is suppressed or acclaimed.

These writers derive from countries and communities across the globe: Canada, USA, England, the Netherlands, South Africa, Samoa, Australia and New Zealand. What makes the first volumes of this series different from most other series in this field is the proportion of scholars from the Southern hemisphere, in particular, Australia, New Zealand and South Africa. I regret that we could not locate writers from South America for these first volumes. The Earth Bible Team hopes that as this project becomes widely known, more writers from other countries and contexts will contribute to the Earth Bible series.

I appreciate the way in which the Earth Bible Team has collaborated in developing the hermeneutical principles employed in this project, and in recommending constructive improvements to the articles submitted, including my own. The core members of the team for the first two volumes are Vicky Balabanski, Charles Biggs, Norman Habel, Duncan Reid, Michael Trainor, Marie Turner and Shirley Wurst, with contributions from several others. This group also represents a plurality of perspectives, religious affiliations and exegetical view-points, but is united in a common goal of learning how to read the text from the perspective of Earth.

This project is indeed a 'learning exercise' as we gradually work towards a greater understanding of Earth, learn to listen to Earth, and finds ways to read the text with this growing awareness. We do not presume, therefore, to have discovered the one and only way to interpret the text from Earth's perspective. We are explorers together on a journey that is vital for the future welfare of our home, Earth. For this reason future volumes in the series will include conversations with key voices in the field.

Perhaps my deepest debt of gratitude in this project is due to Shirley Wurst who has edited the manuscripts for the series to date. Her painstaking and rigorous work reflects her commitment to the project and the ecojustice principles we espouse as a team. She is an editor's editor and a biblical scholar in her own right.

I am very grateful to those who have supported the project in various ways, whether with funds, in kind or in person. The project is now located in the Centre for Theology, Science and Culture, associated with the Adelaide College of Divinity and Flinders University of South Australia. The body whose financial support has under-written the project to date is the Charles Strong Memorial Trust. This trust is named after Charles Strong, the founder of a denominational body known as the Australian Church (1885–1955). The Trust promotes the sympathetic study of all religions and fosters dialogue between religion and other disciplines. This project is the result of a dialogue between religion, especially Christianity, and ecology. Other supporters of this project include Flinders University, Adelaide College of Divinity and the Columban Mission.

I also wish to thank those scholars who have promoted this project as international consultants in various countries. These include Heather Eaton (Canada), Gerald West (South Africa), Ellen van Wolde (Netherlands), Keith Carley (New Zealand), Diane Jacobson (USA) and Gene Tucker (USA). We would welcome the support of representatives from other countries and communities who are willing to act as sponsors as the project expands.

I enjoyed working with the staff of Sheffield Academic Press in the publication of the Earth Bible, especially David Clines and Philip Davies the publishers, Jean Allen, Judith Willson and Lorraine Bottomley among others. Their professionalism and commitment to this new venture has been very welcome.

A special word is in order about the logo for this series. The artist who worked with me in developing this logo and drafting its final form is Jasmine Corowa. Jasmine is a young Indigenous Australian whose art reflects traditional Aboriginal techniques of communication. Her father, Dennis Corowa, is one of the Rainbow Spirit Elders whom I supported in their publication *Rainbow Spirit Theology*. A set of Jasmine's paintings appears in *The Rainbow Spirit in Creation: A Reading of Genesis I* published by The Liturgical Press in 2000.

The logo is a symbol of Earth. The land dots are in Earth colours forming that maze of shimmering life we call the Earth community. The white dots of the sky rise from Earth. The surface of the land/earth is an open book. This is a double symbol: not only is the land/earth read like a book (as Australian Aboriginal peoples do), but when we read 'The Book' in this project we do so from beneath, from the perspectives of Earth.

Finally, I want to thank Veronica Brady, an eminent Australian scholar, for her creative and inspiring preface to the first volume of the Earth Bible series.

Preface

Veronica Brady

The biblical word, we believe, is not a mere sound or breath and not just an arbitrary designation, but an aspect of the continuous and continuing power of the divine reality which goes on revealing itself to us.

It is thus a word of power, reality in its most concentrated, compacted, essential form. In this sense the world and its future as well as our individual lives can be said to depend on it. Today, however, this belief is becoming increasingly difficult to sustain, for a whole range of reasons. The Earth Bible Series confronts one of these reasons: the challenge offered by the ecological crisis and by the accusation that the lack of care for the earth and its creatures—the arrogant assumption that they exist merely for us to use and exploit—can be traced back to the Bible and, in particular, to God's command to increase and multiply, 'fill the earth and subdue it; and have dominion over… every living thing' (Gen. 1.28). In this view, far from being the word of life, the Bible brings a word of death and has little or nothing positive to contribute to the struggle for Earth and for the future of humanity.

This is a profoundly important challenge—as important perhaps as the one that challenged the first Christians when they were called to move beyond the frontiers of the Judaism in which they had been nurtured, and move towards a more universal vision of the creative work of God's spirit and power at work in the world. What is at issue is not only the nature of the God revealed in the Bible but also where that God is to be found. For centuries Christianity has been associated with Western culture—sometimes almost exclusively—so that being converted to Christianity often meant renouncing one's own culture and embracing Western ways. As a child, for example, I remember being told that 'the faith is Europe and Europe is the faith'. But nowadays it is becoming increasingly clear that European culture is not synonymous with Christianity: imperial expansion and the invasion of other countries, the deaths, dispossession and domination of their peoples, the destruction of their cultures and the exploitation of

the natural world in the name of profit, to say nothing of the material-
ism, brutal competitiveness and worship of mindless pleasure which
are the marks of Western culture today hardly square with the gospel.

The Earth Bible Project takes up this challenge in two ways. The
first is to note that we may suspect some texts of being anthropocentric, focusing exclusively on human interests rather than incor-
porating the concerns of the Earth. The Bible, after all, was written by
human beings, even if they viewed themselves as agents of God. The
second way is to argue that the problem lies not with the Bible but
with the ways in which it has been read or, to put it more properly,
misread. These tactics will not please everyone. Some Christians will
disapprove of the turn away from concern with personal redemption
and the new attention given to Creation, while on the other side critics
of Christianity will not accept the implicit premise that the Bible still
represents a word of life and hope for this world and for our human
future.

Being a Christian, however, does not mean turning away from the
world and the moment of history in which we live and it does not
excuse us from the work of love. It is all too easy to make a God to
suit our own needs, forgetting that, as one theologian, J.B. Metz, has
put it, the best short definition of God may be 'interruption', that God
is always Other, the one who calls us to a largeness of life beyond our
selfish dreams (1980: 171). This God speaks in the Bible, but what God
says can never be reduced to a pious formula, and has to be responded
to in terms of the word of power that it speaks. This word is ancient
but ever new since it is part of the ongoing love of God for this world.
That is why these essays respond to the books of Scripture in the context of the crisis facing us, attempting to match their words to the
needs of the human community and the creation God loves and wills
to transform.

The Earth Bible Series is scholarly work, but it speaks to us here and
now with some urgency—which is all to the good. A disinterested
approach is of little use in a crisis. What is needed is passion—though
this is a passion controlled by reason and respect for what is the case.
In effect, the writers here belong to the long tradition of Christian
thinkers who have through the ages attempted to give a rational
account of the faith which is in them, to take their place in what Elaine
Wainwright, in the title of her essay in this volume, calls the 'transformative struggle towards the divine dream'.

The assumption persists that the Bible remains a word of power,
that its still has things to say to us in the crisis which confronts us,
that the gospel is still 'good news'—and that it is so because it

challenges commonsense in the name of the God who continually calls us to live more richly, fully and lovingly, and to work with God to bring about the new heaven and earth which is our destiny. The writers take Earth seriously; they do not focus their attention on 'heavenly places'. Here they find themselves on common ground with the ecologists who also care for Earth because it is sacred and speaks to us of our place in a larger scheme of things, in what Judith Wright calls 'the whole flow' of existence.

For the last four or five centuries, Christianity has focused on the individual human being; the ecological movement recalls us to this flow, reminding us of the sense of the glory of God in creation which runs through many of the books of the Bible, especially the Psalms and the book of Job. A poem like Judith Wright's 'Rainforest', for example, expresses this sense of worship and the need for human beings to take our place as part of creation with a responsibility to, as well as for, it:

> The forest drips and glows with green.
> The tree-frog croaks his far-off song.
> His voice is stillness, moss and rain
> drunk from the forest ages long.

But it also reminds us of the limits of our knowledge, echoing Pascal's humble yourself, proud reason, his call to worship beyond ourselves:

> We with our quick dividing eyes
> measure, distinguish and are gone.
> The forest burns, the tree-frog dies,
> yet one is all and all are one.[1]

This sense of a power at work in this world, far from diminishing it, expands our sense of the mystery of God. In the past some Christians turned away from this world and from history into a merely individualistic and sometimes solipsistic world of their own. The essays in this series read the Bible to find what it has to say about the mystery of Creation and of God's ongoing power at work in the world we inhabit, and not just in the past but moving us into the future. This is a God whose being, in Eberhard Jungel's fine phrase, 'is in coming' and who 'goes on ways to himself through this world even when [these ways] lead to other places, even to that which is not God' (1983: 158).

---

1.   Judith Wright, 'Rainforest', from *A Human Pattern: Selected Poems* (Sydney: ETT Imprint, 1996), p. 230. Reprinted by permission of ETT Imprint.

This dynamic sense of God also puts biblical faith more in tune with the insights of contemporary science and mathematics in which space is seen both as an energy and as a medium and visible tangible reality is not complete in itself but resembles a holographic image under which lies another order of existence, a vast and primary level of energy which gives birth to objects and appearances. One scientist has characterized this as the 'scientist's nightmare': having scaled mountains of ignorance and pulled him or herself over the final rock, finding a band of theologians who have been sitting there for centuries. But for those who believe that Christian faith may have a creative response to offer to our situation it is perhaps a dream come true.

There is another challenge which the Earth Bible Project may help us to meet, a challenge which is particularly troubling for us as Australians: the question of our relation with the indigenous peoples of this land and with the land itself. We have tended to dismiss their culture as 'pagan', and asked them to give up their culture and spirituality and embrace ours. As an Aboriginal Christian puts it:

> Jesus was thrust down my throat. I was not encouraged to think for my-self or allow a theology to grow from within me as an Aboriginal... I was told what to do, what to think, where to live. I was not free. I now need to think things through, to feel my own needs, work through my own faith, and develop my own theology (Rainbow Spirit Elders 1997: 4).

If God is to be found at work everywhere in the living world around us and not just in places officially labelled 'Christian', then we may have a great deal to learn from the culture of the first peoples of this land who had a deep sense of this God and whose lives were organized around worshipping God. Through them we may find the 'latent meaning' Joseph Furphy discerned in the land and which he believed it was our task as newcomers to discover (Barnes 1981: 65) fulfilling the promise of the early name for this land: 'the Land of the Holy Spirit'.

Just as significantly, the Aboriginal peoples' sense of the holiness of the land and of the community of life we share with it and with all living things will bring us to a deeper appreciation of our need to change our ways. A theology of Creation is thus deeply bound up with a theology of redemption.

The people we rejected as less than human and the land we have ravaged reflect to us the mystery of the suffering servant, 'wounded for our iniquities and bruised for our sins' (Isa. 53.5), and their story calls us to the change of heart, the death and resurrection which is the preliminary to genuine faith, the move into the centre which has always fascinated yet also frightened us as a people.

These are perhaps large claims to make for a collection of scholarly essays on the Bible. However, if we are to be true to the belief that Scripture speaks a word of power, a word which not only recalls the great acts of God but also makes all things new, we must begin to explore the challenges the writers in the Earth Bible Project take up. What is at stake here is more than the outcome of a purely academic debate. It has to do with the future of Creation and the possibilities of Christian belief in the new millennium, and our ability to join in the great chorus of life as a whole and play our part in the wider Earth community.

Abbreviations

ABD	David Noel Freedman (ed.), *The Anchor Bible Dictionary* (New York: Doubleday, 1992)
AnBib	Analecta biblica
BA	*Biblical Archaeologist*
BAGD	Walter Bauer, William F. Arndt, F. William Gingrich and Frederick W. Danker, *A Greek–English Lexicon of the New Testament and Other Early Christian Literature* (Chicago: University of Chicago Press, 2nd edn, 1958)
BARev	*Biblical Archaeology Review*
BDB	Francis Brown, S.R. Driver and Charles A. Briggs, *A Hebrew and English Lexicon of the Old Testament* (Oxford: Clarendon Press, 1907)
Bib	*Biblica*
BIS	Biblical Interpretation Series
BJRL	*Bulletin of the John Rylands University Library of Manchester*
BSac	*Bibliotheca Sacra*
BTB	*Biblical Theology Bulletin*
CBQ	*Catholic Biblical Quarterly*
CBQMS	*Catholic Biblical Quarterly*, Monograph Series
CTJ	*Calvin Theological Journal*
EBib	Etudes bibliques
EKKNT	Evangelisch-Katholischer Kommentar zum Neuen Testament
FOTL	The Forms of the Old Testament Literature
HR	*History of Religions*
HTR	*Harvard Theological Review*
HUT	Hermeneutische Untersuchungen zur Theologie
JBL	*Journal of Biblical Literature*
JJS	*Journal of Jewish Studies*
JRelS	*Journal of Religious Studies*
JSNT	*Journal for the Study of the New Testament*
JSNTSup	*Journal for the Study of the New Testament*, Supplement Series
JSOT	*Journal for the Study of the Old Testament*
JSOTSup	*Journal for the Study of the Old Testament*, Supplement Series
JSPSup	*Journal for the Study of the Pseudepigrapha*, Supplement Series
NCB	New Century Bible
NIBC	New International Biblical Commentary
NICNT	New International Commentary on the New Testament
NIDNTT	Colin Brown (ed.), *The New International Dictionary of New Testament Theology* (3 vols.; Exeter: Paternoster Press, 1975)

NIGTC	The New International Greek Testament Commentary
NovT	*Novum Testamentum*
NovTSup	*Novum Testamentum*, Supplements
NTG	New Testament Guides
NTR	*New Theology Review*
PG	J.-P. Migne (ed.), *Patrologia cursus completa…* *Series graeca* (166 vols.; Paris: Petit-Montrouge, 1857–83)
SBLDS	SBL Dissertation Series
SJT	*Scottish Journal of Theology*
SNTU	Studien zum Neuen Testament und seiner Umwelt
TDNT	Gerhard Kittel and Gerhard Friedrich (eds.), *Theological Dictionary of the New Testament* (trans. Geoffrey W. Bromiley; 10 vols.; Grand Rapids: Eerdmans, 1964–)
TTod	*Theology Today*
WBC	Word Biblical Commentary
WUNT	Wissenschaftliche Untersuchungen zum Neuen Testament
WW	*Word and World*

List of Contributors

Vicky Balabanski, member of the Earth Bible Team, is a Lecturer in New Testament at Parkin Wesley College, Adelaide College of Divinity at Flinders University of South Australia. She has recently published *Eschatology in the Making: Mark, Matthew and the Didache* and *That We May Not Lose the Way.* Her current research is on the Jewish queen Alexandra Salome.

Dianne Bergant, CSA is Professor of Biblical Studies and Director of Doctor of Ministry Studies at Catholic Theological Union, Chicago. Her publications include *Israel's Wisdom Literature: A Liberation-Critical Reading* and *Song of Songs: The Love Poetry of Scripture.* Her current research is in preaching from the new lectionary, an Old Testament introduction and studies in several biblical books.

Brendan Byrne is Professor of New Testament at Jesuit Theological College, Melbourne and President of Melbourne College of Divinity. His major publications include *Romans* (Sacra Pagina 6) and 'Sons of God—Seed of Abraham' in *Analecta Biblica* 83. His current research is on Paul in relation to Judaism and Gospel narrative and history.

Keith Carley is a Lecturer in First Testament Studies at the Joint Theological Colleges of St John's and Trinity, Auckland and Honorary Lecturer in Theology at University of Auckland. His major writings include *Ezekiel Among the Prophets* and 'Psalms for Worship—An Assessment' in *Journeyings* 3 (1989).

Edgar Conrad is a Reader in Studies in Religion at the University of Queensland. He has written *Reading Isaiah* in the *Overtures to Biblical Theology* series and *Zechariah. Readings: A New Biblical Commentary.* His current areas of research involve forms of prophetic speech in relation to new canonical criticism.

Heather Eaton is Assistant Professor at St Paul University, Ottawa. Her major publications include 'Ecofeminism and Theology: Challenges, Confrontations and Reconstructions', in *Christianity and Ecology: Wholeness, Respect, Justice, Sustainability*, edited by Dieter Hessel and Rosemary Radford Ruether, and 'The Edges of the Sea: The Colonisation of Ecofeminist Religious Perspectives', in *Review of Books in Religion* 11. Her current research lies in the fields of ecofeminism and globalization, biotechnology and theological ethics.

Terry E. Fretheim is the Elva B. Lovell Professor of Old Testament at Luther Seminary, St Paul. His major publications include *The Suffering God: An Old Testament Perspective* and *Exodus* in the Interpretation series. His research currently focuses on Jeremiah and the God of the Old Testament.

Norman Habel, the Chief Editor of the Earth Bible Project, is Professorial Fellow at Flinders University of South Australia and Adelaide College of Divinity. His major works include a commentary on Job in the Old Testament Library, *The Land is Mine: Six Biblical Land Ideologies* and *Reconciliation: Searching for Australia's Soul*. His current research extends to ecoliturgy and ecojustice writings for the wider community.

David Jobling is Professor of Hebrew Bible, St Andrew's College, Saskatoon. His major publications include *Samuel* in the *Berit Olam* series; he is also a co-author of *The Post-Modern Bible*. He is currently researching postmodern and political reading of the Hebrew Bible.

Nathan Loewen is a Master's student at St Andrew's College, Saskatoon and Director of the Shekinah Retreat Centre, Wadheim, Saskatchewan.

Duncan Reid, a member of the Earth Bible Team, is a Lecturer at St Barnabas Theological College, Adelaide and Head of the School of Theology, Flinders University of South Australia. *Energies of the Spirit: Trinitarian Models in Eastern Orthodox and Western Theology* is one of his major works.

Iutisone Salevao, who originates from Samoa, is Honorary Tutor in Theology at University of Auckland and a barrister and solicitor of the High Court of New Zealand. He has a work currently in press entitled *Legitimation and the Letter to the Hebrews: An Examination of the Correlation between Theology, Social Situation and Strategy*. His current research is in the Corinthian correspondence and constitutional law and jurisprudence in relation to land law in Samoa.

Michael Trainor, a member of the Earth Bible Team, is Senior Lecturer in the School of Theology at Flinders University of South Australia. His major publications include *Jesus in Luke's Gospel* and *According to Luke: Insights for Contemporary Pastoral Practice.* His research currently is in early Christianity, hermeneutics and biblical education.

Paul Trebilco is Associate Professor and Head of Theology and Religious Studies at University of Otago in Dunedin. His major publications include *Jewish Communities in Asia Minor*, Society for New Testament Studies Monograph Series, 69 and *Considering Orthodoxy: Foundations for Faith Today.* His research at present is concentrated on the early Christians at Ephesus, the Pastoral Epistles and the Diaspora of Judaism.

Desmond Tutu is former Archbishop of Capetown, South Africa, and currently Archbishop Emeritus of the same city. Two of his major publications include *The Rainbow People of God* and *No Future Without Forgiveness.*

William J. Urbrock is Professor of Religious Studies at University of Wisconsin, Oshkosh, Wisconsin. His publications include 'Blessings and Curses' in the *Anchor Bible Dictionary*, Volume I. Since 1992 he has been editor of *Transactions*, the annual scholarly journal of the Wisconsin Academy of Sciences, Arts and Letters. His current areas of research are Psalms and Job in the Hebrew Bible.

Elaine M. Wainwright is a Lecturer in Biblical Studies and Feminist Theology in the Brisbane College of Theology and Adjunct Fellow in the School of Theology at Griffith University, Queensland. Her publications include *Towards a Feminist Critical Reading of the Gospel according to Matthew* (BZNW, 60) and *Shall We Look for Another? A Feminist Re-reading of the Matthean Jesus.* Her current research is on the genderization of healing in the Graeco-Roman world.

Six Ecojustice Principles

1. *The Principle of Intrinsic Worth*
The universe, Earth and all its components have intrinsic worth/value.

2. *The Principle of Interconnectedness*
Earth is a community of interconnected living things that are mutually dependent on each other for life and survival.

3. *The Principle of Voice*
Earth is a subject capable of raising its voice in celebration and against injustice.

4. *The Principle of Purpose*
The universe, Earth and all its components, are part of a dynamic cosmic design within which each piece has a place in the overall goal of that design.

5. *The Principle of Mutual Custodianship*
Earth is a balanced and diverse domain where responsible custodians can function as partners, rather than rulers, to sustain a balanced and diverse Earth community.

6. *The Principle of Resistance*
Earth and its components not only differ from injustices at the hands of humans, but actively resist them in the struggle for justice.

The principles listed here are basic to the approach of writers in the Earth Bible Project seeking to read the biblical text from the perspective of Earth. For an elaboration of these principles see Chapter 2, 'Guiding Ecojustice Principles'.

Introducing the Earth Bible

Norman Habel

Why the Earth Bible?

Earth is facing an environmental crisis. This *Earth crisis* threatens the very life of the planet. The atmosphere we breathe is being polluted. The forests that generate the oxygen we need to survive are being depleted at a rapid rate. Fertile soils needed to provide food are being poisoned by salinity and pesticides. Waters that house organisms essential to the cycle of life are being polluted by chemicals and waste. Global warming has become a frightening threat. The list goes on.

The depth and danger of this ecological crisis are well documented in reputable scientific sources. This crisis is so pervasive, destructive and insidious that academics, biblical scholars, theologians and religious practitioners can no longer ignore it. This crisis challenges the very way we do theology in the twenty-first century (Hessel 1996: 1-20), and, as the writers in this series will argue, the way we read the Bible. Jürgen Moltmann, who can hardly be called an alarmist, speaks of this crisis as 'the beginning of a life and death struggle for life on this earth' (1904. xi).

> The **Earth crisis** challenges us to read the Bible afresh and ask whether the biblical text itself, its interpreters—or both—have contributed to this crisis.

A close analysis of the way in which many Christian traditions, especially in the West, have read the biblical text reveals a strong tendency to devalue Earth. These readings, based on the assumption that human beings have divinely sanctioned 'dominion' over Earth and a mandate to 'harness nature', support attitudes and perspectives that contribute to a devaluation of Earth.

Earth devaluation, in turn, provides an intellectual justification for exploitation of the environment. This history of interpreting the text in the selfish interests of humanity—often only from the perspective of a chosen group within humanity—challenges us to return to the text to discover whether the relevant texts of the Bible are environmentally friendly or not.

> Our history of **Earth devaluation** confronts us with the question of whether the Bible, in key places, does indeed devalue the Earth and render it little more than disposable matter.

One of the significant developments of the current environmental crisis is *a new Earth consciousness* in a growing segment of humanity. We are now aware, as never before, that to survive as human beings on this planet we require more than human ingenuity. We are dependent on a continuous and complex interaction between a vast labyrinth of subtle forces, many of which remain a perplexing biological and physiological mystery. As humans, we are but one group in the diverse 'household of planet Earth', a community of ecosystems that dazzle our comprehension in their delicacy, complexity and resilience. Whether our new Earth consciousness is intellectual, emotive or spiritual, it affects the way we see the world of the text.

In the human community, there are numerous modes of Earth consciousness represented by everyone from green activists to political opportunists, from organic farmers to landscape artists. Many indigenous peoples, like the Aboriginal Australians, have a profound Earth consciousness, a sense of kinship with the land as a spiritual source of their being. This emerging—or perhaps partially regained—Earth consciousness in the global community provides both an impetus and an invitation to read our religious traditions from a fresh perspective: the perspective of the Earth community.

> This **new Earth consciousness** invites us, a members of the Earth community, to return to the Bible, and in dialogue with the text, ascertain whether a similar kinship with Earth is reflected there.

The concern of humanity for the planet's ecosystem can be viewed as but another form of enlightened self-interest: we want a sustainable environment in order to survive. We need, however, to go beyond enlightenment to empathy, beyond consciousness to resistance. Our planet is an Earth community and much of that community has been violently oppressed by one species—humans. The rights of our planet have been violated and the time has come for humans, in their role as advocates for Earth, to join in resisting this violation of our planet. The time has come for *Earth justice*.

One group which illustrates this mood is the Earth Charter Movement. The inaugural Australian Earth Charter Forum was held in Canberra in February 1999. Similar assemblies will be held in many countries as the central committee of the movement seeks to formulate a document to be submitted to the United Nations in 2002. That document, it is hoped, will serve as a moral charter for Earth, similar to the Declaration of Human Rights.

The Earth Bible series reflects a similar moral concern as writers seek to reread our biblical heritage so as to discern whether the relevant texts support ecojustice or view Earth as property to be exploited, with God's blessing, in the interests of human beings.

> **Earth justice** obligates us, as members of the Earth community, to be advocates for Earth and to interrogate our biblical heritage to ascertain whether Earth is silenced, oppressed or liberated in the Bible.

The Earth crisis, Earth devaluation, Earth justice and a new Earth consciousness are some of the compelling reasons why we have initiated the Earth Bible Series. These reasons demonstrate that we are undertaking this project not as merely another fad in biblical interpretation, but as a contribution to resolving a crisis that affects all members of the Earth community.

At this juncture it is appropriate to say a word about our usage of the term 'Earth' in this series. The primary meaning of this term in the Earth Bible Project is planet Earth, that living system *within* which we humans live in a relationship of interdependence with other members of the Earth community. In some cases, 'earth' may refer to the ground or land-mass we inhabit, a part of the Earth that represents the whole. In this context, 'earth' does not represent the polar opposite of heaven in a religious sense.

Biblical usage differs somewhat from contemporary usage. The Hebrew אֶרֶץ and the Greek γῆ can both have a variety of meanings: the earth as distinct from the sky or in some cases heaven; the inhabited land-mass; ground or dirt; a particular land, that is, a region of Earth where a particular group of people live. Each writer in the Earth Bible Series will indicate where a distinctive meaning is being used. Unless otherwise specified, Earth refers to planet Earth and to its closest biblical equivalent, the inhabited world.

Earlier Approaches

Before I outline the orientation and aims of the Earth Bible Project in detail, it is helpful to recognize approaches and developments that have contributed to our particular approach.

The first of these is a renewed interest in creation as a central theme and theology in the Bible. This interest arose partly in reaction to a dominant approach known as 'Salvation History', as espoused by renowned scholars such as Gerhard von Rad and Oscar Cullmann. These scholars viewed the history of salvation as a governing theme that was used to organize both the Hebrew and Christian Scriptures. Genesis 1–11 was read as but a prologue to the central story: the salvation history of God's people.

According to von Rad, creation was secondary to redemption. He claimed that the doctrine of creation never attained the stature of a relevant independent doctrine (1966: 131-48). Creation, he argued in this very influential article first published in German in 1936, was incorporated into the Israelite concept of redemption. The effect of this thinking was to support, perhaps inadvertently, the devaluation of nature as God's domain in favour of history as the arena of God's mighty acts of salvation.

This revival of interest in creation-thinking developed independently of the ecological movement, but provided a basis on which many ecotheologians grounded their writings. Especially significant is the work of Westermann who traces this progressive negation of creation back to the Enlightenment, and to a defence of the Bible as an ancient book that, after all, 'had nothing to do with scientific knowledge' about the origins of the universe (1971: 91). The result of this development, says Westermann, is disastrous.

> Once theology has imperceptibly become detached from Creator–Creation, the necessary consequence is that it must gradually become an anthropology and begin to disintegrate from within and collapse around us (1971: 92).

Popular writers like Matthew Fox (1981) made creation theology and creation spirituality accessible to a much wider audience. This rise of interest in creation thinking and spirituality may have prevented theology from devolving into mere 'anthropology', but it did not necessarily avoid the trap of anthropocentrism—the assumption that humans were really the central concern of the text.

However, an appeal to creation theology in a given biblical text or tradition does not necessarily imply a genuine ecological concern for Earth or creation. Scholars like Zimmerli, for example, argued that 'Wisdom thinks resolutely within the framework of a theology of creation' (1964: 148). This led to the assumption that wisdom literature in general is a legitimate source for an environmental ethic (Johnson 1987). A close reading of the classic ancient proverbs of Israel collected in Proverbs 10–24, however, reveals very few allusions to creation; those that do appear demonstrate that the Earth community is viewed as being in the service of humanity. These proverbs may be 'down to earth'; they may reflect everyday human experience—but they also reflect the experiences of humans in society, not as members of the Earth community. They are anthropocentric, focusing in the needs and aspirations of humans. They are summed up in the self-centred axiom,'To get wisdom is to love oneself; to keep understanding is to prosper' (Prov. 19.8).

Some wisdom literature, like Job 38–39 and the Wisdom of Solomon, does focus on creation; the notion of creation as the foundation for all wisdom literature, as asserted by many scholars, is not obvious in the texts we have available.

If it does exist in the background, this underlying principle of creation clearly does not protect much of the literature from anthropocentric attitudes—either on the part of the authors or the interpreters. Johnson, for example, notes that wisdom in Proverbs offers humans 'a path of life', 'length of days', 'a good name', as well as 'riches and honour' (1987: 73). There is nothing here about Earth or the voice of Earth. Wisdom in these references is a means for humans to prosper in human terms; human prosperity is not inevitably linked to the prosperity of Earth.

We applaud this renewal of interest in creation and Earth as a part of creation, but our approach in the Earth Bible Series is also concerned with listening to Earth as a subject in the text—rather than as a topic in the text, or as the backdrop to human history.

A second contributing factor in the development of our approach is the challenge posed by those who have sought to explain the origins of the ecological crisis. Some have pointed the finger of blame at our classical Greek roots; others have blamed the Enlightenment period, while some scholars have accused the Industrial Revolution of contributing significantly to our contemporary ecological crisis.

Christianity, and its sacred text, the Bible, have not been exempt from the search for a culprit. The now famous article of the historian Lynn White, Jr claimed that 'especially in its Western form, Christianity is the most anthropomorphic religion the world has seen' (1967: 1205). He argued that Christianity grounded its anthropocentric orientation in the text of Genesis where 'God planned all of this explicitly for man's [sic] benefit and rule: no item in the physical creation had any purpose save to serve man's [sic] purposes' (1967: 1205).

Since White's article appeared, biblical scholars have been on the back foot seeking to disprove his allegations. White has done us a favour by challenging us to consider whether in fact the anthropocentric orientation of Western Christianity is based on the Scriptures. Is there a measure of truth in his assertion? Are Loader and other schol-

ars correct when they contend that it not the Christian or biblical faith
that is to blame, but interpretations and emphases of modern Christianity? (1987: 9).

Another outcome of this ecological awakening was the realization
that much of the destructive action directed against Earth was
grounded in a set of underlying hierarchical dualisms typical of
Western thought, many of which the feminist movement had by then
already exposed as dangerous (see Plumwood 1993: 41-68). These
dualisms are assumed to be part of reality: the 'natural' and 'normal'
division of the world into male and female, mind and matter, reason
and emotion, spiritual and material, heaven and earth, culture and
nature. This way of thinking assumes a hierarchy in which the first
component of the duality is superior and more valued than the second, and frequently leads to the domination of the second by the first.

Post-colonial studies have also highlighted the way the Bible was
used as a justification for 'conquering' new lands as Joshua had once
conquered Canaan. Prior traces the use of the Bible in the colonization
of South America, South Africa and Palestine (1997: 48-170). I can testify to a similar usage in the colonization of Australia. On a hill over-
looking the lush vineyards of the Barossa Valley in South Australia,
there is a plaque with a biblical quotation that once justified Joshua's
conquest of the land: 'The Lord has given us this land. Jos. 2.9'.

Under colonialist imperialism, the conquest of the peoples of the
land was coupled with the conquest of the land itself. Many European
colonists believed that God had indeed 'given the land into their
hands', and with those hands they were obligated to clear that land
for cultivation and colonization 'as God intended'.

This growing consciousness of colonial and contemporary crimes
against Earth and the indigenous peoples of Earth demands that we
are honest with our past readings of biblical texts and seriously ask
whether these texts, at least on the surface, are part of the problem. In
our approach in this series we are willing accept the challenge of
Lynn White, Jr and entertain the suspicion that the Bible, too, may
have contributed to the current crisis. Are most biblical texts basically
anthropocentric? Do they assume an underlying dualism—implicit or
explicit—that devalues Earth? Or are there forgotten traditions within
the biblical text that reflect a kinship with Earth?

A third consideration in the development of our approach in the
Earth Bible Series is a large array of works on ecotheology that have
flooded the market in the past 20 years. The vast majority of these
works assume that the Bible is environmentally friendly and quote
biblical passages uncritically to support the contention that an ecolog-

ical thrust is inherent in the text. But are contemporary ecological values genuinely supported by many of the biblical texts cited?

Serious studies seeking to promote an ecological thrust in the Bible are represented by Moltmann's work *God in Creation*, which claims to explore the ecological doctrine of creation (1985). Moltmann maintains that God is not only the Creator of the universe; the presence of God is also the Spirit of the universe. Through the Spirit, God indwells all creation. Earth is valued not only as God's creation but by virtue of God's presence in creation. The problem, says Moltmann elsewhere, is a one-sided view of God as omnipotent Lord and ruler, who owns Earth as property and does with it as God pleases (1999: 98). Moltmann, however, still maintains a highly anthropocentric orientation to the role of humans as God's stewards on Earth. According to Moltmann, human beings, 'rule over other creatures as God's representatives'. They are described as nothing less that 'the appearance of God's splendour' and God's 'glory on Earth' (1985: 220-21).

Perhaps the most frequently defended text in the ecological debate is Gen. 1.26-28, where humans are made in the image of God and given an explicit directive to rule over and dominate all living creatures and to subdue Earth. This is also the passage that critics of the Christian heritage cite as the basis for our Western impulse to exploit Earth. The common argument of those defending this passage (e.g. Dryness 1987: 54) runs as follows:

- the term 'rule' reflects royal language;
- the first humans are thus depicted as ideal 'kings';
- as rulers representing God they should reflect God's just rule;
- the ideals for God's rule through a chosen king are given in Psalm 72;
- these ideals include judging the poor with justice;
- this is interpreted as 'taking care' of the poor;
- 'ruling' Earth therefore means 'taking care of' Earth.

Whether or not one believes that this text can be interpreted in the light of select verses from Psalm 72, the focus of the Genesis text lies on the power of human beings over nature. The thrust remains anthropocentric. Moreover, to soften the force of the verb 'rule' to mean 'take care of' does not follow from the text of Psalm 72. When the verb for 'rule' does appear in Ps. 72.8, it refers explicitly to ruling over a domain in which all conquered foes have been forced to lick the dust. This is hardly an image of caring!

Another factor which has influenced our way of reading the text in this series are the basic approaches of feminist scholars. Feminists have highlighted, first of all, how pervasive and powerful the Western dualistic view of reality has been in influencing the way we have interpreted the Scriptures. The significance of these dualisms, outlined in the next chapter, is summarized neatly by Rosemary Radford Ruether:

> From bible and tradition, Christian theology has inherited an understanding of natural reality that often views God over creation, more than in and with the natural world, and humans as other than part of the biotic community. Classical Western cultural traditions, codified between 500 BCE and 800 CE, of which Christianity is a major expression, have sacralized relationships of domination. The bible has more promising leads, but our inherited view of God's relationship to creation, and our relationship to nature, have modelled certain patterns of (male white) domination of women, slaves, Indians, blacks, and so on (1996: 6).

Fundamental to feminist readings of the text is the stated assumption that both the biblical text and its interpretation have been dominated by a patriarchal orientation to the world. Feminist scholars have led the way in identifying and making explicit the bias or orientation they hold *before* reading the text. The ground of this assumption, moreover, lies not in an a priori rational argument, but in the lived experience of women. The lived reality of women suffering under male domination and finding ways to survive by resisting this domination is a truth that is declared in advance of the act of reading. Feminists challenge us to be honest with ourselves and our readers before we embark on a dialogue with the sacred text.

Similarly, in the approach we are espousing in this series, we are committed to identifying and progressively making explicit our relationship to Earth and the Earth community. We not only recognize that an anthropocentric mindset has dominated Western readings of the text, but we also seek to move beyond that orientation to stand with the oppressed Earth community as our kin in this crisis. The degree to which any one of us as members of the Earth community have personally experienced the 'lived reality' of Earth's domination and suffering may vary.

With a growing 'Earth consciousness', as noted above, more and more human beings are becoming sensitive to the suffering of non-human members of the Earth community and of Earth itself. We seek to increase this sensitivity within ourselves as we continue our conversation with both the Earth community today and the biblical text of yesterday.

Based on these stated assumptions, feminists such as Schüssler Fiorenza have developed a specific hermeneutic of suspicion and retrieval (1985). Given that the biblical texts are generally written by— and until recently interpreted by—men with a patriarchal view of the world, feminist readers may *suspect* that the role, status and voice of women in a given text have been negated or suppressed. Or, as Fiorenza writes,

> [while] a liberation-theological interpretation affirms the liberating dynamics of the biblical texts, a feminist critical hermeneutics of suspicion places a warning label on all biblical texts: *Caution! Could be dangerous to your health and survival* (1985: 130).

The dynamics of a feminist hermeneutic, however, are concerned with more than evaluating the text critically in terms of its patriarchal and oppressive aspects. This same approach is used to 'detect anti-patriarchal elements and functions' in the biblical text. Clues are sought within the text that point to traditions where the suppressed voices of women resisting a patriarchal society can be detected and the tradition itself can be *retrieved*. Ultimately, writes Fiorenza,

> [r]ather than abandon the memory of our foresisters' sufferings, visions and hopes in our patriarchal biblical past, such a hermeneutics reclaims their sufferings, struggles, and victories through the subversive power of the 'remembered' past (1985: 133).

This technique of retrieval has been developed in a more 'revo-lutionary' way by feminists such as Pardes and Bal. Pardes, for example, discerns countertraditions—subtexts that read against the grain of the dominant rhetoric of the main text. The patriarchy of the Bible is 'continuously challenged by antithetical trends' that need to be uncovered (Pardes 1992: 51). Pardes' goal is 'to reconstruct, in the light of surviving remains, antithetical undercurrents which call into question the monotheistic repression of femininity' (1992: 2). In a simi-lar way, Mieke Bal seeks to discern 'countercoherent' traditions within the text (1988: 1-7). In the Earth Bible series we welcome simi-lar counter-readings that identify undercurrents from the perspective of the Earth that challenge the dominant anthropocentric voices of the biblical text.

A New Way of Reading the Text

In the light of the preceding factors, we have sought to formulate a fresh approach to reading the Bible. Rather than reflecting *about* the Earth as we analyse a text, we are seeking to reflect *with* Earth and see things from the perspective of Earth. Liberationists stand with the oppressed poor as they read; feminists stand with oppressed women as they read; we stand with oppressed Earth in our dialogue with the text. We are concerned with ecojustice: justice for Earth. Our approach can therefore be called an ecojustice hermeneutic. This change in perspective is achieved by two crucial moves.

The first involves a move away from searching the text to study the theme or topic of Earth, as part of a creation theology or any other theology. Rather, we are identifying, as far as possible, with Earth or the Earth community, as we converse with the text. We no longer consider ourselves readers within the hierarchy of creation, but fellow members within the community of Earth. We are no longer reading as stewards over creation, but as kin, relatives within the Earth community. We no longer see ourselves as pilgrims *on* Earth, but as a species *in* Earth, beneath a common protective skin called the atmosphere. This move from reading about creation to reading as members of the Earth community, as reflected in recent titles like *Theology for Earth Community*, is central to the enterprise (Hessel 1996).

This new perspective implies that when we are reading the text we are sensitive to whether it reflects an orientation where humans act *with and within* Earth, or where humans act *upon* Earth. Put simply, we read Earth as a subject rather than an object in the text. Therefore we ask the following questions. Is Earth an active character with a voice in its own right? Is Earth a passive recipient or a subject whose voice is suppressed? Are all the members of the Earth community invited, directly or indirectly, to celebrate together, praise together, lament together or resist evil together? Is celebrating with Earth encouraged or negated? (Habel 1996: 17-30). Are Earth and its components merely lifeless entities upon which God and humans perform greater or lesser deeds?

The second move involves assuming a similar perspective, but with a declared consciousness of ecojustice. It involves asking whether Earth is being treated unjustly. Justice for the oppressed and marginalized in society is a strong concern in many biblical traditions— whether they be the Israelites in Egypt, the widow and the landless or the leper and the harlot. Is there a similar concern for Earth and its community? Is there demonstrable resistance by non-human members of the Earth community when humans devalue, desecrate or destroy Earth? Or is this concept of exploitation and oppression of Earth strictly a contemporary one?

Santmire, in *The Travail of Nature* (1985), calls for a new option in biblical interpretation. Santmire argues that biblical theology allows—

and perhaps requires—us 'to develop an ecological reading of biblical faith, focusing on themes now familiar to us' (1985: 189). Santmire's challenge is important and emphasizes central ecological themes in creation theologies throughout the Bible, especially when reading through the eyes of theologians like Iranaeus, Francis or Luther—and we would add, Hildegard von Bingen.

Our approach in this series attempts to move beyond a focus on ecological *themes* to a process of listening to, and identifying with, Earth as a presence or voice in the text. Our task is to take up the cause of Earth and the non-human members of the Earth community by sensing their presence in the text—whether their presence is suppressed, oppressed or celebrated. We seek to move beyond identifying ecological themes in creation theology to identifying with Earth in its ecojustice struggle.

Hessel, as editor of the volume *Theology for Earth Community* (1996), maintains that McAfee's article on 'Ecology and Biblical Studies' can be classified as 'state-of-the-art' in this respect.

McAfee does take a number of significant steps toward an ecojustice hermeneutic. He recognizes, as noted above, that an ecological approach to the world is distinct from the theological concept of creation (1996: 31). After reviewing some of the current debate about the scope of redemption, McAfee poses a number of key questions for future readings of the biblical text. Like Hiebert (1996), he argues that we need to discern, where possible, 'the actual physical environment of the writers of biblical texts and the ideologies reflected in these texts' (McAfee 1996: 42).

We would argue, however, that we also need to discern whether the text actually reveals the links between the writer and a given location, or whether the ideas in the text reach for ideals that transcend the writer's physical reality.

McAfee warns against discerning ecological relevance in texts that tend to focus on the events of history and regard creation merely as a background, the 'scene' for the action.

We would add that it is also legitimate to ask whether Earth, in fact, is simply in the background of the text, or whether it is actively being suppressed and hence devalued as secondary to the realm of history (McAfee 1996: 42).

McAfee moves closer to the approach we have espoused when he cites Wieskel (1993) and questions whether a theology based on a fundamentally 'anthropocentric Scripture' can really help us live 'on the planet's terms and not our own'. As Wieskel suggests, we may well approach the biblical traditions with an a priori suspicion that the text—and most of its interpreters—are 'anthropocentric', and that any claim to the contrary would need to be justified by a close eco-justice reading (McAfee 1996: 43). Accordingly, a hermeneutic of suspicion in this context is quite legitimate. Just as feminists have adopted an approach of reading the Bible primarily as a collection of texts with an androcentric and patriarchal orientation, so we would suspect that the Bible, being written by humans for humans, would be not only patriarchal and androcentric but also anthropocentric. Even when scholars seem to skirt the issue by declaring a text theocentric (Bergant 1991: 13), the treatment of Earth may reflect something far less than justice or concern for the Earth community.

Our approach in the Earth Bible Series does not exclude a corresponding hermeneutic of retrieval; we allow for the possibility that, in a given tradition, Earth or members of the Earth community are valued in their own right and invited to be part of a worshipping community with God's people (e.g. Hinsdale: 1991). Or, as Santmire (1985) has demonstrated, in the case of Francis, Irenaeus and others, there are several Christian traditions which are not anti-nature, and may serve as a guide to alternative readings of the text.

Especially significant is the potential contribution of ecofeminists who seek to discover clues to the Earth resisting its suppression by dominant human voices. The claims of ecofeminism are summarized by Lois Daly:

> (1) The oppression of women and the oppression of nature are interconnected; (2) these connections must be uncovered in order to understand both the oppression of women and the oppression of nature; (3) feminist analysis must include ecological insights; (4) a feminist perspective must be part of any proposed ecological solutions (1990: 89).

Heather Eaton, for example, challenges the way Genesis has been read by ecotheologians, claiming the methodology has been 'revised rather than revolutionised' (Eaton 1996: 84).

If, as the ecofeminists have shown, the oppression of Earth is interconnected with the oppression of women, the way feminists have learned to discern the suppressed voice of women may assist us in discerning the suppressed voice of Earth.

Aims of our Approach

In the light of the preceding discussion, it is now possible to outline the basic aims of the approach we are espousing in this series. We are seeking to

- acknowledge, before reading the biblical text, that as Western interpreters we are heirs to a long anthropocentric, patriarchal and androcentric approach to reading the text that has devalued Earth and that continues to influence the way we read the text;
- declare, before reading the text, that we are members of a human community that has exploited, oppressed and endangered the existence of the Earth community;
- become progressively more conscious that we are also members of the endangered Earth community in dialogue with ancient texts;
- recognize Earth as a subject in the text with which we seek to relate empathetically rather than as a topic to be analysed rationally;
- take up the cause of justice for Earth to ascertain whether Earth and the Earth community are oppressed, silenced or liberated in the biblical text;
- develop techniques of reading the text to discern and retrieve alternative traditions where the voice of the Earth community has been suppressed.

To guide us in achieving these aims, we have articulated a set of ecojustice principles. These principles are outlined in Table 1 and discussed in detail in the next chapter. In pursuing this ecojustice approach, we take into account both the aims of our approach as outlined in this chapter and the ecojustice principles discussed in the chapters that follow.

Guiding Ecojustice Principles

The Earth Bible Team

Introduction

The principles enunciated in this chapter are the basic understandings about ecojustice shared by the group of people who have developed the Earth Bible series. This set of principles has been developed over several years in dialogue with ecologists and their writings, some of whom, like Thomas Berry, have developed their own distinctive sets of ecological principles (Berry 1988). The principles formulated here have been refined in consultations and workshops concerned with both ecology in general, and the relationship between ecology and theology or the Bible.

These principles serve several purposes. First, they identify the ecological orientation of the Earth Bible series—though writers are free to dialogue with these principles and offer variations relevant to a given text or topic. Second, they embrace specific ecological values consistent with the basic approach, the aims of which are presented at the end of the previous chapter. Third, they provide a basis for articulating the key questions we pose as we seek to read and interpret the Bible. These principles are the starting point for our exploration of biblical texts.

One feature of these principles—immediately obvious to those with a theological interest—is that the specific terms 'God' and 'creation' are not employed in the wording of the principles. This formulation has been chosen to facilitate dialogue with biologists, ecologists, other religious traditions like Buddhism, and scientists who may not function with God or God's creation as an a priori assumption. This formulation also forces the interpreter to focus on Earth itself as the object of investigation in the text, rather than on Earth as God's creation or property.

These principles are not intended to be exhaustive and writers may wish to complement them with additional principles—there is no principle, for example, which explicitly links the plight of oppressed peoples of Earth with the plight of Earth. Clearly social justice and ecojustice are closely connected in many contexts.

Nor will writers find all of these principles useful in reading a given biblical text afresh. Any one of these principles, however, may provide the stimulus needed to pose new questions as we converse with the text, become conscious of Earth's presence in the text or join the Earth community in a struggle of justice for Earth.

Suspicion and Retrieval

A helpful way of using these principles to pose questions of the text is to adapt the basic hermeneutic of feminist scholars introduced in the previous chapter: suspicion and retrieval (Schüssler Fiorenza 1985, 1992). The suspicion aspect of this approach means that we may legitimately suspect that biblical texts, written by human beings, reflect the primary interests of human beings—their human welfare, their human relationship to God and their personal salvation. In short, we may suspect that biblical texts are anthropocentric. As these texts were also written by men, we can expect them to be androcentric, and probably patriarchal.

Even where scholars have insisted that texts are theocentric rather than anthropocentric in character, the writer may ultimately be more concerned about God's relation to humanity—or a group within humanity—than about God's relation to Earth or the Earth community as a whole. The Bible has long been understood as God's book for humans. And for those of us who have been reading biblical texts that way for years, this understanding has come to be self-evident, normal. Should we not then, with a new ecological consciousness, legitimately suspect that the text and its interpreters have been understandably anthropocentric?

The second aspect of this approach involves detecting features of the text that facilitate our retrieval of traditions about Earth or the Earth community that have been unnoticed, suppressed or hidden. The task before us is to reread the text to discern where Earth or members of the Earth community may have suffered, resisted or been excluded by attitudes within the text or the history of its interpretation. The task demands a strategy for reclaiming the sufferings and struggles of Earth, a task that involves regarding the wider Earth community as our kin.

There is a strong possibility that biblical texts may be more sympathetic to the plight and potential of Earth than our previous interpretations have allowed—even if the ecological questions we are posing arise out of a contemporary Earth consciousness. This is suggested by the very title of Gene Tucker's presidential address to the Society of Biblical Literature in 1996: 'Rain on a Land Where No One Lives' (1997: 3). Some texts may even celebrate Earth in a way that our contemporary anthropocentric eyes have not detected, or that we have regarded as the quaint language of ancient poetry. Is it 'only poetry' when the psalmist asserts that 'the heavens/skies are telling the glory of El' (Ps. 19.1)? The verses that follow speak of a genuine communication between parts of creation in a form that is other than human 'words' (Ps. 19.1-4).

We also need to consider the possibility that there are suppressed Earth traditions that resist the dominant patriarchal anthropocentric orientation of the text. By counter-reading the text, we may identify alternative voices that challenge or subvert the normative voice of the dominant tradition, and discern within the text countercoherent readings.[1] Whether these subtexts point to the continuing voice of Canaanite traditions still in touch with Earth, or whether these alterative perspectives arose as a mode of resisting the patriarchal orientation of monotheistic Yahwism, is a task for further exploration.

Western Dualism

One of the reasons for this blind spot in our interpretive work as readers of an ancient text is that we are influenced by our Western dualistic perceptions of reality. This view of reality has developed since biblical days; because these dualisms, or binary oppositions, are so much part of our Western view of reality, we tend to assume that they are necessarily part of the ancient worldview in the biblical text.

Plumwood (1993: 43) outlines the key elements of the hierarchical dualisms underpinning Western thought. These pairings include, among others, the following sets of contrasting pairs:

culture	/	nature
reason	/	nature
male	/	female
mind, spirit	/	body (nature)
reason	/	matter
reason	/	emotion (nature)
rationality	/	animality (nature)

---

1.   Editor's footnote: 'countercoherent' is a term that describes alternatives readings of the text that both make sense—cohere—and challenge the dominant reading and/or the tradition of interpretation associated with this reading.

human	/	nature (non-human)
civilized	/	primitive (nature)
production	/	reproduction (nature)
freedom	/	necessity (nature)
subject	/	object

To this listing, in the context of our project, we would add the following closely related pairs:

animate	/	inanimate
spiritual	/	material
heavenly	/	earthly
heaven	/	earth
sacred	/	profane

These dualistic pairs are deliberately listed here as background for the following discussion of the six ecojustice principles, each of which articulates an ecological view of reality challenging at least one of these traditional pairings. It is immediately apparent from these pairings that the realities associated with the human and male pole of the pairing have long been understood to be superior in some way to the nature and female pole of the pairing. These dualisms necessarily devalue Earth as belonging to the weak or subordinate side of the pairings.

Do these pairings reflect genuine dualisms in the ancient biblical text, or are they complementary opposites within the structure of the cosmos in the ancient worldview?

Perhaps the most destructive form of this dualism in relation to our perception of the natural world developed as a result of the mechanistic approach of Descartes and his successors. Ponting quotes Descartes and analyses his position in the following way:

> This tendency was reinforced by a mechanistic approach to natural phenomena, which can again be traced back to Descartes who wrote, 'I do not recognise any difference between the machines made by craftsmen and the various bodies that nature alone composes'... His mechanistic view of the world seemed to be vindicated by the spectacular success of Newton in the late seventeenth century in applying physical laws, such as that governing the force of gravity, to explain the workings of the universe (1991: 147).

Philosophers and scientists of the seventeenth and eighteenth century pressed the dualism of mediaeval Christianity to its logical conclusion. They viewed Earth as a machine, God as the great designer of the machine and humans as beings fashioned to determine the workings of the machine and run it for the benefit of human beings. As modern interpreters, we are still influenced by this heritage. We are obliged to make a conscious paradigm shift if we are to view the world in terms of complementary opposites rather than some form of monism, or as antagonistic and hierarchical Western dualisms.

Before discussing the principles in detail, it is important to recognize that because Earth and women have traditionally been associated on the same side of these dualistic pairings, this has resulted in a disregard for the importance and rights of both Earth and women. When Earth has been viewed as female, as 'Mother Earth' or as 'Mother Nature', Earth has often been oppressed and abused, and denied any status as a subject in its own right.

As participants in the Earth Bible Project, we are clearly denying the secondary status of both Earth and women advocated by Western dualisms. Because they view avoiding any such equation as axiomatic in Earth Bible readings, some writers in this series refuse to refer routinely to the Earth as 'she'. Many of us believe that to regard Earth as 'she' as a matter of course is to impose the language of social domination on a part of our physical world—the Earth community we are claiming to be our kin.

We also recognize that some writers may wish to use the 'feminizing' of Earth in their work, seeking thereby to challenge Western hierarchical dualistic thinking, require a re-evaluation of the feminine and retrieve the female as a positive category in Western eyes. In addition, where writers are analysing a tradition where Earth is explicitly feminine—for example, where Earth is depicted as a goddess—the use of 'she' is quite appropriate.

The task of transcending this dualistic form of Western thinking may not be easy, but the Earth Bible Project is designed to facilitate that process. This task is consistent with our stated aim to recognize our kinship with all members of the Earth community, and to assume a posture of empathy and partnership with Earth, rather than assume dominion over Earth in partnership with a hierarchal deity represented as being above Earth. In so doing, we will also seek to retrieve biblical traditions that may be consistent with the Earth Bible Project's six ecojustice principles.

Six Ecojustice Principles

1. The Principle of Intrinsic Worth
The universe, Earth and all its components have intrinsic worth/value.
This ecological principle is fundamental for developing an ethic, a theology or a hermeneutic that seeks to promote justice for Earth. This

principle asserts that Earth and its components have value in themselves, not because they have utilitarian value for humans living on the planet, nor because they are vehicles to reflect the Creator's handiwork. Nor is this intrinsic value to be confined to sentient or living beings. The whole Earth as a complex of ecological systems, and all the components of those systems—from rocks to rainbows—have worth because they are part of these systems. The question before us as we approach the text is whether Earth understood in this way is respected and honoured by the voices in the text.

Given the history of Western thought, we may assume that biblical interpreters have read the text in terms of the dualities dominant in Western society. In this context, heaven is viewed as spiritual, superior, pure and eternal; Earth is correspondingly viewed as material, inferior, corrupt and transitory. We may suspect, from the outset, that the biblical materials reflect a similar dualism—especially if we have imbibed the spirituality of hymns based on the book of Hebrews, where heaven is apparently depicted as our true home and Earth is a 'motel' for passing pilgrims (Heb. 11.13-16). In such hymns, this earthly domain is 'very evil', a place where 'exiles mourn', and a 'vale of tears', while heaven is a 'sweet and blessed country', an endless 'land of rest' (Ewing 1941: hymn no. 605).

Using the principle of intrinsic worth as our guide, we ask whether a given biblical text reflects the kind of dualisms we have inherited in the Western world, or whether a different cosmology is assumed. If an alternative cosmology can be discerned, we ask whether it honours Earth and its components in terms of intrinsic worth, or whether Earth in that cosmology is negated and relegated to a position of secondary value.

The process can be illustrated by the language used in the first verse of Genesis. The Hebrew expression השמים והארץ has been traditionally translated 'heaven and earth'. This expression has the potential for being read as a dualism embracing two opposing cosmic domains. If, however, the expression is rendered 'sky and land', the meaning is radically different. Land and sky are two complementary parts of the known physical world of the ancient Near East. According to our reading of Genesis 1, Earth is honoured, and not represented as inferior to the sky.

Can the same be said of the cosmology of Isa. 66.2, where sky/heaven is declared to be God's throne and Earth/land is God's footstool? In this passage the sky (שמים) is no longer the sky as a part of the physical world, but the locus of God's presence and power as ruler over Earth.[2] The secondary status of Earth is represented by the image of Earth as a 'footstool' under the feet of the ruler. In the ancient Near East, the imagery of a person or nation as a footstool is an image of subservience. In this tradition, Earth is demeaned even if we are hesitant to admit it. Even if the emphasis in the text lies on the limited perspective of those who viewed the temple as God's abode, Earth is devalued in relation to heaven. Heaven is God's abode; Earth is God's property—it is the place where God puts God's feet.

A close reading of Genesis 1 also illustrates how we can retrieve positive traditions that emphasize the intrinsic value of Earth. In many interpretations, Earth is understood to be valued or 'good' precisely because God has invested Earth with value. The expression 'and God saw that [X] was good' in Genesis 1 is often viewed as a formula of divine pronouncement: Earth is good because God pronounces it good.

If, however, we recognize that the text speaks of a narrative event, and a corresponding divine reaction, we can discern a rather different understanding. God 'sees' the light (1.4), or Earth emerging from the waters (1.10). God reacts to what God sees, and what God sees is good. Earth and the components of Earth in Genesis 1 are valued as 'good' by God when God discovers them to be so, not because God pronounces them to be so. In Genesis 1, Earth is 'good' of itself; this is a reality that God discovers (see also Welker 1991–92: 60).[3] Are there other biblical passages where the same affirmation of Earth can be retrieved?

2. *The Principle of Interconnectedness*
Earth is a community of interconnected living things that are mutually dependent on each other for life and survival.
The ecological movement, influenced by quantum physics and other sciences, has increased our awareness that Earth is not a controlled or mechanical structure consisting of independent parts governed by the so-called laws of nature. Every species and every member of every species are connected to others by complex webs of interrelationships. Humans, too, are dependent on the fields, the forests, the trees, the air and the wide diversity of life that inhabits these domains. Humans are an integral part of what has come to be called the 'Earth community';

---

2.   Editor's note: 'locus' is the appropriate term because it refers to the perceived or effective placement or location of something abstract.

3.   Welker refers to this recognition as God's 'evaluative perception'.

humans are Earth-bound. All breathing creatures inhale the same air. According to Birch, '[e]very molecule of oxygen in the planet comes from plants. All the oxygen is completely recycled by living organisms every two thousand years' (1993: 18). We breathe today the same air once breathed and recycled by the cedars of Lebanon. Or, as Denis Edwards puts it, all humans are composed of the same star dust as Jesus of Nazareth (1991: 81).

Traditionally, Western thought has assumed that male humans are creatures of a different order than other life forms. In terms of this human/nature dualism, male humans are superior beings possessing mind, reason, soul, language and spiritual consciousness; male humans are the creators of culture. Other forms, whether animate or inanimate, are believed to be inferior, possessing, at best, certain basic natural instincts but lacking the higher faculties given to male humans.

One way of highlighting the interconnectedness of Earth's ecosystems is to focus on the kinship between these systems. Philip Hefner argues that such kinship is integral to our very identity as humans. Science, he argues, has demonstrated quite clearly that humans are 'indissolubly part of nature, fully natural' (1995: 121).

> On the basis of these scientific perspectives, there can be little doubt that homo sapiens is nature's creature. How are we related to the rest of nature? We flourish only within an intimate ecological fabric, and within the relationships of that fabric, we are kin to the other citizens of nature's society. Our interrelatedness is best conceptualised according to the model of genetic relatedness. Nature's processes have produced us, we are constituted by our inheritance from its past and we live in the ambience of its created balances today. There is a kind of non-negotiability to the message that science delivers on this point. Our kinship with nature is not a matter of our preference, nor is it an issue that calls for our acquiescence. It simply is (Hefner 1995: 122).

As we apply the principle of interconnectedness, we may suspect that the history of interpretation of a given text has been anthropocentric—the rest of the Earth community, and Earth itself, have been regarded as inferior creations. We may suspect that male interpreters have massaged their own egos by highlighting references to the higher standing and nature of humans, especially men. We may expect that biblical texts themselves exalt humans over other creatures even if their writers do not reflect the sharp dualism of later Western thought.

In Psalm 8, for example, the psalmist's reflections on the nature of humans seems to be unequivocally anthropocentric. The order of things seems to be a carefully structured hierarchy in which humans are 'a little less then the gods', and the animal world is under their domination. Is this orientation assumed in most biblical passages that deal with the connection between humans and the wider Earth community?

As we read a given text in the light of this principle, we may also retrieve alternative traditions that affirm an interconnection and interdependence between the domains of the biological world as well as between this world and human beings. Does the figure of wisdom in Proverbs 8 and elsewhere point to an underlying principle that integrates the physical, social and spiritual realms? Is there a similar concept of an integrated cosmos behind Romans 8? Are there texts that indicate that humans are one with Earth, kin with the animals, and an integral part of an integrated Earth community?

3. *The Principle of Voice*
Earth is a subject capable of raising its voice in celebration and against injustice.

There is a growing consciousness among many biologists, ecologists, feminists and theologians that Earth is a living entity, both biologically and spiritually. Deep Ecologists argue that Earth functions more like a living organism than a machine governed by rigid laws. According to James Lovelock's Gaia hypothesis, Earth is itself alive, sustaining and regulating its own environment. Sallie McFague (1993) uses the metaphor of the body of God to describe Earth as a living entity. Theologians like Jay McDaniel speak—as we do in this eco-justice hermeneutical process—of the need to identify with planet Earth as a whole. In doing so, he views Earth as a total community of subjects 'like a forest whose "spirit" is the sum total of each of its living beings' (cited in Hessel 1996: 15). The interconnectedness of all living ecosystems amounts to a super ecosystem—Earth is an all-embracing organism.

Whether or not one opts for a particular view of Earth as a living entity, our growing consciousness of Earth as a subject can no longer be dismissed. Those who have experienced Earth in this way are committed to hearing the voices of Earth—whether they are those of the various species inhabiting Earth or the voice of Earth itself. In this context, it is valuable to recall how 'how nature has grown silent in our discourse, shifting from an animistic to a symbolic presence, from a voluble subject to a mute object' (Manes 1996: 17).

It may be argued that to speak of Earth as a subject or living entity is to impose human categories upon a non-human reality. Not so!

When we speak of the voice of Earth, we are not implying that Earth speaks with a human voice or uses human language. The modes of self-expression or communication by Earth and non-human members of the Earth community reflect their distinctive natures. Just as humans may communicate through body language, the various components of Earth may communicate their presence and intent through alternative forms of language we might call 'Earth language'. Like human body language, this may be physical and a consequence of orientation—rather then aural, and a consequence of sound waves. Scientists have already studied the 'language of birds', and the 'language of animals'—for example cats, whales and chipmunks; both groups use combinations of sounds and physical demeanour to convey their messages. Members of the Deaf community also use physical signs and their body orientation to communicate with each other and members of the 'hearing' community.

An awareness of Earth as a subject or community of subjects presents a formidable challenge to our traditional conceptions of Earth and the non-human components of the Earth community as objects, devoid of the consciousness, soul, mind, and the form of language that humans possess. This form of Western dualism extends to the belief that humans have genuine feelings, a spiritual consciousness and a capacity to worship—all of which are absent in other living creatures or inanimate parts of creation. From this perspective, only humans have the sensibility and language to praise God. Non-humans are dumb brutes or mere physical matter with no agency, sense or feeling.

When applying the principle of voice we may suspect that the history of biblical interpretation has, by and large, tended to silence the language of Earth. When we approach a given text we may suspect that the language of the text gives rise to this kind of differentiation between 'voiced' humans and the presumed 'voiceless' members of the wider Earth community. Given this dualistic mindset, passages referring to God's creation blessing or praising God (as in Ps. 103.22), have been dismissed as poetic license. But do these texts reflect more than poetry? Do they reflect an understanding of the common bond between humans and non-humans as worshippers before God?

We may look afresh at the text and ask whether the voice of Earth and the members of the Earth community can be retrieved in many passages in a way that views them as subjects with their own languages—entities with non-human voices and a capacity for worship. Or we may ask whether the voice of the Earth has been suppressed because it is a threat to the authority of anthropocentric writers, just

as the voices of women and other oppressed minority groups have
been silenced and ignored for similar reasons?

We also allow for the possibility that Earth-sensitive humans may
mediate the voices of Earth to the rest of humanity. Ecologists like
David Suzuki, who claims to be in tune with Earth, echo the cries of
the denuded forests and the polluted seas in our hearing. Indigenous
poets, like Mary Duroux, hear the land crying and confront us with
the pain of their mother, the crucified land.

> My mother, my mother
> what have they done?
> Crucified you
> like the Only Son!
> Murder committed
> by mortal hand.
> I weep, my mother,
> my mother the land (1992: 20).[4]

As we read the words of the storytellers, prophets and poets in the
Scriptures, we ask if they are mediating the voice of Earth or members
of the Earth community? Are they suppressing those voices as they
strive to hear the voice of God? Is Jeremiah—who hears the land
mourning—typical (Jer. 12.4, 11)? Is the author of Job simply being
rhetorical in urging us to 'Ask the animals and they will teach you'
(Job 12.7)? Or are most biblical writers happy to announce curses—the
consequence of human behaviour, but experienced by the ground,
trees, animal life or rivers—without any sense of the anguish felt by
Earth as a result? We are invited in this ecojustice hermeneutical process to stand with Earth and retrieve the silenced voices of Earth and
the Earth community.

4. *The Principle of Purpose*
The universe, Earth and all its components, are part of a dynamic cosmic
design within which each piece has a place in the overall goal of that design.
Earth is a complex of interacting ecosystems; it functions according to
an in-built design or purpose. These mysterious patterns of balancing
interdependent life forces are still being explored by scientists and
philosophers, and evoking wonder in poets and prophets. Whether
one views these patterns as being developed by an evolutionary
impulse, an immanent energy, a living Spirit or a Creator God, the
reality remains: all the pieces of these ecosystems form a design and
reflect a direction. The design is a magnificent green planet called

---

4.   Reprinted by permission of Heritage Publishing, Moruya, NSW.

Earth and the direction is to sustain life in all its diversity and beauty.

What is the future of this design, this complex pattern of ancient life cycles still operating to keep planet Earth alive? Charles Birch, in *Confronting the Future*, demonstrates not only the wonder of this design but the tragedy of how modern human society has smashed ancient patterns, broken complex life cycles, and thereby placed the future of the planet in jeopardy. Birch reminds us that the

> closing circle is the image or metaphor of the way nature deals with things. It closes the circle. It takes nutrients from the soil, turns them into something else and puts them back, so that it is a completely circular process... Traditional economists seem to think that the economy is a flow in a single direction between two infinities: infinite resources on one side and an infinite hole on the other side into which we can dump all our wastes. There is no account of recycling and reuse of wastes. Nature doesn't work that way. There is no pollution is nature's ecosystems. This is Garrett Hardin's 'law' of ecology, 'There is no away to throw to' (Birch 1993: 18).

This growing concern for understanding the design of Earth's life systems is motivated not only by those who now revere Earth for its wondrous life patterns, but also by those who, out of self-interest, seek to create a 'sustainable society' in the future.

Within much of traditional Western Christianity, we learned to view the wonders of Earth as but a foretaste of the glories to be experienced in heaven. We paid relatively little attention to whether natural resources or non-human life cycles were declining. After all, Earth was disposable matter—Earth would eventually be become waste, destroyed in God's cosmic incinerator.

As we relate the principle of purpose to the text, we ask whether the writer reflects this stark dualism about the end times. Is the Earth disposable? Or does Earth have another ultimate purpose and design? Is the destruction of the elements by fire in 2 Pet. 3.10 the dominant orientation of the New Testament? When we view the text from the perspective of Earth, is the death of Earth considered inevitable in a book such as Revelation—and, if so, is that death part of a natural cycle of birth, death and renewal? What does 'renewal' in this sense mean?

When we step back into the Hebrew Scriptures, we need to ask afresh how the life cycles of Earth are understood. Is the grand 'design' that confronts Job anything like the pattern of ecosystems that we marvel at today? How do the biblical approaches differ from the mechanistic model outlined above (Ponting 1991: 147). Is the purpose and direction of life on Earth to sustain the pattern of life estab-

lished by God? Given the violation of life cycles by humanity—even
in the biblical period—do biblical texts tend to focus on a restoration
of past life systems, or lean towards a liberation and transformation
into a new system?

5. *The Principle of Mutual Custodianship*
*Earth is a balanced and diverse domain where responsible custodians can
function as partners, rather than rulers, to sustain a balanced and diverse
Earth community.*
This principle is designed to reflect the role of human beings in the
Earth community. Understandably, there is a widespread recognition
today that the language of human dominion over Earth is not acceptable. It is, in fact, one of the factors that has led to our contemporary
ecological crisis. A considerable mass of literature advocates the concept of humans exercising responsible stewardship over Earth.
According to this model, the household (οἰκός) of Earth has been
entrusted to humans by God, the owner of the house. The fact that
humans have been unfaithful stewards in the past does not nullify the
usefulness of the model.

I have critiqued this model elsewhere as one which retains an
inherent anthropocentrism and a hierarchy of power that is based on
an economic model of the ancient world (Habel 1998). The steward
(οἰκονόμος) has responsibility for the planning and administrating
(putting in order or νομός) the affairs of the household (οἰκός). Thus
the steward is responsible for the economy (οἰκονομία) of the house
(Hall 1990: 41).

The anthropocentrism of the model is exposed by Clare Palmer
when she writes that

> perceptions of stewardship have great difficulty in accommodating the
> idea of God's action or presence in the world. God is understood to be
> an absentee landlord, who has put humanity in charge of his [*sic*] pos-
> sessions... Within the framework of this model, God's actions and pres-
> ence are largely mediated through humans. This is so both in the feudal
> perception, where God the Master leaves man [*sic*] in charge of his [*sic*]
> estate, and also in the financial perception, where God, the owner of
> financial resources, puts them in the trust of humanity, the investor, to
> use for him [*sic*] as best it can (1992: 74).

As we relate the principle of custodianship to the biblical text, we
may suspect that key texts—such as Gen. 1.26-28 and their interpreters—represent humans as stewards ruling on behalf of God, but
nevertheless ruling. Do these passages reflect an underlying antago-
nism between humans and the rest of creation? Are humans repre-

sented as creatures of a different order from the rest of creation and destined by God to rule over the Earth community for God?

An alternative ecological model views humans as a species which is an integral part of the Earth community, inevitably interconnected with other species and ecosystems, and dependent upon these systems for survival. Humans, therefore, have a natural kinship with members of the Earth community—a kinship that reaches beyond pure biological dependency (see Hefner, quoted above). Many indigenous peoples testify to this sense of kinship. George Tinker describes a ritual among his people where the community is assembled in a circle.

> In fact the circle is a key symbol for self-understanding, representing the whole universe and our part in it. We see ourselves as coequal participants in the circle, neither standing above nor below anything in God's creation. There is no hierarchy in our cultural context, even of species, because the circle has no beginning or ending (1992: 147).

The indigenous tradition cited by Tinker is reminiscent of the indigenous traditions of Australia where kinship with Earth and with the community of the Earth is a fundamental understanding of reality. Through the appropriate rites at sacred sites, human custodians are responsible for sustaining a particular species of the natural world who are close kin to members of their community. They are the custodians of the sacred, in tune with sacred presences in Earth (Rainbow Spirit Elders 1997: 29-42).

Custodianship is a mutual partnership. Earth and the Earth community have, in spite of the assumed rulership of humanity, been the custodians of human beings. Earth has provided food, shelter, beauty and many other riches to sustain the body and the spirit of humanity. In return humans have assumed these riches as their right rather than the contribution of their partners in the Earth community.

As we explore the text in search of alternative traditions that reflect a kinship between humans and the rest of Earth, we ask whether Earth is ever considered sacred in the Scriptures? Are humans ever viewed as custodians of their non-human kin, and of a sacred Earth? Is the role of Earth as custodian reflected in biblical texts? Do these kinds of ideas reflect suppressed Canaanite traditions that are frequently denounced as 'nature religion'? Does the hierarchical stewardship model persist as normative in spite of these alternative traditions? Are there texts that can be counter-read so that Earth-affirming traditions within the text can be identified?

6. Principle of Resistance
Earth and its components not only suffer from injustices at the hands of
humans, but actively resist them in the struggle for justice.
This ecojustice principle is not as widely disseminated as the previous
five, but is, in our opinion, integral to the process of ecojustice. In the
struggle of social groups for justice—whether they be indigenous
peoples, Dalits, women, people with disabilities or some other category—members of the group do not necessarily view themselves as
helpless victims, but as oppressed human beings who find ways to
survive and resist their oppressors. Victim construction by oppressors
is itself part of the process of maintaining power over those being
marginalized, exploited or disempowered. Victims are even blamed
for their condition as part of this oppressive conditioning process.

Those who belong to such groups—and those who dare to identify
with them and espouse their causes—recognize that oppressed
groups use numerous means of resistance in order to survive oppressive situations. There are powerful resistance stories in the Scriptures,
including the account of the Gideonites who tricked Joshua (Josh. 9)
and the record of the midwives who defied Pharaoh (Exod. 2.15-22).
Are there explicit or oppressed resistance stories that relate to Earth or
non-human members of the Earth community? Is Earth constructed
by anthropocentric writers into a passive victim? Or are there Earth
voices in the text resisting this construction of Earth as victim?

We may well suspect that a given text is likely to focus on sins
against God and wrongs against other humans, but ignore the injustices committed against Earth, because Earth is viewed as a passive
object without feeling or voice. When God sends plagues or curses on
Earth, Earth seems to suffer because of human misdeeds. Is this just?
Is this considered natural? Or is there a hint that Earth resists this
injustice? Is Earth destined to suffer for humans?

If we assume a posture of empathy with the wider Earth community, can we ignore the way Earth seems to suffer unjustly because of
human behaviour? The curses of the covenant in texts like Deuteron-
omy 28 involve numerous domains of Earth that have played no part
in the human sin against God. When the sky turns to bronze and
Earth to iron (Deut. 28.23), the people may indeed suffer. But does
Earth not suffer too? Is this suffering just? Do these texts portray a
deity who simply 'uses' Earth to punish humans (cf. Amos 4.7-9)? Or
is this a form of corporate suffering—does Earth suffer in sympathy
with humans?

Suggestions that Earth or Earth community are sensitive to these
injustices can be found in prophets like Jeremiah, who hears the land

mourning because Israel's sin has made the land desolate (Jer. 12.4, 7-11; cf. Hos. 4.1-3). In the book of Jeremiah, God, too, seems to suffer in sympathy with the land.

Is the groaning of creation in Romans 8 also part of the resistance of Earth to the injustices to which it has been subjected? Is there more than poetic imagery in the assertion that the land will 'vomit out' those inhabitants who defile the land? (Lev. 18.24-30).

Biologists and ecologists have made us aware that the ecosystems of Earth are not necessarily fragile. They have a remarkable capacity to survive, regenerate and adapt to changing physical circumstances, in spite of human exploitation and short-sighted greed. Do any of the biblical traditions reflect a similar awareness of Earth as a subject with the power to revive and regenerate?

There is, however—as contemporary ecologists assert—a limit to this ecological healing. Earth is a finite body of ecosystems, resources and species. The time has come for ecosensitive humans to join Earth in its struggle against these injustices that now threaten the total ecosystem of Earth. If we, as people who still find the Bible relevant, recognize that we have been involved in the ecological crisis, we also need to recognize that we have a moral obligation to help find a solution.

Ecofeminist Contributions to an Ecojustice Hermeneutics

Heather Eaton

The Bible, of all books, is the most dangerous one, the one that has been endowed with the power to kill (Bal 1991: 19).

To read the Bible with Earth consciousness—a fragile resurgence of awareness of our radical dependence on and indeed emergence from within the Earth's complex life processes—is to stand with the oppressed Earth and from there dialogue with the Bible. This liberationist stance taken by the Earth Bible Project is advocational: it does not pretend neutrality or objectivity.[1] The twin perspectives, of identifying with the Earth community and claiming the centrality of justice, are made explicit in the six ecojustice principles which act as the hermeneutical lens through which we may see the Earth as a subject—oppressed, silent or liberated—within the biblical text.

The question posed in this chapter is 'How can we approach the Earth Bible Project from an ecofeminist perspective, and develop ecofeminist hermeneutics? Two interconnected tracts will be followed; one is the range of socio-political critiques deemed necessary for an adequate biblical method. The other is the larger issue of changing world views, and from what world view the reader is located in her/his reflection. The preliminary task is to define what is meant by an ecofeminist perspective. A second task is to enter into the methodological maze of biblical interpretation, and indeed probe the daring and deceptive art of reading the Bible. These discussions will become the dialogue partner for each ecojustice principle. The chapter concludes with comments concerning the aims of the Project; that is, taking up the cause of justice for the Earth in response to the ecological crisis.[2]

---

1. All liberation theologies are advocational and begin their reflection from the perspective of the oppressed. The one context that has been neglected is the context of the Earth. See McFague 1993: 84-98.
2. Although the word 'crisis' is contentious to some, I accept the analysis that it is appropriate and that often social issues are related to ecological stress. See

Ecofeminist Perspectives

Ecological-feminism (ecofeminism) emerged in the 1970s predominantly in North America, although the term was coined by French feminist Françoise d'Eaubonne (1974). It has expanded rapidly from numerous origins such as social and ecological activists and academics, and from diverse fields such as feminism, socialism, anti-racism, critical theory and ecology.[3] Ecofeminism is a third wave of feminism: a convergence of ecology and feminism into a new social theory and political movement (Sturgeon 1997: 24; Plumwood 1993: 39). Feminist theologian Rosemary Radford Ruether suggests that there can be no liberation for women and no solution to the ecological crisis within a society whose fundamental model of relationships is one of domination (1975).

Ruether describes ecofeminism as the symbolic and social connection between the oppression of women and the domination of nature (Ruether 1992b). The mistrust or hatred of women (misogyny), and a fear of dependency on the natural world are the interlocking forces and underpinnings of a patriarchal world view. As Eurowestern societies developed, the combined influences of the rise of science, the dualisms of the Christian world view, the philosophy of modernity and the industrialization of the economy became the cultural forces that entrenched the feminizing of nature, the naturalizing of women and their inter-entanglements in theoretical, historical and cultural webs. The influence of hierarchical dualisms, a core piece of patriarchal ideology and described by Habel in this volume, is central to ecofeminist critiques. Carolyn Merchant's (1980) study of the historical development of Eurowestern ideas and beliefs about the Earth has shown that these dualisms were, and continue to be, foundational to Eurowestern thought, values and attitudes. Ecofeminism challenges a patriarchal, hierarchical and dualistic world view and holds that the domination of the Earth is enmeshed with the oppression of women. Ecofeminists claim that all oppressions, such as those based on class,

Brown 1999. A 1996 United Nation's report suggests that between 150 and 200 species become extinct every day. See 'We're Killing the Planet Even Faster than Feared: U.N.', *The Toronto Star*, 20 April 1996. John Livingston states that the present period of mass extinction is comparable to those 65, 94, 213 and 248 million years ago. See Livingston 1994.

3.   A recent list of primary publications can be found in Sturgeon (1997: 28-32), and it is not exhaustive.

ethnicity, gender, orientation, ableism and the Earth are interconnected within a logic of domination (Warren 1987).

Feminist theorists using liberal, cultural, social, socialist, radical and postmodern critiques perceive differently the relationship between women and the natural world, and between misogyny and the ecological crisis (Merchant 1992). In addition, ecofeminist positions embrace distinct ecological paradigms, including resource-based environmentalism, social ecology, deep ecology and/or cosmology. These variations within ecofeminism reflect not only the differences in the analysis of the woman/nature connection, but also differences on such fundamental matters as the origin of and the solutions to women's oppression, the theory of human nature, as well as the conceptions of freedom, equality and epistemology on which various feminist theories depend (Warren 1987).

Ecological feminism is *feminist* because of a commitment to the recognition and elimination of male-gender bias and the development of practices, policies and theories which do not reflect this bias. It is *ecological* due to an understanding of and commitment to the valuing and preserving of ecosystems, broadly understood (Warren 1990). Far from being reductionist or simplistic, ecofeminism is a textured field of theoretical and experiential insights, encompassing different forms of knowledge, and is embodied in the concrete. Ecofeminism is international in scope, and is analysis, critique, vision and action (Eaton 1996: 77).

Ecofeminism and Religion

The ecofeminist challenge to religion is profound and permeates all layers of religious reflection and praxis (Eaton 1998b). Ecofeminist perspectives are developing within classical religions such as Judaism, Buddhism, Christianity, Islam, within new movements such as Wiccan, Goddess or New Age, and in some indigenous traditions. As Ruether points out, the cultural-symbolic level of the relationship between sexism and ecological exploitation is the ideological superstructure that reflects and sanctions the social, economic, political and religious order (Ruether 2000). Challenging foundational presuppositions and reshaping the infrastructure of religion are substantive hurdles (Eaton 1996, 2000). Cherished notions, such as the inferiority of women, need to be rejected. Religious ecofeminists also claim that the Earth is sacred, and this sacrality is neither explicit nor accepted in some traditions.

Given that ecofeminism embodies diversity and is evolving continuously, the implications are impossible to delineate. There are lively debates concerning essentialism, romantic or utopic dreams of a harmonious past or future, apolitical spiritualities, and the relationship between theory and social transformation (Eaton 1995). Nonetheless, ecofeminists desire to heal the wounds caused by the splits between nature and culture, mind and body, women and men, reason and emotion, spirit and matter, theory and action, and ultimately between humans and the Earth.

Ecofeminism and the Bible: A Methodological Maze

The implications of ecofeminist biblical readings have yet to be explored in depth. Currently there are few samples to study (Eaton 1996: 84-85). Although there are ecofeminist interpretations of some biblical passages (Primavesi 1991: 222-44; Clifford 1995: 178-84), and many (non-feminist) ecological readings of the Bible, there have been neither discussions of ecological or ecofeminist Biblical *methodologies* nor deliberations about the *function* of the Bible in ecological-feminist inquiries. To explore an intersection between ecofeminism and the Bible, the first task is to develop some methodological and hermeneutical parameters which could guide ecofeminist readings of biblical texts. This is the basic goal of this chapter.

Feminist biblical methods are a primary resource in developing ecofeminist biblical tools. The evolving sophistication in analytic instruments emerging from feminist biblical scholars over the past 30 years is unparalleled in biblical scholarship. Although feminist methodologies are not ecofeminist, and an ecological standpoint is not an addendum to feminism, they are a reasonable place to begin to develop ecofeminist strategies for reading texts. Further, it is evident that the 'merest fragment of feminist biblical scholarship constitutes a challenge of established assumptions' (Bal 1989: 15; Milne 1995: 47-52). Therefore, the following reflection relies on feminist analysis to guide ecofeminist biblical reflection, as the ecofeminist challenge will be at least the same as, if not greater than, the feminist one. From the bountiful opus of feminist scholarship, I am selecting three issues, which although interwoven will be presented separately. These are the sacrality and authority of the text, location of meaning and ethical accountability. The purpose of this discussion is to accentuate some of the issues related to interpretation which must be addressed prior to delving into the texts.

Sacrality and Authority of the Bible

Few texts, if any, have been as formative to Eurowestern consciousness and world view as the Bible. The simple weight of biblical influence suggests an accountability to the ecological crisis. A direct
causality is far too naive, Lynn White notwithstanding. Among the
myriad causal possibilities, the issues of the sacrality of the text and
the canon are germane.

Feminist scholarship has revealed that the formation of the religious canon is foremost a question of power; texts became authoritative first, then were deemed sacred and canonical (Kwok 1995: 17).
The naming of a text as sacred, thus holding some intrinsic power,
revelation, truth and divine authority is culturally conditioned and
involves a complex interplay of processes at both the level of formation and for the reading community (Kwok 1995: 16-19). To engage
with an ancient text on such crucial issues as the ecological crisis, and
to listen for the Earth voice, indicates that these texts hold some
sacrality/authority, even if one eventually stands in resistance to
them.

Given two assumptions of the Earth Bible Project, that this project
does not endorse ahistorical, dogmatic and bona fide interpretations,
and that the Bible, although revelatory, is neither a document of revelation nor revelation itself, then the authority of the Bible cannot be
direct, binding or absolute (Schüssler Fiorenza 1985: 25). Although
within the Earth Bible Project there will be divergent positions, an
ecofeminist perspective would insist that the issue of biblical authority and sacrality must be addressed to avoid ideological maneuvers
(Kwok 1995: 29).

Feminists have been engaged with the canonical debate (Milne
1995: 69).[4] Most feminist scholars refuse, in one way or another, the
validity of an authoritatively closed canon. The Bible may be accepted
in essence but not in its totality. In some instances distinctive principles or motifs/themes are retrieved as pivotal hermeneutics and
criteria for approbation, such as the prophetic–messianic tradition, the
Bible as a historical and structuring prototype (Schüssler Fiorenza

---

4.   Feminists have addressed the (neo-orthodox) canon within the canon, and
the limitation of closure which prevents eliminating anti-women and anti-earth
texts and adding women-authored texts, as in other disciplines. Further, the closed
canon functions to safeguard a kind of truth, yet can repress other truths, forms of
the sacred and freeze our imagination (Kwok and Schüssler Fiorenza 1998; Kwok
1995: 18).

1992: 149), or as a poetic classic (McFague 1982: 54-60). Feminist communities may claim interpretive authority by affirming liberative elements, adding sacred stories, and limiting or negating the authority of sexist texts. Some distinguish kinds of biblical authority (accepted, imposed, illustrative [Gebara 1998: 7-19]). Others refuse to give the Bible authority, because 'women's voices have been virtually silenced and have to be teased out, if they can be found at all' (Milne 1995: 69). These insights from feminist research bear directly on the development of ecofeminist hermeneutics. Many biblical texts are not only androcentric but anthropocentric, meaning that the Earth is quasi-absent as the drama of human (male) life takes center-stage.

Since feminists are not able to incorporate an authoritative sacred canon into a feminist paradigm (Milne 1995: 70), the same is likely to be true of ecofeminists. Since the Bible has served ideologies and practices which have led to the exploitation and destruction of the Earth, it is necessary to be cautious when approaching it with Earth consciousness. For ecofeminists, as long as the Bible is accorded authoritative status, we accord authoritative status to patriarchy. Patriarchy, as a cultural ideology and phenomenon, depends upon the dual dominations of women and nature/Earth. For ecofeminists, the choices are explicit: to accept the patriarchal Bible as sacred and authoritative and be content to expose its patriarchy, or expose its patriarchy and reject it as sacred and authoritative (Milne 1993: 167). From an ecofeminist perspective, the Bible can be accepted only as contingent and provisional (adapted from West 1993: 89).

Location of Meaning
The biblical scholarly question is no longer *what* the Bible means, or even *why* it means, but *how* it means (Milne 1995: 66). Historical-critical methods have been displaced by interest in untangling the dynamic interaction between reader(s) and text. The innumerable cultural-religious matrices of texts and readers, multiple historical consciousnesses, different hermeneutical traditions and reasons for engaging with texts have resulted in an abundance of biblical methodologies, which have led to a melange of meaning-making patterns that defy the postmodern imagination.[5] The Bible is a multi-discoursed and multi-structured entity catalyzing a diversity of meanings

5.   *The Postmodern Bible* details seven current postmodern approaches to biblical study; postmodern pointing to, at the least, a crisis of legitimation of meaning, authority, and of tools for searching for knowledge and meaning, an incredulity towards metanarratives (Bible and Culture Collective 1995).

which emerge as different communities create meanings from their distinct and plural social, political and contextual identities. The postmodern biblical literature is vast. The present discussion is limited to highlighting the nexus of concerns for feminist scholarship about the location of meaning, drawing primarily from reader-response hermeneutics.

Reader-response approaches claim that meaning is a property of the act of reading and is located predominantly in the reader (Bal 1989: 13). 'Reading is no more than actualizing possibilities in one's own mind and projecting them upon the object named "text" '. A text cannot lend itself in a direction that is not within the reader. This is not to say that the reader may personally agree, but that it is the reader who makes—not takes—the meaning from the text. Although to study a text for its intention, social background, political-historical impulses, social events or ecological consciousness reveals something of its origin, meaning cannot be derived primarily from this stand-point.

There is disagreement as to how far the reader is responsible for meaning-making. Some post-structuralist feminists relocate all mean-ing in the reader(s). For Mary McClintock Fulkerson, meaning is a social signifying process that neither resides in, nor can be derived from, the text (1991: 53-73). Meaning is to be found in discursive practices and in the differently configured community(ies) of inter-pretation (Fulkerson 1991: 60-61). Fulkerson asserts that it is inade-quate to claim that a text is itself oppressive or pernicious, and that such epistemological claims are not only incoherent but are ultimately inadequate politically (1991: 61).

Others, myself included, argue that both the text and the reader are accountable for meaning, and although meaning is a product of the reader, it is rooted in the possibilities of the text (Bal 1989; Milne 1995: 67). The text is constrained by the historical, biographical and ideolog-ical reality of the author reflecting on the context within the conven-tions of the time. Readers engage in meaning production by reflecting upon the text with her/his plural identities, eco-social locations, commitments and subject positions, directed also by the conventions of the time (Bal 1989: 13-15).

The patriarchal stamp of the Bible is a further insidious constraint (Milne 1993, 1995). Milne's view is that reformist feminist hermeneu-tics are not viable because the patriarchal bias of the text is integral to the very structure of the biblical tradition (Milne 1993: 168). The Bible cannot be reread, refurbished, rehabilitated or reinterpreted into an adequate spiritual source for women (Milne 1993: 148). Milne's position is that feminist poststructuralist approaches can transform the way we relate to, interpret and understand the Bible, but they cannot rescue the Bible itself from patriarchy (Milne 1993: 164). In fact, she would argue that the hierarchical dualisms that are a source of the current socio-ecological problems and critiqued by ecofeminists are inherent in the biblical sources of Christian theologies. Dualistic interpretations have not been imposed upon the Bible, but derived from them (Milne 1993: 166). This is a valid challenge to ecofeminist readings of the Bible.

It is evident that such culturally founding texts as the Bible have been, are and will be used to shape social reality (Bal 1989: 13). The Earth Bible Project is based on the premise that a refreshing read of the Bible with Earth consciousness will reveal some necessary and useful insights to shape social reality in resisting ecological ruin and reclaiming a sense of sacrality of the Earth. However, to approach the Bible, even using the hermeneutical lens provided by the six ecojustice principles, does not circumvent the reader ordering and reworking the collection of possible meanings in the encounters with the text. Reader-response theory insists that the reader take the bulk of the responsibility in this reshaping of meaning. Therefore an ecofeminist reading would be very different than, for example, Maori, indigenous North American, patriarchal or Russian Orthodox reading position(s).

Ethical Accountability

Few scholars address directly the ethical responsibility for, and the political consequences of, reading the Bible (Bal 1989: 13). If one reads texts from overt 'politicized' positions such as feminist, gay/lesbian, black, indigenous, mujerista,[6] 'the poor'—and ecological—the readerly quality of *all* interpretation is glaring. The most significant question in biblical inquiry is 'who constitutes the reader(s)?', because their interpretative acts, historical and ideological biases and the blindness inherent in privileged positions have a radical impact on the social and ecological consequences of their interpretations.

Many claim that the Christian tradition and elements of the Bible have been used to foster ecological ruin. Given the apparent validity of this claim, to continue to turn towards the Bible means that the dance between the constraints of the texts and the parameters of the reader is one where the steps need to be utterly clear, conscious and

---

6.   Mujerista refers to theology from the perspective of Latinas as an intrinsic element of Hispanic/Latino theology, creating a public voice for Latinas in which they can hear, find and express themselves. See Isasi-Díaz 1996.

explicit. The ethical implications are decisive. As Mieke Bal states: 'The Bible, of all books, is the most dangerous one, the one that has been endowed with the power to kill' (Bal 1991: 14).

However, the ethical implications are not readily apparent because they are hidden in the reader-text dynamic: these fluid movements of meaning-production. Some questions help expose what is camouflaged, such as, 'Who has the right and power to speak'? This is true for the narrator and reader(s) of the text. What would be her/his social location? From what position or event is the narrator speaking when the Earth is the agent referred to, such as in Hosea, Jeremiah, Job, and so on? For the reader(s)? From what privilege is the narrator/reader acting and interpreting? What is the ecological consciousness of the readers? How knowledgeable are they of the ecological crisis, the critique of modernity, global economic systems and ideologies, hierarchical dualisms and how they function, gender analyses, liberation movements and biblical methods? What are the commitments of the narrator and the reader(s) which revealed in which way she/he represents the subject—the Earth? What communities are and are not represented by these views? Who acts in the text, and for/against whom? Who takes actions from the interpretations, and for/against whom? Clearly the gender of the reader is as significant as the gender of the author, for a plethora of reasons (Milne 1993: 171). Mieke Bal elaborates further on why this method greatly assists attending to ethical accountability (Bal 1989: 15-19).

Biblical interpretation necessitates a multi-axial, multi-dimensional framework of evaluation, an integrative method and many hermeneutics of suspicion and analysis. Because the Bible has been used to legitimate myriad oppressions (ethnocentrism, classism, sexism, colonialism, cultural imperialism) we need multifaceted tools to work with these texts. Similar to the ecojustice principles, Kwok suggests ten theses to address racism, ethnocentrism and sexism in biblical interpretation (Kwok 1995: 84-95). Unfortunately she, and the majority of feminist (biblical) scholars do not address the ecological crisis. Equally problematic is that most eco-biblical scholars do not use multifaceted or feminist frameworks, and thus the hydra-headed forms of patriarchal domination reside overtly or covertly within their interpretations. Herein lies the necessity of adequate ecofeminist biblical methods.

Ethical accountability of biblical interpretation is central to an ecofeminist perspective. Further, and given the multiples of multiples of interpretations possible and the inevitable conflicts that emerge, ethical accountability acts as a restraint. Bal blandly states the problem: 'one can easily disagree with my readings, if only [because] one does not share my interests' (Bal 1987: 132). Even if some interpreters of textual passages condone the oppression of women, ecological ruin, elitism—and many do—those with an Earth consciousness and understanding of how oppression functions will refute, perhaps not the interpretation, but the praxis. Still, some texts are irredeemable.

The six ecojustice principles provide an ethic of accountability for the Earth Bible Project. Each fine-tunes the lenses through which the reader is to look at and engage with the text. The six principles of intrinsic worth, interconnectedness, voice, purpose, custodianship and resistance not only orient the reader, but constrain the ethical impact of the interpretations of the text. In an implicit and appropriate way, the principles have priority over the text.[7] However excellent guides they may be, they are not addressing the issues mentioned above, that of sacrality, location of meaning and ethical accountability. These cannot be added as principles. They function as dynamics within the dialogue among the principles, readers and text to insist on an adequate biblical method, to address the over-arching and subtle influence of one's world view, and to stress the significance of the location of the reader.

Ecofeminist Reflections on the Ecojustice Principles

The Earth Bible Project awakens the reader to the Earth through its focus on the six ecojustice principles. Each will be considered in light of the preceding deliberations. The two tracts of the article—adequate biblical methodologies and the need for alternative world views— merge in this discussion. My emphasis throughout has been to stress the contextual nature and location of the interpreter and to apply this also to the principles. The goal is to elaborate on and support the principles, while indicating where there are interpretive dangers from an ecofeminist perspective.

---

7.   This is entirely appropriate. In the same vein as the liberatory experiences of women have priority over misogynist texts, earth consciousness is the stance from which one is reading the text. As all advocational, liberation theologies are about praxis, the Earth Bible Project is oriented towards the liberation of Earth from oppression, and reading the Bible to see what is there. If the Bible asserts that the earth is irrelevant, such a position will be refuted from the perspective of the principles.

1. *The Principle of Intrinsic Worth: The universe, the Earth and all its components have intrinsic worth/value*

The perspective that the Earth and every form of life have intrinsic worth/value is an ethic currently developing and debated within ecological discourse. Seemingly simple, this ethic or stance has textured layers of complexities. How one actually gives, recognizes, argues for, appraises and implements 'intrinsic value' is ambiguous. To speak of intrinsic value with a broad understanding is to accord or recognize an innate freedom and values to Life-processes; noting that to accord or recognize are two distinct ethical theories, world views, experiences, value judgments and teleologies.

A dilemma for ecofeminists has been that 'intrinsic value' can be applied to the Earth community and be oblivious to the associated political, sexist, ethnocentric and class issues. Ecofeminists insist on making this connection explicit. Several environmental philosophers and adherents of deep ecology, a movement that has championed the cause of intrinsic value, have been noted for their lack of critical, political and/or (eco)feminist analysis.[8] Others do not ground ecological ethics in notions of the intrinsic value of the natural world and they contend that there are no objective values in nature (Callicott 1994). Many ecofeminists would share the position that values and knowledge are relational, and originate in the experience of the beholder(s). Postmodernism reveals that facts are theory-laden, theories are value-laden, and values are shaped by particular contextualized questions and issues.

It is impossible here to delve in detail into the complexities of 'intrinsic value'.[9] The inherent 'goodness of Earth' is a foundational pretext to the Jewish and Christian traditions. However, the antithesis is also present in Christianity, in both teachings and praxis. Therefore, how will the retrieval of texts supporting a principle of intrinsic worth yet embedded within anti-Earth interpretations, attitudes and actions *function* to resist further ecological ruin? How will new and very necessary reinterpretations *function* within the ebb and flow among texts, communities of interpretation, patriarchal world views and praxis? How will a retrieval of the intrinsic value of Earth join with the struggles for freedom of others oppressed, namely most women? Here a social/political ecofeminist analysis is an integral element.

8.   For discussions of ecofeminism and deep ecology, wherein ecofeminists are distancing themselves from the latter, see Eaton 1997b; Plumwood 1993; Slicer 1995.

9.   As an example this discussion see Rolston 1994.

2. *Principle of Interconnectedness: The Earth is a community of interconnected living things that are mutually dependent on each other for life and
survival*

Ecofeminists, deep ecologists and many working in the natural, ato-
mic and cosmological sciences affirm the principle of interconnectedness. Ecofeminists and feminist theorists have done extensive work
with interconnectedness and relational paradigms. If relationality is
the lens through which one reflects, it is possible to see a vital-intere-
lational creativity existing on every level of reality, both creative and
salvific (Ruether 2000). It may be possible to detect interconnectedness
as the basic dynamic of life, and evident within biblical texts.

Nevertheless there are difficulties in developing an ethic based on
the principle of interconnectedness, specifically if it is based in the
new physics. Many environmental theorists and increasingly theologians use interconnectedness as an overarching framework.[10] Some
maintain that such an environmental ethic can claim universality
because it is based in science, and 'scientific foundations are universally endorsed' (Callicott 1994: 189). However, there is no consensus
on the metaphysical implications from the new physics, such as hol-
ism, interconnectedness, and intimacy with all life (Eaton 1997b: 114-
19). More so, the entangled interpretations among physics, God and
hierarchical dualisms, and the gender bias and 'priestly (male) culture
of physics' are, to some, simply a new form of misogyny (Wertheim
1997: 13-16). Yet, a sense of intimacy and felt connectedness with all
life is intuited by many people, and is supported with some ecosystems science.

Last, principles of interconnectedness and intrinsic worth should
not be grounded only in science, and cannot provide an objective base
to which all parties can appeal equally. Differences and disagreements
will prevail because they are often about the access to, and the
distribution and use of knowledge and power. Unequal power relations are often accepted as 'common sense'. Ecofeminists are adamant
about the need to analyse power, and how it affects cultural structures, values, ideals and goals and the creation of knowledge.

10. For example see Cooper and Palmer 1998; Rasmussen 1996; Oelschlaeger
1995; Tucker and Grim 1993; Haught 1993; Ruether 1992; Primavesi 1991; Berry
1988; Griffin 1988.

3. *The Principle of Voice: The Earth is a subject capable of raising its voice in celebration and against injustice*

The notions of the subjectivity and agency of the Earth are an intellectual minefield. It is a manner of communicating the sense that the Earth is alive and has an integrity larger than the sum of the parts. A consciousness of the Earth as a living entity is increasing worldwide. Although through both science and religion/spirituality, the insights of the wholeness of the Earth and its vitality are emerging into human consciousness, it is not in the same form for all. Meanings and implications differ. I will not debate the point, as this fragile and tentative consciousness is barely present, and intense systematic scrutiny is not helpful.

To experience the Earth as a 'speaking' subject, a living entity, is to engage all of the senses (Abram 1997). To articulate this is to move into the realm of poesies;[11] vivid and intense imagery being the only metaphoric language that can contain and mediate these experiences. This is also an effective terrain of transformation. However, there are some questions that need answering, such as 'Who will speak for the Earth? With what power and for whom do they speak? How can humans speak for the Earth? With what knowledge and looking through which lens?' The Earth Bible Team writes of 'Earth-sensitive humans'; I wonder who would qualify, and who would decide. They suggest that they could mediate the voices of the Earth. Who would listen? Why would they listen? The reader may refer to the questions suggested above in the section on ethical accountability. I am not denying the authenticity of what the Earth Bible Team claim, but rather engaging in the process of concretizing them into complex, differentiated and postmodern realities where power-differentials are operative.

For example, the interconnections among population, consumption and ecological ruin are serious, highly volatile and convoluted. If some Earth-sensitive voices claim power in the conversation around population control, the direction is frightening. Currently, in China, where population controls exist for Earth-sensitive reasons, over 90 percent of fetuses aborted are female. The projected future use of the

---

11. The term 'poesies' refers here to the realm of expression for the deepest realities that defy description. A literal interpretation of the earth as a speaking subject is impossible, thus to illuminate the reality of which this principle is addressing is to engage in deep symbolic language which mediates the reality and experience. That the earth is alive is a profound truth, albeit difficult to prove in an age of linear science. There remains something ineffable and elusive about this claim.

Human Genome Project is anyone's guess, and could easily become a form of eugenics. The current power/decision lines follow patterns based on ethnic, gender, class and sexual orientation.

Further, the global economic climate of corporate rule and a green backlash to environmentalists are not favourable to the challenges of the 'voice of the Earth'. The discrimination against and the deaths of the Earth-sensitive humans are ongoing everywhere in the world, which reveals that there are deep-seated and frightening reasons for, and efficacy in, silencing voices (Karliner 1997; Rowell 1996). An analysis of power and how it functions must accompany the principles.

Another example of the potentially pernicious plasticity of this principle can be found in popular interpretations of ecological disasters. Headlines in national papers read 'God has abandoned us' and 'The Earth strikes back!' referring to recent hurricanes and tornados. These interpretations of the capability of the Earth reveal much about the operative world view and belief systems. The ensuing actions will differ depending on the interpretations. I am not suggesting that such trite interpretations are inevitable, but that they are occurring. It is true that the voice of the earth has been silenced and needs urgently to be heard. However to acknowledge a subjectivity of the Earth and to give it voice, means a mediated voice through human understanding and prejudice filtered through whatever is the operative world view. Ecofeminism is a great tool for examining surreptitious world views and belief systems. Therefore, to reread the Bible with this principle may open new horizons, but it would be naive to assume that all voices will be benevolent to life on Earth.

4. *Principle of Purpose: The universe, the Earth and all its components are part of a dynamic cosmic design within which each piece has a place in the overall goal of that design*
This principle functions to provide a fundamental orientation to the whole. To accept fully a comprehensive ecological, Earth-based approach is to situate the genesis and specific histories of each religion within the history of the Earth and to perceive that the entire religious enterprise is an emerging process of human development within the evolutionary processes of the Earth (Berry 1988). This prevents our religious frameworks from being the definitive references. The insights/teachings remain of ultimate value, but some become relativized within a new understanding of our radical dependence on Earth and the evolutionary processes (Eaton 1998b, 1999). This opens the possibility of a new religious moment because, in Thomas Berry's words, we may begin to see the universe as:

> the primary sacred community, the primary revelation of the divine, the
> primary subject of incarnation, the primary unit of redemption, the pri-
> mary referent in any discussion of reality or of value. Any human activ-
> ity must be seen primarily as an activity of the universe and only secon-
> darily an activity of the individual (Berry 1985: 6).

Adopting this principle challenges the prevailing and dysfunctional
cosmologies in which patriarchal religious traditions are immersed.
Several ecofeminist theologians are engaged in recovering the significance of cosmology (Eaton 1998a, 1996; McFague 1993a; Ruether 1992;
Primavesi 1991). Reflection on cosmology is only beginning, and the
dialogue among world views, cosmology and biblical work will be an
effective avenue to follow. The great danger of this principle is its
potential to function as a hegemonic metanarrative, and it is difficult,
verging on impossible, to combine it with postmodernism.[12]

5. The Principle of Custodianship: The Earth is a balanced and diverse domain
where responsible custodians can function as partners with, rather than
rulers over, the Earth to sustain its balance and diversity
The shift here from stewardship to custodianship is subtle, and
addresses the difficult concept of anthropocentrism. There is much
discussion about these terms, and more significantly, the dilemma of
how we imagine, (re)discover or create sustainable human-Earth relations not based on exploitative domination. Further, there is no avoiding the enormous human accountability and responsibility for, and
impact upon, the Earth.

The problems with stewardship are being addressed, yet I think
some remain with custodianship. Apart from the fact that steward-
ship/custodianship are the easiest ecological/ethical frameworks for
anthropocentric-minded people to accept, there are reasons to be leery
of these models, even as a strategy. They can keep the hierarchal
dualisms in place, preserve a human–Earth division, and miss the
fundamental reality of human dependence on the Earth. They signify

---

12.   Some are developing reconstructive postmodernism, basing their work in a
viewpoint similar to this (Spretnak 1991: 17-2; Toulmin 1985: 217-75; Griffin 1988:
passim). However appealing this paradigm is to Eurowestern-minded individuals,
it has a culturally hegemonic element that has not sufficiently been addressed.
Indigenous cosmologies, East Indian, Chinese and Andean (for example) may
share some elements in common with this principle, but they tend to resist the
imperialist form of this new cosmology. Further, the location of the problematic is
not only the world view in question and its derivation, i.e. which cosmology, but
how it has been used and to what ends. The same hermeneutic of suspicion applies
to this principle.

a shift within the present system rather than a vision of a new and different order, and are not a feminist ethic (Clifford 1995: 184-85). Some suggest solidarity as an option (Clifford 1995: 185).

To encounter an anthropocentric ethic in Scripture is inevitable. The Bible is a patriarchal document. Yet, all texts are not fully anchored in the dualisms; Job, for example. Still, I am not persuaded that any language will take us from the current patriarchal world view without first addressing, in a sustained manner, the issue of world view itself. For example, John Haught considers that much of the reluctance of theology to address the ecological crisis in depth stems from a prior reluctance to think about evolution (Haught 1993: 32). My worry is that until the larger evolutionary world view is acknowledged, custodianship (even solidarity), may be merely the same poison in new wrappings.

6. *Principle of Resistance: The Earth and its components not only suffer injustices at the hands of humans, but actively resist them in the struggle for justice*
This principle is very interesting, as it requires imagining the Earth not only as a subject capable of agency, but one that has a sensitivity toward justice for the Earth and to the human community. Factions within the human community register with the Earth, according to some interpretations of texts/readers, and the Earth responds. My concerns are not necessarily with the validity of the principle, and although I am sure that the earth is not a passive victim, I am not sure that the Earth 'fights back'. To construct the Earth as either victim or as an active agent of resistance is just that: a construction. I am concerned about issues of power: 'Who will interpret the actions of the Earth, with which tools and through what lens/world view?' Similar concerns were raised earlier.

Evaluation

This article has followed two tracts: methodology and world view, both intertwined within the location of the reader. The methodological maze of biblical interpretation from an ecofeminist perspective, and commentaries on the six ecojustice principles of the Earth Bible Project were presented. The results of the Earth Bible Project are in the preliminary stages. Given the significance of the Bible for cultural constructs, it must be studied, investigated and challenged when needed. That the Bible is a patriarchal document is undeniable, and quite reasonable given that it was formed within a patriarchal period.

In addition, most contemporary readers are also formed by this world view, thus the biases are hard to ferret out. Patriarchal world views are very powerful, and most so when they are accepted as reflecting reality. Patriarchy is the operative world view virtually everywhere in the world, although not always shared by those who benefit least. Pillars of patriarchy are the women–nature construct and the denigration of both. For many, to read the Bible from an anti-women and anti-Earth perspective is to enjoy a comfortable read. Therefore, there can be no simple application of these principles to biblical interpretation. First, the location of the reader is pivotal to their interpretations and applications. Second, the principles themselves are not, and cannot be, self-evident. Five further comments are in order.

First, some ecological theologians have stated that the aim of biblical scholarship is to reveal the authentic definition and purpose of the text, and given this, that the Bible has clear and consistent positions on environmental issues (Beed and Beed 1998: 66). This statement, to me, reveals a substantial lack of awareness of the methodological and interpretive issues raised in this article. An ecofeminist perspective requires explicit and ethically accountable methods of biblical readings to assist in responding to the ecological crisis.

Second, there are some specific commitments within the Christian tradition that act as impediments to developing an Earth consciousness, and one is the biblical dedication. Because our sense of the divine is encouraged to be derived extensively from biblical sources, an awareness of the revelation of the divine in the natural world has been all but lost. The emphasis on biblical authority, coupled with an ignorance of the nature of religion in general, have caused the basic perception, that our sense of the divine comes from the grandeur of the universe and from the resplendent modes of expressions of life on Earth, to be engulfed and distrusted.

Third, the biblical-redemptive story rather than the creation story has been chosen as the primary context of understanding the Christian tradition, and indeed life itself. The tradition has made commitments to biblical revelation over against the revelation of the natural world, to the salvific over the creative process, to the human over the Earth community as the norm of reality and value, to male supremacy, and to progress meaning an increased human well-being over a sense of progress of the advance in the well-being of the entire life community (Berry 1986: 7).

Fourth, it is urgent that the biblical tradition not only engage in inter-religious dialogue, but interpret itself in light of the worlds' religions within a tapestry of revelations (Berry 1986: 7). With collective efforts, the transformative and prophetic insights and particular values of distinct traditions can be identified and affirmed, and assist with collaborative responses to the socio-ecological crises. Berry suggests that we need to read the four scriptures which reveal the true dimensions of the real: that is, the cosmic, verbal, historical, and the scriptures written in the very structure of the Earth (Berry 1977). To revive such a rich notion of Scripture and revelation would allow room for new religious sensitivities to develop. The central task, from an ecofeminist perspective, is to align religious efforts within the rhythms and limits of Earth processes.

Fifth, and most difficult, is the unresolved tension between the need for a unifying vision that is ecologically sound, and respect for diversity, cultural specificity and distinctiveness. The Eurowestern tendency for (enforced) homogeneity is imperialistic and oppressive, and is often criticized by ecofeminists. Further, the relativism and nihilism of some postmodernism makes normative ethical and ecological claims impossible. To develop an ecological meta-narrative and, at the same time, to accept subjectivity and particularity is an enormous challenge. Paradoxically, neither is suitable, yet both are necessary.

In conclusion, the Earth Bible Project is an appreciated and desired initiative. There are no facile solutions to the dilemma of the ecological crisis and its causes. The Bible is an influential book nestled within a forceful tradition and an anti-women/anti-Earth world view that has impacted the world—for good, bad and much in between. Its relationship to the ecological crisis is ambiguous at best. We must understand its power, authority, insights, limitations and potential for transformation in the current era of immense difficulties. We must also re-realize that the Earth is sacred, and that a sense of the sacredness of the Earth and life has been constitutive of spiritual awareness from time immemorial (Eliade 1959: 11-13).

The promises and the problems of biblical Earth consciousness will be a necessary voice in the coming decades. I welcome and support the Earth Bible Project and its principles, acknowledging that the derivations, explanations and implications are not straightforward in a postmodern world. Nonetheless, apprehension persists. Ecofeminist biblical scholarship unveils that all interpretations are positional and political. This is why the Bible is such a dangerous text. 'The feeling that there is a text in support of one's view makes texts such efficient ideological tools' (Bal 1987: 132).

Sketches for Earth Readings of the Book of Amos

David Jobling and Nathan Loewen

Introduction

The book of Amos is not among the 'classic' biblical texts for ecotheo-logical or 'Earth' reading, as are texts like the beginning of Genesis, Psalms 8 and 104, or Job 38–41. We see our readings here as contribut-ing to the development of Earth reading as part of a method for reading *any* text.

Feminist reading of the Bible, by analogy, focused in its beginnings on texts that were directly relevant to its concerns. Only later was the critical question asked: what is a feminist reading of a text that is not by, for or about women? So Earth reading, too, needs to move beyond the 'obvious' texts.

New ways of reading the Bible enter an already full, complicated and conflicted scene. Earth readings must take their place—indeed make their place—in relation to many other readings, including many kinds of 'liberation' readings. The more conscious we are of these relationships with other kinds of readings, the better. It is in part in response to this situation that we offer here not a single Earth reading of Amos, but rather some sketches or points of departure, with an eye also to linkages with other methods.

It is widely accepted that the Bible and 'biblical religion' have been complicit in the long history that has led to our current ecological cri-sis. The advent and development of the Israelite world view had the effect of demythologizing nature. Radical monotheism posited a god whose powers overarch all known phenomena, and hence placed dis-tance between God and 'nature'. The Earth became mainly a stage for God's historical action (Baker 1990: 19). This was a major step on the way from ancient Near Eastern mythology to the de-divinized thought of modern times. In the Bible, the Earth is only rarely personi-fied as an autonomous subject, and it is rarely spoken of in a decid-edly mythological way (Eulinger 1995: 45).

The main theological tradition has followed this lead. Western theology has been as much an artefact of the culture of dualism and domination as any other product of human consciousness. This history has culminated in an

> ultramodernist technological utopianism…willing to accept apocalyptic consequences for the earth while transferring traditional progress-optimism into the heavens…we may call this the eschatology of progress, an apocalypse without judgment (Keller 1997: 89).

There are in the Bible exceptions to this tendency, just as in subsequent history there have been outstanding exceptions; for example, St Francis of Assisi and Teilhard de Chardin perceived the world and its inhabitants as sacred in themselves rather than merely a means to human perfection and salvation (Boff 1995: 152); their views were not representative of the views of their contemporaries.

We need to start any Earth reading by admitting that the Bible is part of the problem before it is part of the solution. As with feminist readings of the Bible, the impulse to Earth readings has come less from the Bible and mainstream theology than from outside—from voices that warn us of impending disaster, and convict our religious traditions of complicity in it.

Those who have pioneered 'ecotheology' see their work partly as a critique of traditional theology, ethics and scriptural analysis. Catherine Keller neatly characterizes this as a theological practice of recycling (1997: 92). In our pursuit of Earth readings, we also need to discern the toxins at work in religion that break down the interrelationships of organisms and habitats on Earth. We must cleanse theology of late capitalist deterioration and compost it so that it enhances life and interrelationship.

For this task, the Earth Bible Team has proposed six ecojustice principles: intrinsic worth, interconnectedness, voice, purpose, custodianship and resistance, based on the

> axiom of social justice that the true nature, depth and force of any injustice can only be understood by those experiencing that injustice… We need first to hear the suffering of the earth and all those pieces of the earth's ecosystem that have been violated and abused (Habel 1998–99: 118).

Human sin has created alienation from the biosphere, as well as from other humans and God. Redemption must come through the establishment of solidarity with the world. Theology and biblical studies can contribute to this, but only through a thorough recycling of the biblical texts and our understanding of them.

Any use of the Bible in ecological discussions must respect the gigantic distance between the ancient experiences and views of the world and our own. The Bible will not directly warn us about wrong decisions, still less guide us to right ones; rather, its importance lies in the way it illuminates for us the formation of our most fundamental attitudes towards the Earth. Though the Bible itself forms part of the path that has led to Earth-unfriendly attitudes, its influence lies at a very early stage of that path. It speaks to us from a time before the most critical choices in the development of Western civilization were made. The Bible is the most culturally authoritative document still speaking to us from that time.

Hearing what the ancient text tells us about the making of those— mostly unwitting—choices, and learning how these choices were intertwined with developing understandings of God and humanity that we may still wish to affirm, will help us undo the fundamental attitudes underlying inappropriate contemporary choices—a task which, in the long run, is as important as facing the immediate crises.

Though not considered a classic text for discerning Earth readings, the book of Amos is an inviting one. It *is* a classic text for discovering in the Bible class analysis and resistance to the oppression of the poor; an Earth reading of Amos is a vital addition to work being done on the interface between human justice and Earth justice, notably by Leonardo Boff (see our second sketch, below).

A close reading of the book of Amos reveals a deep knowledge of both urban and rural life in Israel; there are a multitude of specific references to both environments in the text. The book of Amos presents the two as fundamentally in conflict, and affirms the rural interest. Our interest in the book is a direct development of our attempts to find a *rural* reading of Amos. We know better than to assume that the rural bias in the book of Amos will necessarily make the text more Earth-friendly—but at least it means that the issues tend to get raised.

The prophet Amos, the key figure in the book, is constructed as someone who *knows the Earth* in more than the rural sense. Within the constraints of his world view, Amos takes a *global* view of things. To judge by the extraordinary variety of geographical locations mentioned in the book, he was a travelling man—traversing the Canaanite highlands and beyond—and a deeply interested and shrewd observer of all that he saw. He also knows about history: recent events and the traditional interpretations of the history of his people. At the level of the text of the whole book as we have received it, this global perspective extends to the workings of the whole cosmos. The insistence of ecologists that we view the world comprehensively as a complex set of relationships receives support from the book of Amos.

Sketch One: Ecology as Prophecy

Ecological resistance belongs to the tradition of biblical prophecy, in the sense that any form of resistance in Western culture belongs to that tradition. Prophetic resistance to power and the status quo is part of the culture to which we belong, and we sometimes call notable resisters 'prophets'.

Rosemary Radford Ruether (1983: 20-33) argues that we can appropriate the biblical prophets for feminist resistance even when they ignore or respond negatively to women's concerns, because what we are appropriating is the 'prophetic principle'. We also draw on the same theology of resistance to oppression that the prophets did to resist the different oppression that we face. Thus ecotheologians may claim the power of biblical prophecy. Read in this way, the prophets highlight the significance of the principle of resistance. Potentially, they may be found to resist not only with and for the oppressed peoples of the Earth, but also with and for the oppressed of the Earth community and the Earth.

The prophet Amos and ecological prophecy are linked in a specific way. The eighth-century prophet Amos was a prophet of total doom. Contemporary ecologists, too, often predict total doom. Unless the public can be made to see that their actions may result in total disaster, they are apt to be indifferent.

Prophecy of total doom, however, cannot be the last word. If there are no other possibilities than doom, prophecy is pointless. The redactional history of the book of Amos provides an example of what we may call the 'management of doom prophecy'. Doom prophecy is legitimate and necessary—but only if it can be usefully received and applied.

Of particular interest for our purposes is the redactional scheme proposed by Robert B. Coote. He demarcates three stages: Amos A, Amos B and Amos C. Amos A includes the identifiable oracles of the eighth-century prophet, who castigated a specific class in northern Israel: royalty and the powerful. His message is single, specific and categorical; he announces impending inevitable catastrophe to this class.

Amos B stems from the southern Israelite kingdom, Judah, long after the fall of northern Israel's ruling classes. It includes new material constituting the main bulk of the book, as well as a reframing of Amos A. Amos B takes Amos A's doom prophecy seriously; part of its audience are refugees from the northern kingdom who have indeed

lost everything. Amos B still sees total doom as a possibility for the
new audience. But unlike Amos A it addresses a wider rather than a
specific audience; Amos B urges and warns, appeals for a decision,
and keeps the future open. It draws heavily on the resources of the
wisdom tradition.

Amos C is postexilic. It consists of a reframing of the whole book—
which was virtually complete after the changes in the Amos B redaction; Amos C looks for a conditional reversal of the doom (e.g. the
ending, 9.7-15). God's ultimate will in Amos C is a future of peace,
autonomy and fullness of life, not doom. But this future is for those
who hear and believe the prophecy; for those who do not, the doom
of Amos A awaits.

The turn from doom to hope requires a complete purging and
restructuring of society. Amos C comes from a highly polarized community, perhaps from people who see themselves as the faithful ones
who are oppressed by the powerful.

It is to Amos B and C that we owe the preservation of Amos A.
Their existence shows that people experienced Amos A's doom
prophecy as *true* beyond the situation that provoked it, and that different people experienced it as differently true.

All three of Coote's stages resonate with people concerned about
ecological issues today. Stage A evokes a 'green apocalypse' of the
inevitability of the demise of life on Earth—human life in particular—
due to human abuse of the environment. Amos A's references to the
unpredictability of weather (4.7) and to natural disasters like plague
or blight reverberate with the contemporary ecological community's
despair over industrial society's refusal to change. As in the time of
Amos, the wealthy and powerful—both nations and individuals—
seem oblivious to the danger ahead. 'Who can afford to experience
"nature" as banal, exterior, outside of immediate importance, if not
those urban elites who seem to have severed the immediate bonds of
dependency upon weather conditions?' (Keller 1997: 85). The first job
for the ecological prophets is to announce doom, to affirm that the
stakes are absolute, and that the potential loss is total.

As we have already observed, an ecotheology that stopped at total
doom would be unusable; however, different subsequent stages are
possible. A 'stage B' ecology would stress the irreversible devastation
that has happened already (cf. the fall of northern Israel), using this to
exhort the nations to ecological responsibility in the hope of preserving the integrity of what remains. The 'wisdom' of Amos B might
model the broader perspective that people will have to achieve if this
'last chance' is to grasped.

Stage C ecology—the survival of the *remnant*—might, in a radical form, note that humans are not the only inhabitants of the Earth, and be resigned to the possibility that we are not the ones who will survive. Humans as a whole, in such a view, constitute the 'ecological oppressors'! A less radical option might posit the survival of the 'ecologically righteous' humans—those who continue to dwell lightly on the Earth, after the exploiters have destroyed themselves by making demands that the Earth could no longer meet.

Sketch Two: Earth Justice and Human Justice

The link is frequently made between the current ecological crisis and the exploitative practices of global capitalism. According to Leonardo Boff (1995: 27), for example,

> There is a form of socio-economic and political violence directed against peoples, nations, and classes; the consequences are ruined relationships, hunger, disease, and death, and ecological crime against the most complex beings in nature. Violence against nature leads to contamination of the biosphere and degradation of ecosystems... The present dominant model of society is a social sin (the rupture of social relations) and an ecological sin (the rupture of relations between humankind and the environment). It is not only present-day classes and ecosystems that are exploited, but future classes and ecosystems. We are all responsible for the mechanisms that comprise a threat of disease and death to social life, in fact to the entire system of planetary life.

This link between social justice and ecojustice demonstrates that the Earth Bible Project's principle of interconnectedness is not confined to biological interdependencies, but also includes social, political and economic interactions.

The Bible sometimes also links these two concerns. A classic example is the Sabbath legislation. Just as the Sabbath day is a time of rest for all people, regardless of social status, so is the seventh year a time of rest for the land, to the benefit of the poor and even the wild beasts (Exod. 23.10-12, Lev. 25.2-7), as well as a time of release from debt slavery (Deut. 15.7-11). Prophetic literature also links the fate of the Earth to social justice (e.g. Hos. 4.1-3).

The prophet Amos is the foremost champion of social justice among the prophets. Should we then anticipate that he will perceive and pursue the link with ecological concerns? Hardly, when this link is far from obvious or uncontroversial even in our own time and situation. Socialist systems have been among the worst offenders against the Earth. Whereas the correlation between ecology and the many strands of feminism has generally been positive (notably apparent in contemporary ecofeminisms), the correlation between ecology and the liberation of the poor has been much less clear. Marxist theory has usually made a wide separation between relationships among humans ('social relations of production') and relationships with the Earth ('material relations of production'). Only through the work of people like Boff are we beginning to see how necessary it is to bring these struggles together.

The passion of Amos for the poor makes the prophet a classic forerunner of socialism; perhaps he is also blind to Earth issues. Even his rural identity does not guarantee his concern for ecology. We know how ecological abuse is often intensified by the desperate efforts of the rural poor to wring a living from the land when they have no other option for survival; these desperate attempts bring them into damaging conflict with bourgeois Earth activists.

Given all these issues—and the great distance separating us from the period when Amos lived—we should not expect to find positive ecological resources readily usable by late twentieth-century Westerners. By careful reading, however, we can make connections which at least will enable us to reframe the questions.

We begin by examining the socio-economic system of which Amos was a part, and conclude by probing how the book presents the system metaphorically.

The book of Amos presents a situation in which a wealthy urban class live in luxury at the expense of the rural poor. The prophet rails against this luxury and the class division that allows it (e.g. 4.1; 5.11). In the memorable vignette of 6.4-6, the rich revel in their class 'superiority' over the rural peasants by 'conspicuous consumption' of agricultural produce, livestock, oil and wine. If this is a depiction of a funerary festival (King 1988: 139), they even give religious sanction to class differences.

The systemic foundation of this society was the monarchy—in the time of the prophet Amos this was still a recent development. For both topographical and sociological reasons, the monarchy was much harder to maintain in northern Israel than in Judah. The land was far less geographically manageable—the tribes were spread out over a large territory split by mountain ranges. The region's topography was ideal for groups who valued their independence (Hopkins 1985: 75).

To be successful under these conditions a king either had to evoke popular loyalty—which rarely happened—or enforce his rule by military means, with the support of special interests (Gottwald 1985: 347). The latter was achieved by a shift in the system of land tenure, from patrimonial to prebendal domain (Coote 1981: 27-28).

In early Israelite times land tenure in the highlands was patrimonial—land was held by kinship groups who maintained ties and cooperation within each region with members of their group linked to each other through the male/patriarchal line. This system was expressed ideologically as Yahweh's gift of land to each tribe and family. In the prebendal system, a government official was assigned the control of a region, and in exchange for enforcing the king's rule received grants of income from the land he administered. Such income could come only from the taxes paid by those working the land, so that peasants fell into debt and were gradually forced to cede their patrimonial lands in order to survive. The king gave these lands—lost through indebtedness—to his officials to consolidate their loyalty and his power (Gottwald 1985: 345).

Though he scathingly describes the system at work, Amos has oddly little to say about monarchy as such, and does not display a clear understanding of its being the underlying cause of the situation he confronts. It is true that his description of luxury in 6.4-6 includes an apparent swipe at King David in his traditional role of musician (6.5), but there are very few references to the monarchy or its attendant abuses.

We can now return to the question of a link in Amos between class oppression and the treatment of the Earth. Land use was determined by absentee urban landlords rather than by those who worked the land; this typically puts pressure on the Earth. More specifically, agricultural land was being diverted from subsistence to luxury crops, as well as to the pleasure pursuits of the rich. Wine and oil, which are frequently mentioned (2.8; 5.11; 6.6), are not luxury goods per se, but when they are 'the finest' (6.6), and when they are associated with obvious luxury goods like ivory (6.4; cf. 3.15), we may assume that the urban elite were determining land use in ways that did not take account of the subsistence needs of the peasants.

The king himself is implicated in these dynamics. Amos 7.1 refers to his right to the first of the season's crops. Interestingly, the context is a natural disaster: locusts. Royal privilege does not bring the locusts, but it does, we might conclude, make their plague more devastating for the unprivileged (cf. Psalm 72—see Jobling 1992).

We can find further suggestions of the monarchy's complicity in the rich world of metaphor in the book of Amos. Compare Amos 2.7 with 2.13: in 'trampling the head of the poor into the dust of the earth' (2.7), the rich treat the poor simply as part of the Earth they till. Dominating the poor becomes part and parcel of dominating the Earth. But a more complex metaphor in Amos 2.13 reverses this: 'I will press you down...just as a cart presses down when it is full of sheaves' (NRSV; the Hebrew is unclear). The rich are now 'pressed down' (cf. 2.7, 'trampled')—by the agricultural produce they have sought to monopolize! This reminds us of the tumbril—the farm cart—used, in the French Revolution, to carry the former exploiters to the guillotine! In this revolution, the Earth turns against the oppressors of the Earth and the poor.

Most interesting is the use of metaphors that evoke monarchy. In 1.1, Amos, who is 'among the shepherds', is linked to kings of Israel and Judah. In the ancient Near East, 'shepherd' is a stock metaphor for a king. This juxtaposition of shepherd and 'shepherd' looks forward to the prophet's confrontation with King Jeroboam in 7.10-17—Amos claims the identity of 'shepherd', and disowns that of 'prophet'. He invites comparison between himself as a real, productive shepherd, and the king as a false and parasitical 'shepherd' of the people.

Shepherds and kings are also connected in Amos 1.2, though it is hard to assess what this verse intends. Yahweh, operating from Jerusalem, the very centre of royal and urban culture, devastates 'the pastures of the shepherds'. Probably this is an affirmation, at a redactional level, of Judah and the Davidic monarchy over northern Israel; perhaps 'shepherds' plays on the northern 'shepherd–kings' and their failure to protect after their human 'flocks'.

From an ecological perspective, Amos 1.2 strikes a distinctly negative chord, and a hermeneutic of suspicion is appropriate. The text implies that the royal urban system devastates the shepherds, the countryside, the Earth—and that Yahweh is implicated in the devastation. But which 'Yahweh' is this? This is the Yahweh of the Jerusalem ideology, who may be a very different deity, with different implications for ecological debate, from other constructions of 'Yahweh', including that of the prophet Amos!

Amos 3.12 rings yet a third change on the theme. Here the shepherd appears as a figure of futility; he manages to preserve little from the lion's attack. The importance of this verse lies in its obvious allusion to David in 1 Sam. 17.34-36. It parodies David's ability to rescue his sheep, much as Amos 6.5 derides another of David's traditional accomplishments: music-making. Raw nature in the form of the lion (see our third sketch, on the ecology of danger) fights back against the oppressive royal system. The 'leonine' claims of the Jerusalem monarchy (Gen. 49.9) only add to the irony.

Sketch Three: Ecology, Theology and Metaphor

What patterns of human relationship to the Earth do we find in the book of Amos? Most basically, humans are farmers, living as best they can from what the Earth yields. This basic reality seems relatively absent from the prophet's discourse—everyday farming seems rarely the source of his language (contrast, for example, Isa. 28.23-29). Beyond this, we may identify three specific ecological perspectives.

Most dominant is an ecology of danger: a sense that nature is an unpredictable source of peril for humanity. Many violent natural images help build a picture of imminent destruction and death. The text serves up lions roaring, bears attacking, snakes biting, earthquakes, consuming fire, dismembered sheep, swarming locusts and sweeping disease. Amos knows the power of his environment to strike fear into humans. Even the agricultural metaphors are sometimes violent—notably the threshing (pulverization) and sieving (suggestive of rejection) that are part of every harvest.

At the opposite extreme is the 'Edenic' ecology of plenty (9.13-15): the natural world can endlessly and effortlessly supply all human needs and wants. The passage is not consistent; in 9.14, human agricultural work is seen as still necessary, yet the metaphors of 9.13a, in which work cannot keep pace with nature's fecundity, deconstruct this idea. Finally, 9.13b presents a picture similar to Greek myths of the golden age (Lovejoy and Boas 1935): nature producing without human effort.

Finally, the 'doxologies' (4.13; 5.8-9; 9.5-6) offer an ecology of contemplation. These passages evoke the cosmos as totality, 'the heights of the earth', 'the waters of the sea', 'Pleiades and Orion'. The world becomes an object of rapt contemplation, a sphere of mystery. We find ourselves in the world of wisdom, adopting the wisdom tradition's habit of looking at and learning from the world. This vision extends to other prominent wisdom themes in the book: the universalism (1.3–2.3; 9.7), and the impatience with the traditional cult.

How do these ecologies in the book of Amos strike a modern ecological consciousness? The ecology of danger, though one-sided, is a positive reminder that nature does not exist for us: it obeys its own rules—sometimes with disastrous consequences for us if we get in the way.

The 'Edenic' ecology, on the other hand, rouses our suspicion. The assumption that the Earth is endlessly productive and exploitable has brought us where we are today; in terms of our second sketch, this assumption is bound up with royal ideology, both in Amos 9.11-15 and, classically, in the Solomon traditions (see Jobling 1991).

However, many would hesitate to reject ecologies of plenty from the debate entirely. In some historical forms these ecologies have been part of pro-Earth attitudes. One strand of Greek golden age thinking stressed the primal fruitfulness of the Earth and saw this as having been spoiled by human agricultural aggression.

At this point the principle of intrinsic worth is relevant. Does the Earth have value of itself? Or is it viewed as a wild natural domain that must be tamed by humanity? Or again, is it considered a rich resource given for humans to plunder? Does the ecology of contemplation move the reader beyond these orientations to a re-valuing of the earth?

It is probably to the wisdom ecology of contemplation that we react most positively. It meshes well with theologies of the type sometimes known as 'panentheism', being espoused by ecotheologians. Boff comments:

> A spirit…is every being that draws breath; hence spirit refers to all liv-
> ing beings… The whole earth and the universe are experienced as bear-
> ers of spirit, because they are sources of life and furnish all the elements
> that are needed for life, yet also sustain the thrust of creation (1995: 36;
> see also 50-51).

Panentheism reframes the divine, and brings it from the other-worldly metaphysical confines of the theistic model into a state of participation in the mysterious dynamics of the universe. The divine becomes the synapse of continuity that enables the movement of one moment to another, and the interaction of the various forms of energy with each other. God intimately enlivens the interaction of these autonomous elements. This approach bonds theological discourse to the Earth and the universe.

> The world is not only a bridge to God. It is also the place where God is
> honored and worshiped, and the place where we meet God…if the soul
> could know God without the world, the world would never have been
> created (Boff 1995: 51).

An integral part of the world view of the doxologies of the book of Amos is that God 'reveals his thoughts to mortals' (4.13). Humans relate to this ecology through a special kind of participatory knowl-edge.

We must remind ourselves, however, that, in the book of Amos, the monotheistic God insists on being a presence in the relationship between humans and the Earth. This is no less true of the ecology of contemplation than the others—in the doxologies, the cosmos which invites contemplation is invariably the creation of the one God. The Edenic ecology is equally dominated by the God's omnipotent presence. It is, in fact, from the ecology of danger that divine intrusion is most often absent.

In most instances, certainly, nature is dangerous because God is using it to punish people. Divine control of weather, fertility and disease (4.6-10) provides a major example (see also 5.16-17; 7.1-2; 8.7-10; 9.3). In these examples, through direct divine action, human sin leads to ecological failure. In the case of fire—one of the most frequent sources of danger in Amos (1.3–2.3; 5.6; 7.4)—we seem scarcely to be dealing with a natural phenomenon, but rather with a special divine fire. At any rate, the view of 'nature' here is purely instrumental rather than as having intrinsic worth. Even the doxologies tend to drift into this form of the ecology of danger (5.9; 9.5).

There is, though, another side to it. Sometimes the non-human world comes into view as dangerous without reference to a specific divine intention. Lions *qua* lions are dangerous (3.4, 8, 12). In Amos 5.19, the point is not that bears and snakes are dangerous because God uses them for punishment, but rather that the punishing God is dangerous in the way these animals are dangerous. We might say, in this instance, that the experience of 'nature' is prior to the experience of God.

The sheer perilousness of the world is visible even in passages where God is formally the agent. In Amos 9.5, earthquakes expressly come from God, but in 1.2 they may be just a fact of life, while 8.7-8 lies somewhere between these two views. It is noteworthy that the unequal rainfall that God sends on different cities (4.7-8) is not correlated with different levels of sinfulness. How then are people supposed to discern the agency of God behind the capriciousness of the weather?

Behind a theology of retribution attributing all our experiences in the world to God's agency, we see, then, traces of the wisdom ecology in which humans must adapt as they can to the world as they find it.

We used to celebrate the prophets for achieving a transition from magical, priestly religion to the rational religion of the divine word. In the current era of ecological consciousness, this seems less of an achievement—in effect it distanced people from the Earth. The book of Amos, considered as a whole, represents an extreme case of this transition. It would be interesting to do a full comparison with his twin, Hosea. The prophet Hosea, of course, engages in direct combat with the gods of the Earth and agriculture—but at least he is still in contact with these gods. Perhaps Hosea is forced, by the terms of his struggle, to turn Yahweh into something like a nature god (Hos. 2.18-23; 2.20-25 in Hebrew).

One of the most interesting ways in which we can trace the widening of the distance between humanity and the Earth in the book of Amos is through the use of metaphor. We can observe the world becoming a metaphorical picture of humanity's—or Israel's—situation, rather than being metonymically linked with that situation. In fact, this is another way of expressing the transition from priestly to prophetic. The world, rather than sharing in human reality, becomes merely an instrument for thinking about human reality.

For example, both agriculture (1.3) and husbandry (4.1-3) provide metaphors for military defeat, but there is no exploration of the real effects of war on farming and the usability of the land. Likewise, in 2.9, defeating an enemy is *like* destroying trees: 'Yet I destroyed the Amorite before them, whose height was like the height of cedars, and who was as strong as oaks; I destroyed his fruit above, and [even] his roots beneath'. But the actual destruction of trees—for example, to produce the materiel of warfare—goes unnoticed. Where are the real cedars and oaks that used to flourish in Syria-Palestine?

Amos 8.1-2 is word-play rather than metaphor, but the dynamics are similar. 'This is what the Lord God showed me—a basket of summer fruit (*qayits*)... Then the Lord said to me, "The end (*qēts*) has come upon my people Israel" '. Again, the phenomena of nature exist simply *to mean something else*. Contrast Amos 9.13, where the people's destiny is not just *like* a harvest, but *is* a harvest: 'The time is surely coming, says the LORD, when the one who plows shall overtake the one who reaps'.

Perhaps no other verse in Amos is more memorable than 5.24: 'But let justice roll down like waters, and righteousness like an ever-flowing stream'. From an ecological perspective, perhaps none is more problematic. Contrast it with Amos 4.7-8: 'I also withheld the rain from you...one field would be rained upon, and the field on which it did not rain withered...yet you did not return to me, says the LORD'. Here the natural world, in its aspect of needing and providing water, both punishes and suffers for human sin. This is a 'primitive' theology, but one to which ecology gives new meaning!

Amos 5.24 also evokes the need for water, but the well-watered environment is here simply a metaphor of a social or religious good. Where, we now want to ask, are those ever-flowing streams? Many dried up centuries ago, through human injustice against the Earth.

Which serves us better in this case—the magical, metonymic theology of Amos 4.7-8 or the metaphoric word-theology of Amos 5.24?

Conclusion

Starting from the text of the book of Amos, these sketches have in different ways probed the deep attitudes toward the ecological crisis likely to be held by people whom the Bible has shaped.

The first sketch suggested that the responses we make to ecological 'prophecy'—for example, collaborative or conflictual responses—are influenced by the lessons our culture has taught us about responding to prophets, and that these lessons have some of their origins in historical responses to the prophets of the Bible. The second sketch, finding little direct connection in the book of Amos between human justice and Earth justice themes, sought a way forward by probing the text's—and hence our own—'ecological unconscious'. The third sketch saw the book of Amos as an early stage on a path leading to the creation of distance between humans and the Earth, and argued for deconstructive and resistant reading.

Messengers in the Sky

Edgar W. Conrad

Introduction

In an essay published in this series, Norman Habel translates שמים as 'sky' rather than 'heavens' in his analysis of 'the earth story' in Gen. 1.1-25. He does this because he understands that שמים 'refers to the sky as part of the visible order of things, and not to some distant celestial place called "heaven" where, according to some biblical traditions, God is said to dwell in distant splendour'.[1]

In this essay I want to explore another way in which translation of the Hebrew Bible has created a celestial 'Other' in biblical texts in place of the visible order of earth and sky. In particular, my essay will focus on the way in which the Hebrew word, מלאך, 'messenger' has been translated as 'angel' in most contexts in which a messenger is sent by YHWH. I will contend that 'angel' conjures up a sharper division between the human and the divine than is appropriate—the passages in which 'messengers of YHWH' appear represent the human and the divine inhabiting a common world; translations of מלאך as angel bring to the text a hierarchical dualism between heaven and earth not present in the original. There is an implicit interrelatedness between sky and earth as the abode of human and divine; YHWH's messengers reside in this interrelated domain, not in the world of celestial otherness. In pursuing this study I seek to explore a cosmic dimension of the principle of interconnectedness, principle two of the Earth Bible Project ecojustice principles.

Messengers, Prophets and Angels

Apparently in an attempt to counter an argument that Haggai was an angel, John Calvin argued that the word מלאך, in Hag. 1.13, could also

---

1. See 'Geophany: The Earth Story in Genesis 1', in the second volume in this series.

be translated 'messenger', and that prophets were often called messengers, מלאכים, in the Hebrew Bible. He asserts,

> The word...*mala'k*, means a messenger; and as angels are called...
> *mela'kim*, some foolish men have thought that Haggai was one of the
> celestial angels, clothed with the form of man: but this is the most frivo-
> lous conjecture; for priests, we know, are honoured with this title in the
> second chapter of Malachi; and God in many other places called his
> prophets messengers or ambassadors (Calvin 1989: 344).

Calvin is correct in saying that priests are called messengers in the
second chapter of Malachi, but his comment that prophets are called
messengers or ambassadors 'in many other places' is overstated. The
Hebrew מלאך is never used as a designation for 'prophet', נביא, in the
part of the canon known as the 'Former Prophets'; in the 'Latter Prophets',[2] Haggai is the only individual designated as both 'messenger',
מלאך, and 'prophet', נביא. He is called a מלאך in Hag. 1.13—the passage referred to by Calvin; in five texts (Hag. 1.1, 3, 12; 2.1, 10) he is
designated as a נביא. The designation of a נביא as a מלאך, contra Calvin, only occurs in Hag. 1.13.[3]

While some in Calvin's day appeared ready to accept that Haggai
was an angel, it is interesting that in our own time, a number of interpreters of Zechariah, the book that follows Haggai in the Twelve,
understand the מלאך (almost universally translated as 'angel') who
spoke to Zechariah to be acting like a 'prophet', a נביא. Joseph Blenkinsopp's view is representative of this position. He says, the *'angelus
interpres* of the visions [in Zechariah] assumes the prophetic role of
intercession (Zech. 1.12) and the giving of oracles (1.14-17; 2.4-5)'
(Blenkinsopp 1983: 239).

In the light of these observations, I will argue in this article that the
distinctions between angel, מלאך, and prophet, נביא—and therefore
between the human sphere and the realm of celestial beings—are
blurred in the textual world of the Hebrew Bible. I maintain that
translators have constructed a textual world for contemporary readers

---

2.   The Latter Prophets is that part of the canon that includes the scrolls of four
prophetic books: Isaiah, Jeremiah, Ezekiel and the twelve minor prophets: Hosea,
Joel, Amos, Obadiah, Jonah, Micah, Nahum, Habakkuk, Zephaniah, Haggai, Zechariah and Malachi. This scroll of the twelve minor prophets is increasingly being
read as a literary whole, as I have done in my recent research, and when it is read
that way it is often referred to as 'the Twelve'.

3.   Indeed, the only other place where these two terms can be interpreted as
synonymous is 2 Chron. 36.15-16; both terms are used in the plural in this passage.

in which a sharp demarcation is created between the earthly and the heavenly other.

The basic meaning of the Hebrew word, מלאך, is 'messenger'. It is rendered this way by most translations when a human figure sends a messenger with a message.[4] However, when YHWH is the one who sends the מלאך, it is common practice for translations to render the word as 'angel'.[5] The exceptions to this practice are found at the end of the Twelve: in Hag. 1.13 where the phrase, חגי מלאך יהוה, is rendered, 'Haggai, the messenger of the YHWH'; in Mal. 1.1 and 3.1 where מלאכי is rendered 'my messenger'; and in Mal. 2.7 where the phrase, מלאך יהוה, referring to the priest, is commonly translated 'the messenger of YHWH'.

The common practice of translating מלאך as 'angel' when the מלאך is sent by YHWH, I maintain, introduces a world view alien to the Hebrew Bible, and contributes to a marked dichotomy between the heavenly realm of supernatural beings and the earthly domain of human beings. Rather than supporting division and distance between the heavenly and the earthly, the Hebrew Bible, in its portrayal of YHWH's messengers, breaks down these distinctions. Biblical translations have created a fissure where the Hebrew Bible portrays an interconnected universe.

Since the Bible has mostly been read in translation in the West, the cleavage between heaven and earth promoted by biblical translation has contributed significantly to the Western devaluation of the earth.[6]

YHWH's Messengers as Humans

A number of stories in the Hebrew Bible suggest that 'messengers of YHWH' often appear as human beings and are indistinguishable from

4. See, e.g., Gen. 32.3, 6; Num. 20.14; 21.21; 22.5; Deut. 2.26; Josh. 6.17, 25; 7.22; Judg. 7.24; 9.31; 11.12-14, 19; 1 Sam. 6.21; 11.3, 4, 7, 9; 16.19; 19.11, 14, 15, 16, 20, 21; 19.20; 23.27; 25.42; 2 Sam. 2.5; 3.12, 14, 26; 5.11; 11.4, 19, 22-23, 25; 12.27; 1 Kgs 19.2; 20.2, 5, 9; 22.13; 2 Kgs 1.2; 3.5, 16; 5.10; 6.32, 33; 7.15; 9.18; 10.8; 14.8; 16.7; 17.4; 19.9, 14, 23; Nah. 2.14; 1 Chron. 14.1; 19.2, 16; 2 Chron. 18.12; 35.21; Neh. 6.3; Isa. 14.32; 18.2; 30.4; 33.7; 37.9, 14; Jer. 27.3; Ezek. 17.15; 23.16, 40; 30.9; Prov. 13.17; 16.14; 17.11; Job 1.14.

5. See, e.g., Gen. 16.7, 9, 10-11; 19.1, 15; 21.17; 22.11, 15; 24.7, 40; 28.12; 31.11; 32.2, 4, 7; Exod. 3.2; 14.19; 23.20, 23; 32.34; 33.2; Num. 22.22-27, 31-32, 34-35; Judg. 2.1, 4; 5.23; 6.11-12, 20-22, 25, 35; 13.3, 6, 9, 13, 15, 16-18, 20-21; 1 Sam. 29.9; 2 Sam. 14.17, 20; 19.28; 24.16, 17; 1 Kgs 13.18; 19.5, 7; 2 Kgs 1.3, 15; 19.35; Zech. 1.9, 11-14, 2.2, 7; 3.1, 3, 5-6; 4.1, 4-5; 5.5, 10; 6.4-5; 1 Chron. 21.12, 15-16, 18, 20, 27, 30; Isa. 37.36; Job. 4.18; Pss. 35.5-6; 34.8; 78.49; 91.11; 103.20; 104.4; 148.2.

6. My reading shares some parallels with Cohen 1985: 12-24.

humans in appearance and behaviour. For example, the messengers who appear to Lot in Gen. 19.1, 15 are introduced into the story in Genesis 18. The narrator consistently refers to them as 'male human beings', אנשים:

> He (Abraham) looked up and saw three men standing near him (18.2).
> Then the men set out from there, and they looked toward Sodom; and Abraham went with them on the way (18.16).
> So the men turned from there, and went toward Sodom... (18.22).

In addition, the narrator portrays them as engaging in human activity. In a show of hospitality for these strangers, Abraham rushes about to bring water to wash their feet, encourages them to rest under a tree, and brings them curds and milk, cakes made from flour, and prepared calf meat to feed them. He does this with their approval—they tell him to 'do as you have said' (18.5). Then Abraham 'stood by them under the tree while they ate' (18.8).

The interaction between Abraham and these figures is like the interaction of human beings attending to each other's needs. Although these 'men' are identified as 'messengers' after travelling on to Sodom (19.1, see also 19.15), their interaction with Lot is portrayed as typically human.

> The two messengers came to Sodom in the evening, and Lot was sitting in the gateway of Sodom. When Lot saw them, he rose to meet them, and bowed down to them with his face to the ground. He said, 'Please, my lords, turn aside to your servant's house and spend the night, and wash your feet; then you can rise early and go on your way'. They said, 'No; we will spend the night in the square'. But he urged them strongly; so they turned aside to him and entered his house; and he made them a feast, and baked unleavened bread, and they ate (Gen. 19.1-3).

These characters are so human that, even in this story, the narrator can refer to them simply as men (Gen. 19.12, 16).

In Gideon's interaction with the messenger of YHWH (Judg. 6.11-24), the messenger is perceived as human—Gideon does not recognize him as a messenger of YHWH until he vanishes from his sight (Judg. 6.21-22).

Finally, in the story of Manoah and his wife, the messenger of YHWH is not easily distinguished from an איש, man/male human being. The narrator tells us that a messenger appeared to the wife of Manoah (13.3, 13); when she speaks to her husband about him, she refers to him as 'a man [איש] of God', and, although she says that he was like a messenger of God, she is not sure that he is a messenger (Judg. 13.6). Indeed, in the ensuing dialogue between Manoah and his wife, they both refer to the being as a man (Judg. 13.8, 10, 11), and the narrator says—in case we miss the point—'Manoah did not know that he was the messenger of YHWH' (Judg. 13.15).

As in the Gideon story, 'the man' is only perceived as a messenger of God when he vanishes, ascending in a flame towards the sky (Judg. 13.20).

Messengers of YHWH, then, do appear as human beings in the Hebrew Bible. They are only perceived as 'messengers of YHWH' when they take part in extraordinary activities.

YHWH'S Messengers and the Sky

Clearly in the Hebrew Bible, then, 'messengers of YHWH' are identified as human by those who encounter them. Indeed, as we have seen, throughout Genesis 18 the messengers of YHWH are referred to only as 'men'; the Hebrew word, מלאך, is not even used in this chapter.

However, while messengers of YHWH appear to be human, it would be wrong to ignore the fact that they often speak 'from the sky' and have their habitation there. Judges 13.20, cited above, reports that the messenger who appeared to Manoah and his wife disappeared in a 'flame going up toward the sky'.

Messengers of YHWH often call out from the sky to help those in distress. The story of Hagar is an example. Hagar, banished from the household of Abraham with her son, was preparing for her own death and the death of her son, because the skin of water she was carrying was empty. The narrator reports that God heard the child's cries and

> a messenger [מלאך] of God called from the sky, and said to her, 'What troubles you Hagar? Do not be afraid... Then God opened her eyes and she saw a well of water. She went and filled the skin with water, and gave the boy a drink (Gen. 21.17-19).[7]

Similarly, when Abraham lifts up the knife to sacrifice his son

> a messenger [מלאך] of YHWH called to him from the sky and said, 'Abraham, Abraham... Do not lay your hand on the boy or do anything to him... And Abraham looked up and saw a ram caught in the thicket by its horns. Abraham went and took the ram and offered it up as a burnt offering instead of his son... The messenger [מלאך] of YHWH called to Abraham a second time from the sky [and promised to bless Abraham] (Gen. 22.9-19).

7.   See the alternative story in Gen. 16.7-14. Here, however, the messenger of YHWH does not call out from the sky.

In Jacob's dream, 'a ladder [or stairway or ramp] set on the earth the top of it reaching to the sky, and the messengers of God were ascending and descending on it' (Gen. 28.12). Jacob had this dream on the way to Paddam-aram, after Isaac had blessed Jacob and charged him to marry a woman from the household of his uncle Laban, rather than a Canaanite woman. In this passage, these messengers of God offer protection to Jacob on his journey in much the same way that the messengers of YHWH, from their position in the sky, offered protection to Hagar and to Abraham's son, Isaac. God promises Jacob, 'Know that I am with you and will keep you wherever you go, and will bring you back to this land; for I will not leave you until I have done what I promised you' (Gen. 28.15).

The theme of messengers offering protection from their position in the sky is found in other places in the Hebrew Bible. For example, 'YHWH, the god of the sky' sends his messenger to protect Abraham's servant who is on a journey to seek a wife for Isaac (Gen. 24.7), and the messenger who goes with Israel's army offers them protection by being present in a pillar of cloud (Exod. 14.19, cf. Gen. 32.2; Exod. 23.20, 23; 32.34; 33.2; Num. 20.16; Ps. 34.8).[8]

The association between YHWH's messengers and the sky is also evident in the messenger's encounter with David in 1 Chron. 21.14-17, regarding a census that David had taken which displeased God. 'David looked up and saw the messenger [מלאך] of YHWH standing between the earth and the sky, and in his hand a drawn sword stretched over Jerusalem' (1 Chron. 21.16).[9]

This association is probably no more evident than in Psalm 148—the sky, including YHWH's messengers, and the earth, including its inhabitants, are all summoned to praise YHWH.

> Praise YHWH!
> Praise YHWH from the sky;
> praise him in the heights!
> Praise him, all his messengers;
> praise him all his host!
> Praise him, sun and moon;
> praise him all the stars of light!...
> Praise YHWH from the earth...

8. Other passages suggest that the messenger of YHWH is present to offer protection, but the theme of his presence in the sky is not made explicit. See Judg. 5.23; 1 Kgs 19.5, 7; 2 Kgs 1.3, 15; Pss. 35.5-6; 78.49; 91.11.

9. Other passages in the Hebrew Bible suggest that the messenger of YHWH is present to punish. See Num. 22.1-36; Judg. 2.1-5; 2 Sam. 24.15-17; 2 Kgs 19.35// Isa. 37.36.

> Kings of the earth and all peoples;
> princes and all rulers of the earth!
> Young men and women alike,
> old and young together! (Ps. 148.1-12)

Just as the messengers, the inhabitants of the sky, are to praise YHWH
so the inhabitants of the earth (kings, princes, rulers, and both young
and old women and men) are to praise YHWH.[10]

Prophets in the Sky

I have argued, then, that YHWH's messengers appear in YHWH's
world as male human beings having human needs and engaging in
human activities. These messengers, however, are also associated
with the sky. They sometimes call out from the sky, and they move
between the sky and the earth.

But is Calvin correct in asserting such a sharp distinction between
Haggai, whom he considers to be a more human מלאך, and YHWH's
other מלאכים, whom he considers to be more angelic? And should
Blenkinsopp be so puzzled that 'angels' in Zechariah are acting like
prophets?

Since prophets, like messengers, can go up in fire to the sky, my
answer to both questions is 'no'. Elijah is a prophet whom YHWH
took up 'in a whirlwind to the sky' (2 Kgs 2.1). The narrator tells us
that as Elisha and Elijah were 'walking and talking, a chariot of fire
and horses of fire separated the two of them, and Elijah went up in a
whirlwind to the sky' (2 Kgs 2.11). We are told in another prophetic
book that Elijah will come again. In the book of Malachi—which
means 'My Messenger'—YHWH says, 'Lo, I will send you the
prophet Elijah, before the great and terrible day of YHWH comes. He
will turn the hearts of parents to their children and the hearts of children to their parents' (Mal. 3.23-24; 4.5-6 in English translation). The
prophet Elijah, then, can go up and come down from the sky—not
unlike the messengers of YHWH in Jacob's dream.

I am arguing, then, that Calvin's and Blenkinsopp's dichotomy
between angels and prophets does not reflect the way YHWH's messengers are portrayed in the Hebrew Bible. There is an implicit and
explicit interconnectedness between the earth and the sky in the Hebrew Bible texts dealing with YHWH's messengers. YHWH's messengers—including prophetic messengers—and even YHWH, too,

---

10. See also Ps. 104.4 where the winds of the sky are used metaphorically as
messengers of YHWH.

inhabit this interrelated realm. This can be clearly seen at the end of the Twelve, where prophets—including Haggai—appear as YHWH's messengers (Conrad 1997: 65-79; forthcoming).

It has become conventional to view the emergence of YHWH's messengers at the end of the Twelve as the beginning of an apocalyptic world view. This interpretation is associated with the translation of מלאך as 'angel'. An apocalyptic world view emphasizes a strong division between heaven and earth; as a consequence the earth is devalued—it will be destroyed at the end of time.

Rather than emphasizing division and distance between the heavenly realm of the divine and the earthly realm of the human, the appearance of YHWH's messengers at the end of the Twelve represents a return to the days of the 'mothers and fathers' or matriarchs and patriarchs. In those days, the presence of a messenger was tantamount to divine presence. This presence had to do with the localization of the divine, not with distance and separation.

There are several ways in which the emergence of messengers in the Twelve echoes the appearance of messengers in the stories of Israel's ancestors.

1. When the messenger is present, YHWH is present 'with' the person to whom the messenger appears. The first time Haggai speaks as a 'messenger of YHWH' his 'message' is, 'I am *with* [את] you, says YHWH'. Such a message of 'presence with' resonates with similar messages conveyed to Israel's ancestors. As a consequence of the appearance of the messengers to Jacob, YHWH says to him, 'Behold, I am *with* [עם][11] you and I will keep you in every way that you go'. When the messenger appears to Moses in the bush that burns but is not consumed he says, 'I will be *with* [עם] you' (Exod. 3.12). When a messenger appears to Gideon, the messenger says, 'YHWH is *with* [עם] you, mighty warrior' (Judg. 6.12). Indeed, the theme of YHWH's presence concludes the chapters in Zechariah after Zechariah's encounter with the messengers of YHWH, chapters in which, as I have argued elsewhere, Zechariah emerges as a messenger of YHWH (Conrad 1999: 132-50). It is anticipated that 'ten men from nations of every language shall take hold of a Jew, grasping his garment and saying, "Let us go with you, for we have heard that God is *with* [עם] you" ' (Zech. 8.23).

2. In many passages in the stories of Israel's ancestors, YHWH's presence is a literal presence—to see the messenger is to see YHWH.

11. The Hebrew prepositions את and עם both have the sense of 'presence with'.

This is stated explicitly in Manoah and his wife's encounter with a 'messenger of YHWH'—they observe, 'We shall surely die, for we have seen God' (Judg. 13.22). This theme is echoed in the story of Hagar in the enigmatic phrase in Gen. 16.13-14 in which she marvels that she has seen God and lives (for similar passages, see Gen. 28.16-17; Exod. 3.6; Num. 23.31; Judg. 6.22-23 and 1 Chron. 21.16-17). In my commentary on Zechariah, I have argued that when Zechariah lifts up his eyes and sees messengers in his world (Zech. 1.6–6.15), he also sees YHWH—with whom he then speaks and interacts (Conrad 1999: 75-76). Zechariah's lack of fear in the presence of YHWH is associated with his own emergence as a messenger of YHWH.

3. When messengers appear, the place becomes a sacred space and altars and temples are built. After Jacob's dream about a ladder extending between the sky and the earth with messengers of YHWH ascending and descending, the awesomeness of the place frightens him; he says, 'This is none other than the house of God, and this is the gate of heaven' (Gen. 28.17). Jacob then takes the stone that has been his headrest, sets it up for a pillar and pours oil on it. He calls the place Bethel ('the house of God') and vows that if YHWH looks after him, 'this stone, which I have set up for a pillar, shall be God's house' (Gen. 28.22). Similarly, when Gideon realizes he has been talking with the messenger of YHWH, 'he builds an altar there to YHWH', and calls it 'YHWH is peace' (Judg. 6.24). When David encounters the messenger of YHWH at the threshing floor of Ornan the Jebusite, the messenger instructs the prophet Gad to tell David to erect an altar on the threshing floor (1 Chron. 21.18). David responds, 'Here shall be the house of YHWH God and here the altar for burnt offering for Israel' (1 Chron. 22.1). The appearance of messengers has the same consequence in the Twelve. When Haggai, the messenger of YHWH speaks the message of YHWH, work begins on the construction of the temple,

> YHWH stirred up the spirit of Zerubbabel son of Shealtiel, governor of Judah, and the spirit of Joshua son of Jehozadak, the high priest, and the spirit of all the remnant of the people: and they came and worked on the house of YHWH of hosts, their God, on the twenty-fourth day of the month, in the sixth month (Hag. 1.14-15).

In a similar way, Zechariah sees, as he interacts with messengers in Zech. 1.7–6.15, the temple under construction.

The appearance of messengers at the end of the Twelve, then, does not represent a transcendent other world, but a world in which YHWH's messengers—including Haggai and Zechariah—represent

YHWH's presence as radically localized in Jerusalem. YHWH the God of all the earth is present in the temple—as the ten men from all the nations say, 'we have heard that God is with you' (Zech. 8.23). This world is not radically different from the world of Israel's ancestors—YHWH and his messengers are present in an interconnected realm of sky and earth.

Conclusion

The translation of מלאך as 'angel' misleadingly suggests the divine as transcendently 'other'—from this perspective, divine messengers are understood as angelic envoys from another world.

I maintain, however, that YHWH's messengers are not celestial beings but human characters, including prophets such as Elijah, Haggai and Zechariah. Sometimes these human messengers, too, can move between the earth and the sky, as Elijah demonstrates. This is a world in which YHWH is not confined to another world. YHWH is present 'with' the people to whom these messengers appear—for example, in the temple constructed in Jerusalem in the days of Haggai and Zechariah, or in Bethel in the days of Jacob (Gen. 28.10-22; Hos. 12.1; 12.4 in the English translation).

Rendering מלאך as 'angel' introduces a dualism characteristic of the Western perception of reality, which makes a sharp demarcation between heaven and earth. This marked separation conceals the convergence between sky and earth, and between the human and divine, that characterizes texts in the Hebrew Bible in which YHWH's messengers appear. The cosmos in these sections of the Hebrew Bible is an interconnected one—as articulated in the second of the Earth Bible Project's ecojustice principles. The translation of מלאך as 'angel' rather than 'messenger' perpetuates the gap between heaven, as superior and spiritual, and earth, as inferior and material.

The alien world view imported into biblical texts when 'messenger' is translated as 'angel' makes the text fit a more familiar construction of reality—one in which our interpretive traditions are more comfortable. To contemporary Western eyes, the material world becomes devoid of divine presence and is seen only as a place of occasional divine visitation by divine envoys in ancient times.

This sharp distinction between heaven and earth also creates an unacceptable divide between the biblical view of the world, and the view of many indigenous peoples. Both views, while clearly different in many respects, encounter the divine in earth and sky; in both world views, the place where that encounter occurs becomes sacred space.

The Earth Story in Jeremiah 12

Terence E. Fretheim

This article focuses on the 'earth story' as presented in Jeremiah 12. I discuss the chapter from three perspectives. First, I will look at issues relating to genre and structure. Second, I reflect on this story from within the context of the book of Jeremiah as a whole. Third, in light of these considerations I work through Jeremiah 12 focusing on the place of the earth,[1] and keeping the guiding ecojustice principles in mind throughout. The principles of interconnectedness, voice, purpose and resistance are sharply evident in this text.

The Structure and Genre of Jeremiah 12

Scholars usually do not treat Jeremiah 12 as either a unit or a unity. Verses 1-6 are commonly linked with 11.18-23; together these texts are seen as confessions/laments of Jeremiah (11.18-20; 12.1-4), followed by divine responses (11.20-23; 12.5-6). Some scholars separate these confessions into two distinct units (on Jeremiah's confessions, see the special studies of O'Connor 1988; Diamond 1987). Because my reading is exploratory and I wish to work with the present form of the book of Jeremiah, I consider 12.1-18 to be a unit with which to work. The history of these verses prior to their present form is very complex (e.g. the prose material in 12.14-17 is probably a later addition).

From the perspective of the speaker, Jeremiah 12 consists of two parts, Jeremiah's lament (12.1-4) and the divine response (12.5-17). I keep 12.7-17 linked to 12.1-6 and interpret them as a continuation of God's response to Jeremiah's lament, begun in 12.5. One good reason for this linkage pertains to the land. Jeremiah brings his lament to a climax in 12.4, not with a concern about himself—though that concern remains—but with an appeal on behalf of the land and its creatures ('How long… ?'). Jeremiah 12.4 has been an interpretive crux, omitted

---

1.   In this paper 'earth' is not capitalized to allow an element of ambiguity.

in whole or in part or linked to what follows, because many have thought it a departure from the argument of 12.1-3.

But if 12.4 is the climactic point of Jeremiah's lament, focused finally on a concern about the land, the verse fits well with 12.1-3 (see below; it is, of course, quite possible for the wealthy to thrive in a time of drought!). God does not respond simply to Jeremiah's more personal issues (12.5-6); God also engages Jeremiah's concern about the present situation of the *land* (12.7-13) and its future (12.14-17). When 12.7-17, with its focus on the land, is included in God's response to Jeremiah's lament, God does provide something of an 'answer' to him in a way that 12.5-6 alone does not. From the perspective of vocabulary, note that the concern for a land that mourns (12.4, 11), and for the land as heritage (12.7-9, 14-15), are interlocking themes across the entire chapter.

Jeremiah's words in 12.1-4 have long been considered as the prophet's confession/lament. The following are often identified as Jeremiah's laments in 11.18–20.18: 11.18-23; 12.1-6; 15.10-21; 16.19-20; 17.14-18; 18.18-23; 20.7-13; 20.14-18. God's responses to Jeremiah are included in some instances (11.21-23; 12.5-6; 15.19-21). Several divine laments have been (or could be) identified, interwoven with the prophet's laments: 12.7-13; 13.15-27; 14.2-6, 17-18; 15.5-9; 18.13-17. Laments of the people are also included (14.7-9, 19-21). Moreover, announcements of judgment are woven within and around the divine laments, for example 13.1-11, 12-14; 14.13-16; 15.1-4; 16.16-18, 21; 17.1-4; 19.1-15. A comparable interweaving of the oracles of judgment and laments is present in Jeremiah 2–10 (see the divine laments in 2.5, 29-31; 3.1-5, 19-20; 4.19-21, 8.4-7, 10–9.3 [ET];[2] 9.10-11, 17-19 [ET]). The laments in Jeremiah 11–20 intensify the laments of the opening chapters and bring them to a screaming climax in Jeremiah's lament in 20.14-18. This interlocking of lament/judgment strongly suggests how the word of judgment is to be interpreted (see below).

Whatever the reader might think of the harshness of the indictments rendered against Israel and the violence of the judgments, the fundamental backdrop of these tumultuous and devastating events for God, Jeremiah and the land is weeping and mourning. The book of Jeremiah is filled with tears.

Jeremiah's confessions/laments have spawned considerable literature. How they are to be interpreted is debated—the options cannot be considered here. Their content and form is similar to the laments of

---

2.   Editor's note: ET in this context denotes English translation; sometimes the Hebrew text has a different verse number.

the psalter (e.g. 13.1-6)—but do they voice the laments of the prophet, the community or God? However much they may be grounded in the experience of the prophet, they have become something more than that in the canonical process. They are no longer (auto)biography—if they ever were—but proclamation; in and through these laments readers hear not only the voice of the prophet but the voice of God. When one considers the prophet's laments alongside the divine laments, readers can see that the prophet not only mirrors the laments of God but also incarnates that divine word (on this understanding, see Fretheim 1984: 156-59).

Hence Jeremiah 12—as is common elsewhere in Jeremiah (e.g. 8.18–9.3)—makes little effort to distinguish between the prophet's words and God's words (explicit only in 12.14); their voices tend to 'bleed' into one another. And in the lamenting in this chapter, there is mutuality in their focus on the land. In Jeremiah 12, the land joins them in one grand 'liturgy' of mourning.

Jeremiah 12 in the Context of the Book of Jeremiah

The book of Jeremiah is a complex, intricately woven tapestry, and the threads of this particular chapter can be observed and understood more clearly from within this larger design. References to Jeremiah 12 are woven into the following paragraphs.

God Made the Earth

God 'made the earth' (Jer. 33.2; cf. 10.12-13=51.15-16; 27.5; 32.17) and continues to uphold the 'fixed orders' of creation (31.35-36; 33.20, 25). Such 'fixed orders' refer to the great rhythms of creation (the sea, sun, moon, stars, day, night; see Gen. 8.22). But, notably, this language does not bespeak a mechanistic world or a divinely determined one, for the land can become desolate and mourn, the animals and birds can be swept away (12.4), and human behaviors can wreak havoc in God's good creation with impunity (12.1). God does not 'control' or micromanage the world, however much God's actions are deemed to be effective.

This perspective regarding the world entails an openness for genuine creaturely decision-making and (lack of) responsiveness. Again and again in Jeremiah, the people are given choices that will shape their future, which in turn will shape the future of all other creatures as well as the future of God—God will do different things depending upon what creatures do. The various 'if/if not' constructions (12.14-17; 17.24-27; 21.8-10; 22.1-5; 38.17-18; 42.9-17) demonstrate an openness to the future. God 'plants' the people, but it is the people who take root, grow, and bring forth fruit (12.2). What creatures 'grow up into' and the fruit they bear make a difference—both for themselves and for their world—for good or for ill. People can make God's 'pleasant portion a desolate wilderness' (12.10); the God who is 'near' and 'far' (23.23) can be 'far from their hearts' (12.2); and Babylonian armies can exceed their divine mandate, with devastating effects upon land and people (12.14; see 8.16; 25.11-14; 51.24). From another perspective, there is room for an incalculable and frustrating randomness in God's created order (e.g. Jer. 12.1—the 'way of the guilty' can prosper; Eccl. 9.11 speaks of 'chance' for such realities), so that no theory of retribution (or any other) can explain the way the world works.

God Fills Heaven and Earth

God 'fills heaven and earth' (Jer. 23.23-24). At the least, this means that God is present and relational to all that is not God, whether 'near by' or 'far off' (in creaturely terms). Inasmuch as God 'fills heaven and earth', the latter exist as creaturely realities to be filled; hence, all creatures are a genuine 'other' to God. Given the comprehensive character of 'heaven and earth', the divine relationship with the other is not limited to the human sphere. God represented as the 'God of all flesh' is one formulation in Jeremiah that moves this relationship beyond the human (32.27).

Moreover, that the desolate land mourns *to* God (12.11; see also 4.28; 23.10; Joel 1.10, 20) demonstrates that it has a relationship with God that is independent of God's relationship with the human (see Job 38–41; Pss. 104.21, 27; 145.15-16; 147–148). That God in turn addresses the land (16.19; see 22.29) also is evidence that such an independent relationship exists.

The language regarding the non-human as subject cannot be reduced to figurative speech, poetic license or worshipful exuberance. Rather, this language of interresponsiveness shows that God's presence to and relationship with the earth and its creatures is more than external; there is an inwardness or interiority characteristic of the earth and its creatures such that a genuine relationship with God exists. To speak in this way does not necessarily lead to a panpsychism or vitalism, only that some kind of *internal* relationship with God is claimed (for detail, see Fretheim 1987).

A Relational God Creates a Relational World

This relational God has created a relational world. An interrelatedness exists among all creatures for Jeremiah—and for Israel. The world could be imaged as a giant spiderweb. Every creature is in relationship with every other, such that any act reverberates out and affects the whole, shaking the entire web with varying degrees of intensity.

This may be illustrated in the virtual drumbeat of Jeremiah: moral order affects creational order—though not mechanistically or inevitably. Again and again, we read how human sin has an adverse effect upon the earth, indeed upon the entire cosmos. Because of human wickedness it does not rain (3.3; 2.12; 5.24-25; 14.4); the land is made desolate (12.10-11; see 23.10); the animals and birds are swept away (12.4; see 4.25; 9.10; 14.5-7; Hos. 4.3; Zeph. 1.3); and the land is polluted (3.2, 9; 16.18; see 2.7; Isa. 24.5) and mourns (12.4; see 4.28; 23.10; Isa. 24.4-7; 33.9; Hos. 4.3: Joel 1.10-20) to God (12.11).

Indeed, the entire 'earth...heavens' seems to be reduced to a pre-creation state of being (4.23-26), though the text (4.27) insists that no 'full end' of the earth is in view. Modern understandings of the interrelatedness of the ecosystem connect well with these biblical insights.

Jeremiah's God Is Not Aloof
This God of Jeremiah is no aloof God: somehow present and related but detached. God in Jeremiah is a God of great passions (pathos); God's deep and genuine divine feelings and emotions are manifest again and again. Sorrow, lament, weeping, wailing, grief, pain, anguish, heartache, regret and anger all are ascribed to God in Jeremiah (see Heschel 1962; Fretheim 1984). While these divine passions are focused on an unfaithful people, the earth and its creatures also get caught up into God's vulnerable heart.

For God, Israel and its land are 'my house...my heritage...the beloved of my heart...my vineyard...my portion...my pleasant portion' (12.7-10; see Ps 50.10-11). This recurrent use of 'my' shows that the relationship God has with people and land is not perfunctory in character; God is deeply involved in their life and is profoundly affected by that engagement.

At the same time, this display of divine emotion is not sentimental or romantic. God manifests not only sorrow (12.7; see 3.19-20; 9.10, 17-18 [ET]; 13.17) but also sword-wielding anger (12.12-13; see 4.26; 7.20 and often).

Indeed, into the midst of this language of closeness and possession comes the strong expression of hate (12.8; see Jer. 44.4; Amos 5.21; Hos. 9.15). As we know from close interhuman relationships, the sharp juxtaposition of love and hate language indicates something of the trauma of this broken relationship for God. These are emotions of great intensity, demonstrating the depth to which God's own 'heart and soul' are affected (see 32.41).

Special attention should be given to divine anger in Jeremiah. This is a difficult emotion for modern readers, not least because God in anger is made responsible at least in part for the environmental degradation. Take 4.23-26, 'I looked on the earth, and lo, it was waste and void...all the birds of the air had fled...the fruitful land was a desert...before the Lord, before his fierce anger' (see also 7.20; 10.10; 21.5-6; 44.22; 51.29, 43; more generally, see 2.15; 4.7, 20; 7.34; 45.4; 50.46; cf. Isa. 13.13; 24.18-20). This connection is also made in 12.11-13. The land is made desolate and produces thorns even though wheat has been sown—because of 'the sword of the Lord' and the 'fierce anger of the Lord'.

God's anger is always *provoked* by creaturely words and deeds (e.g. 7.18; 8.19; 32.29-32; for a fine treatment of this theme, see Heschel 1962). Anger is a divine response not a divine attribute; if there were no sin, there would be no anger. The sin most in focus in Jeremiah is infidelity—Israel's unfaithfulness to their relationship with God. The dominant metaphor is marital, assuming a deep intimacy between God and people; the images used are often graphic (e.g. 3.1-5; 13.20-27). In 'unpacking' this metaphor, the anger—mixed with other emotions—felt by a spouse at a partner's unfaithfulness may be used to signal something of the depth of God's feelings. The juxtaposition of anger over the breakdown of a close relationship, associated with sorrow over its personal and public effects—not least on the land—is evident in 12.7-13 (another striking text is 9.10-11 [ET]; the verb in 9.10 has God as subject, see NRSV footnote). The 'Godward' side of wrath is always grief; and a striking thing about the God of Jeremiah is that both the grief and the anger are revealed to the prophet, who puts both on public display. Readers must distinguish between—but never separate—these two responses in any interpretation of these texts.

These texts insist that this grieving, angry God bears some responsibility for the wasted land; refining this claim is no easy task. Consideration of two additional matters—both are implicit or explicit in Jeremiah 12—will help us sort this out: the relationship between sin and its consequences; and the issue of agency.

Sin and Judgment in Jeremiah

How one thinks about sin and judgment in Jeremiah shapes one's thinkng about the anger of God. The relationship between them is conceived in intrinsic rather than forensic terms. Jeremiah's call account sets the issue: disaster (*ra'ah*) breaks out because of the people's wickedness (*ra'ah*; 1.14, 16). This understanding may be observed in various formulations (note the image of 'fruit', as in 12.2). God brings disaster (*ra'ah*), which is 'the fruit of *their* schemes' (6.19; see 14.16). God gives to all 'according to their ways, according to the fruit of their doings' (17.10; see 32.19). In other words, *ra'ah* issues in *ra'ah*. Like fruit, the consequence grows out of (or is intrinsic to) the deed itself. God introduces nothing new into the situation, and so the consequence can be designated by the same word as the sin/evil.

This reality can also be observed in the use of the verb *paqad*, 'visit'. Its translation as 'punish' in NRSV is often problematic, as in 21.14: 'I will punish you according to the fruit of your doings'. A more literal translation catches the thought more precisely: 'I will visit upon you the fruit of your doings' (see 5.9; 14.10). These formulations show that God mediates the consequences of that which is already present in the wicked situation. The people's sin already has had a significant level of 'negative fallout' on the land, given the interrelatedness of all creatures; God's mediation of the effects brings those consequences to completion, though the agency issues cannot be factored out in any precise way. God's anger and withdrawal is a 'seeing to' the moral order for the sake of justice and a future for the land. It is no favor to the land (or people) to let evil and its ill effects go unchecked.

But God's way of resolving the problem does not entail a flick of the divine wrist—a 'quick fix'. To provide for a positive future for the land God uses another strategy; God enters deeply into the realities of sin and evil—including experiencing the very suffering that the land experiences (see below)—and breaks them open from within.

This understanding of judgment is supported by the fact that, while there is a personal dimension to divine anger, wrath is also impersonally conceived in Jeremiah (and elsewhere, e.g., Num. 1.53; 16.46). Wrath 'goes forth' because of their *ra'ah* (4.4=21.12; 23.19); 'is not turned away' (4.8; 23.20); 'bursts upon' (23.19); or 'is poured out upon' (7.20; 10.25; 42.18)—the effects may include environmental degradation. In this way of thinking, wrath is an effect that grows out of a violation of the moral order of God's creation. God's personal anger may be said to be a 'seeing to' this movement from deed to consequence that is the moral order.

God's Way of Working in the World

God works in the world through means—including human beings (within and without the community of faith) and, potentially, all other creatures. This is the case for both judgment (Nebuchadrezzar) and deliverance (Cyrus). This divine mediation may be observed in several ways in 12.7-13, with respect to both human beings and animals.

The 'sword of the Lord' (12.12; see 47.6), which God 'summons' and 'sends' (25.16, 29) refers to human beings wielding the sword (6.25; 20.4). The judgment of God is mediated through the Babylonian armies or, later, the enemies of Babylon (the 'weapons of his wrath', 50.25). A striking juxtaposition of God and the means God uses is evident in 13.14 and 21.7; both God and Nebuchadrezzar 'will not pity, or spare, or have compassion' in the destruction of Jerusalem (see 27.8, 'I [God] have completed its destruction by *his* hand'). For God, Nebuchadrezzar is 'my servant' (25.9; 27.6; 43.10; elsewhere God's 'servants' are David, Israel and the prophets!) for purposes of judgment in this situation. That God does not 'control' Nebuchadrezzar is shown by the fact he overreaches and exceeds the divine mandate (25.11-14; 51.24; see Isa. 47.5-7); Nebuchadrezzar is no puppet in the hands of God. This decision to work through less than perfect means is a risky move for God because God thereby becomes associated with their (often violent) activity, including the desolation of the land.

Servant language is also used for the birds and animals of the land in Jeremiah; they will 'serve' the king of Babylon in his judgmental work (27.6; see 28.14; they are parallel with the sword in 15.3). Such an understanding is present also in Jeremiah 12.9 (see 7.33; 16.4; 19.7). The animals may be used as metaphors for the Babylonians (e.g. 4.7; see Isa. 56.9), but these texts also speak of the agency of the animals themselves. Note also God's command to cut down the trees to make siege works (6.6) or the use of the hot wind (4.11; 22.22) and fire (5.14). Indeed, desolation of the land as an effect of human iniquity is used by God as an instrument of judgment (3.2-3; 5.24-25; 14.2-12). Using 'victim' language for the land and its animals insufficiently recognizes this 'vocation' to which God calls them in service of the divine purposes, a vocation that may entail suffering. This 'call to suffering' is a significant expression of the principle of purpose in Jeremiah 12. One might compare God's use of wind, waves, clouds and darkness in judgment of the Egyptians in Exodus 14–15; these nonhuman creatures become the *saviour* of the human!

Retelling the Earth Story in Jeremiah 12

Reading Jeremiah 12 from the standpoint of the earth as subject leads to a new appreciation of its place in God's creation. The charge that Jeremiah puts before God (12.1) is focused on the injustice of the prosperity of the wicked and he urges God to give them their just due

(12.3). But the rationale for his argument is not fully apparent until v. 4 (see section on structure above). The lament moves climactically to an appeal to God on behalf of the land and its non-human inhabitants (How long?). God's response to Jeremiah (12.5-17), while initially addressing Jeremiah's personal concerns (12.5-6), moves in 12.7-17 to focus on Jeremiah's concern about the land.

This perspective may be supported by Jeremiah's use of imagery regarding the land in 12.2. The land on which God planted these people (=Israel) is a bountiful land (see 2.7, 21; 11.17). This land has had a life-giving capacity to enable them—even the wicked!—to take root and thrive (12.2; 'it rains on the just and the unjust'). But the 'hearts' of the guilty and treacherous, unlike Jeremiah's 'heart' (12.3a), are bearing the fruits of wickedness (see above; 6.19; 17.10; 21.14). One such fruit is devastation for the land (12.4), a virtual refrain in Jeremiah (e.g. 2.8; 3.2-3; 4.26; 9.12 [ET]; see Hos. 4.1-3). The land is not the problem; the issue is the people who live on it. In the wake of their wickedness, the land—which could take the occasional drought in stride (see 17.7-8)—has become a veritable dust bowl (see 14.2-6). What kind of divine justice is this—that the wicked can have such effects on the land and apparently get away with it?

In this reading, Jeremiah's personal situation is seen as part and parcel of the situation faced also by the land. Both mourn because of the fruits of the wicked. The mourning of the land in Jeremiah provides evidence for the principle of voice in this text; the earth, depicted as subject, mourns in Jeremiah.

Jeremiah, whose wrath conforms to the wrath of God (6.11; 15.17), urges God to pull the wicked out of circulation from among God's sheep—violently (12.3). May they be led to the slaughter as they have led him (11.19)! Remove them from the land—not only for his sake, but also for the sake of the land.

How long must the land mourn? Only by removing this people from the land can the land be saved. Because of the people the land mourns. The grass of *every* field withers. The animals and the birds are swept away. The people deny any connection between this situation and their sin (12.4c; see 5.12). God does take some responsibility for this situation for the land (12.7) as we will see, but only because of the prior reality—'the wickedness of those who live' on the land (12.4b).

The translations of 12.4a vary in view of the fact that the same verbal root may mean both 'mourn' and 'dry up' (see Isa. 24.4). But 'mourn' is the usual focus of the verbal root and it clearly has that meaning with land as subject in 4.28, where it is parallel with the verb 'grow black' (see Joel 1.9-10). Probably both meanings are in view. The verb may pertain concretely to drought and desertification (see the parallel with 'wither', also in 23.10). Yet, that reference does not sufficiently attend to the land as a genuine subject in a larger lament-filled context. The land mourns not only because it is drying up, but also because it has been polluted by Israel's infidelities, devastated by foreign invasions, and forsaken by God. The land joins with Jeremiah and God in lamenting what has happened to the land. Even the people, stretched to the limit, can join in (14.2).

God's response first focuses on Jeremiah's personal situation (12.5-6; cf. 15.19) and then centers more comprehensively on the land and God's response to the wicked about whom Jeremiah has complained (12.7-13). The initial reply contains an enigmatic reference to the land as a 'safe land' (12.5b; or 'land of peace'); it may be a proverbial reference to the land. In 12.12 the land is not at peace ('safe') anymore. The point is that the land is a land of peace compared to what it will become; if Jeremiah has difficulty now, how will he fare when things really get rough (='thickets of the Jordan')? If Jeremiah thinks that family/friends (='foot-runners') have been difficult (see 11.18-23), and God admits they have been (12.6; cf. 12.2b), what will he do when all the wicked in Israel (=riders on horses) descend on him?

Jeremiah 12.7-13 continues God's response to Jeremiah, whose concern for the land (12.4) now becomes the focus of divine consideration; appropriately, the wicked are also in view. As noted, these verses are a divine lament, not an announcement of judgment—which seems to be already in progress (on this text, see Fretheim 1984: 66, 133-34, 157). God's lament over the land matches Jeremiah's lament in 12.4; indeed, the land itself laments and that lamenting has reached the heart of God (12.11). People have not 'laid to heart' the suffering of the land (12.11), but God's heart (12.7) has been deeply touched by it. At the same time, God's forsaking action is also complicit in these developments for the land (see Ps. 107.33-34).

This focus on the land is especially evident in the use of the word 'heritage' (*nahalah*)—God's own possession—used five times in this chapter (on this theme, see Habel 1995: 33-35, 75-96). In Jeremiah, the word usually refers to Canaan as God's gift to Israel or God's own possession (2.7; 3.19; 16.18; 17.4; 50.11). The word may also refer to the people as God's possession (12.8; 10.16; see Deut. 9.29; 32.9). Habel understands the word in terms of a God–people–land 'symbiosis'. In Jeremiah 12 'heritage' usually refers to the land (12.7, 9, 14-15); in 12.8 it refers to the people—whom God hates because they lift up their voice 'against me'. In Jeremiah, 'heritage' is focused on the land, but extended to incorporate the people of the land; both are God's own possession. God's 'house' may refer to temple, land or people (used with 'beloved', it refers to temple in 11.15; see 23.11; 13.11)—in fact, all may be in view.

God's forsaking is comprehensive in scope; God has left temple, land and people. Readers would recall that temple and land are inter-related. From this sanctuary—God's special dwelling place in the land—blessings flow out into all the land (e.g. Ps. 132). But if God forsakes the temple (see Ezek. 8.6), then it no longer has the capacity for blessing.

Jeremiah 12.10 uses 'my' language again—'my vineyard' (2.21; 5.10; 6.9; see Isa. 5.1-7) and 'my (pleasant) portion', a variant formulation of *nahalah* that reiterates that the land is God's land. It is striking that, with all these 'my' references affirming divine ownership of the land, that God cannot take care of the land any better than this. But, as noted above, God's way of possessing does not entail 'control'. God delegates responsibility for the land to others—with all the attendant risks; God will not micromanage their handling of their duties, or intervene to make sure every little thing is done correctly. This way of relating to people and world reveals a divine vulnerability: for God opens the divine self up to hurt should things go wrong—and we hear that hurt expressed here in anguished tones.

God's lament begins with a virtual refrain regarding what God has done with respect to the land and people. God has forsaken (9.2 [ET]; 25.38), but this is not a divine initiative; God has forsaken 'my house' because the people have forsaken God (2.13, 17, 19; 5.7, 19). God has abandoned 'my heritage' (7.29; 23.33, 39), but (again) because the people have abandoned God (15.6). God has given them over to their enemies (as in 21.7) because of their wickedness. Notice the passive language in 12.7—God gives them over to the effects of their sins (see Isa. 54.7-8; 64.7).

It is important, however, not to claim too much for the divine abandonment. It is not that 'God's withdrawal has caused fertility to end and exposes the land...to chaos' (Brueggemann 1998: 122), but that the already devastating effects of the people's wickedness are thereby brought to completion in the moral order which God mediates. Also, to assert that 'Yahweh has withdrawn fidelity' (Brueggemann 1998: 121) suggests that God is not faithful in judg-ment; judgment may in fact be the only way in which God can be faithful in this particular situation.

Jeremiah 12.8 specifies the key factor in this divine move: Israel has become like a lion to God. Heretofore, the lion metaphor has usually been used for the foe from the north that will devour Israel (e.g. 2.15; 4.7; 5.6; see 5.17). But in this text, as in Israel's persecution of the prophets (2.30), Israel has turned on God like a roaring lion, making God its prey. This self-identification of God as prey is remarkable! But in this position God is not a victim—God is not without significant resources. In response God 'hates'; that is, God treats Israel as enemy and sends in the lions and other wild animals.

Inasmuch as these are animals of the land, to call the land a 'victim' in this situation is inadequate—indeed, in this text the land is depicted as resisting the destruction resulting from human activities. In Jeremiah, the animals bring resources to fight for the land (see above: section on animals as servants). Heretofore, other preying animals have been used to speak—literally and metaphorically—of God's instruments of judgment (wolf, leopard, snakes: 5.6; 8.17). That list is expanded with the use of hyenas and birds of prey. Indeed, God calls 'all' the wild animals to be instruments of judgment (12.9). The hyena image in 12.9a (the translation is uncertain) probably implies that the land has been so polluted by its inhabitants (see 2.7; 3.2) that it has become food only for such scavengers. The hyena greedily moves in on its prey while the vultures circle above, and God commands other animals to join in the devouring of Israel (15.3; see 5.17).

A 'what goes around, comes around' understanding informs this text (see above). The people have become lions to God, and hence the lions will attack them. They have made God their prey and hence they will become prey. At the same time, the land gets caught in the middle—it too becomes prey. In God's repetitive, personal and emotion-laden words (12.10-11): the land has become desolate, desolate, desolate, desolate! The land gets hit from several sides:

- it suffers from drought, so that farmers reap only weeds and thorns (12.4, 13; 3.3; 5.23-25; 14.2-6; see Gen. 3.18);
- Israel's wickedness and neglect adversely affect the land (12.8, 11; see 2.7; 3.2-3);
- invading armies (12.10; called 'shepherds' in 6.3; Israel's own shepherds/kings may also be in view, 10.21; 23.1) trample on the land and its vineyards, destroying crops, making the land a wilderness (12.10-11; see 2.15; 4.7, 26-27; 9.10-12 [ET]; 10.22); they have entered into the land across every caravan route (or every hill, 12.12) and plundered it;
- God is active in and through all these desolating events for the land (12.7, 9, 12-13).

'No one is safe' (12.12), perhaps especially not the land.

Readers, who are apt to focus on the effects of these judgments on people, should ponder the sheer force of all of these agents arrayed against the land. The land doesn't stand a chance and becomes prey. In this respect, the land is like the people; but it is even more like God. The land is like God: land and God do not deserve what has happened to them. The land shares with God the status of 'prey'. Land and God are also alike in that both mourn. But, while there is this mutuality in mourning over what has happened, there is a deep inequality as well: the land mourns to God (12.11), but God is able to marshal resources to deal with this moment that the land cannot.

But Jeremiah's (and the readers!) questions in 12.4 now return—at a higher decibel! What kinds of resources does God bring? Doesn't God make things even worse for the land? Given *God's* actions, the land is mourning even more now. God's sword-wielding anger across the length and breadth of the land has resulted in a land that is more devastated and desolate (12.12). How long will the land mourn?

Jeremiah had asked God to pull the people out of the land for the sake of the land (12.3-4). God's response in 12.7-13 is that the resolution of Jeremiah's lament is more complicated than Jeremiah (and often readers) think. Yes, Jeremiah is right, the people must be up-rooted from the land for the sake of the land—but that end cannot be accomplished with a divine flick of the wrist. The enemies of God and land cannot be dealt with in a moment—and there is always 'collateral damage'. God's sword does not cut clean; God has chosen to relate to the world through means that are available—and only violent means may be available—rather than do things alone (see section on agency above). God does not perfect people before working through them, including armies led by 'my servant' Nebuchadrezzar (25.9; 27.6). God responds to the mourning of Jeremiah and the land—but it will take a complex series of often violent events to bring about a 'land of peace' once again.

This divine move may seem suspect, but we are helped in thinking about it by the other dimension of God's response to the situation: God's grief (see above). The personal, emotional, and repetitious language shows how much what happens to the land and people is a genuine loss for God. Given the divine commitment to people and land and the centuries-long relationship with them, God cannot respond indifferently. God is truly caught up in what has happened here and mourns the loss. Abraham Heschel (1962: 112) captures this thought well:

> With Israel's distress came the affliction of God, [God's]...displacement, [God's]...homelessness in the land, in the world... Should Israel cease to

be home, then God, we might say, would be without a home in the
world.

Yes, God forsakes and abandons and gives over the land with its
people—but at tremendous suffering for God. Yet, divine suffering is
the only way into a future for the land (see 31.20; Isa. 54.7-8). This
divine agony is necessary for the sake of a future for the land, and
12.14-17 begins to address that issue.

Jeremiah 12.14-17 speaks to a question that exilic readers may have
asked: will the invaders who plundered people and land get away
with it? As noted, these verses could also be understood as a response
to Jeremiah's lament: how long will the land mourn? In an exilic context, Jeremiah's question about the wicked (12.1) would be expanded
to include the overreaching, proud Babylonians and their allies and
their mistreatment of the land (see 12.14; 25.11-14; 50.29; 51.24). These
marauders have not spoken the last word about the land. God has a
future for the land beyond all of this desolation, and these verses begin
to address that. The book of Consolation will continue this theme, for
example, 30.16, 'All who devour you shall be devoured...those who
plunder you shall be plundered, and all who prey on you I will make
a prey' (more positively, see 31.5, 12, 14; 32.41-44; 33.10-13; 50.19). The
land will become a 'land of peace' once again.

Continuing the use of the personal 'my' (12.14), God announces
judgment on 'my evil neighbors'. These nations surrounding Israel—
especially Babylonia—had 'plundered' the heritage (NAB; the NRSV
translation 'touch' seems weak). Notably, God refers to them as 'my'
evil neighbors; God is included in the Israelite community and is a
resident of its land! The enemies of Israel and its land are God's enemies. The nations that God used to 'pluck up' Israel will now themselves be plucked up (see 1.10; 18.7-10). This verb also refers to the
people of Israel (=the house of Judah) whom God will 'pluck up' (in a
positive sense) from the nations where they have been dispersed. The
third usage of this verb (12.15) seems to refer to all ('everyone') whom
God has uprooted in the past, whether from the nations or the house
of Judah. God will have compassion upon them, and return them
again to their heritage/land. Hence, the focus on land is finally not
simply on the land of promise, but on the heritage/land of all peoples.
God's concern about land has universal dimensions (see the positive
words in the oracles against the nations, 46.26; 48.47; 49.6, 39). Jeremiah is truly a prophet to the nations (1.5, 10).

Then, 12.16-17 seems to refer solely to the 'evil neighbors' upon
whom God has had compassion and whom God has returned to their
homelands. They are to learn the ways of YHWH as assiduously as

they had earlier taught the people of Israel to worship Baal and swear by that god. If they do this, they shall be built up in the midst of God's people (again, see 1.10). If they will not listen, then God will uproot that people from their land and destroy them. This conditional future offered to the other nations is at least in part for the sake of the future of God's own people and God's own land. The implication to be drawn with respect to Israel and the land seems to be this: never again!

God's purposes in the world must be conceived in relation to the story of all of God's creatures, including the land. Using Isaiah's language (65.17-25; see 11.6-9), God is creating a new earth and it will be populated by animals, vegetation and people (see Hos. 2.18-23). Comparably, the salvation oracles of Jeremiah are remarkably inclusive in their orientation, including non-Israelites (e.g. 3.17; 12.14-17; cf. 29.7) and the land itself (31.5, 12, 14, 27; 32.42-44; 33.10-13; 50.19).

When the trumpet sounds, and God rides the cloud chariots into a new heaven and a new earth, the children will come singing, leading wolves and leopards and playing among the snakes. They will not hurt or destroy, for God will, finally, 'give rest to the earth' (50.34; see Isa. 14.7; 51.3).

Psalm 8: An Apology for Domination

Keith Carley

Introduction

Psalm 8 is widely regarded as one of the most inspiring, uplifting poems ever written. By apparently affirming the God-like qualities of human beings irrespective of gender or culture, all humans are accorded equal worth. Since they have authority over the 'natural' world, there is nothing humans need fear.

The psalm also conveys a sense of reverent wonder at the mystery of human existence, as the author contemplates the night sky.

It may seem churlish—even sacrilegious—to question these popular perceptions of the psalm's meaning. But there are features of the psalm about which we can be less than sanguine, particularly with respect to its implications for the environment and social justice.

Earth is portrayed in the psalm as an inanimate stage for the display of divine and human power rather than the vital source of life we now know it to be. The non-human creatures—indeed the whole creation—are seen as subject to human rule. The psalmist's attitude to enemies is also problematic.

Psalm 8 can be seen as an apology for the theme of domination expressed in many parts of the Bible (Wink 1992: 43-44). It raises sharply several issues at variance with ecojustice principles and illustrates the importance of making an imaginative response on behalf of the living Earth—and, indeed, of the whole cosmos.

In what follows, Psalm 8 will be considered in the light of the ecojustice principles of the Earth Bible Project. It must be said at the outset that the six principles are derived from emphases within the biblical traditions. They represent what seem to this author to be the implications of God's love for the whole creation, of God's bias towards the poor and the oppressed and of humankind's task. It is our task, as an integral part of the ecosystem, to act as partners in accepting and extending God's love and justice as the whole creation grows (or groans, Rom. 8.22) to become a place of peace and sufficiency.

Acknowledging the Viewpoint

The New Testament scholar Walter Wink (1993: 477) describes the coining of the term 'ecojustice' as inspired: 'here in a single word the connection is made between social justice and justice to life in all its forms. All justice is now ecological. All species have rights. All life is sacred.'

An ecojustice reading of the Bible is not disinterested. The reader listens carefully to the biblical text, open to what is expressed there. The reader also recognizes the limits of any one passage's point of view and critiques the text in the light of a broader range of perspectives, including perspectives from contemporary study of cosmology and sociology, which the biblical text itself may have played a part in shaping.

This movement from text to interpreter and the reverse is a continuing process. Interpreters struggle under the Holy Spirit's guidance to clarify the implications of texts as they intersect with contemporary wisdom. In his day, Jesus redefined the meaning of ancient texts: 'you have heard it that it was said...but I say...' (Mt. 5.21-48). Daniel Patte notes the change a Gentile woman, who begged healing for her daughter and was at first refused, apparently evoked in Jesus' concept of his mission as limited to the people of Israel (Mt. 15.24). Like this Canaanite woman, we too may have to question accepted meanings of texts on the grounds of what Patte terms 'higher convictions' (1999: 18).

Like liberation, feminist and post-colonialist exegesis, the related ideological perspective of ecojustice encourages us to

> interrogate the Bible as a cultural product...[to] analyse the myriad ways the Bible has been used in the colonial discourse and offer concrete examples of reading strategies from the marginalized communities...; ideological criticism of the Bible has challenged the apolitical reification of the Bible as the Word of God [when it is in fact] 'the product, the record, the site, and the weapon of class, cultural, gender, and racial struggle' (Kwok 1996: 212-13).

We are challenged by the environmental and social context of our own day to read from the marginalized position of the living Earth—its ecosystems are threatened, sometimes by deliberately greedy exploitation, sometimes by simple lack of awareness of Earth's fragility.

Reading Psalm 8 in the light of the guiding ecojustice principles reveals significant differences between the horizon of the text and the horizon of the contemporary ecotheologian. We should not, as

Leonardo Boff has put it, 'keep trying to situate and re-situate such texts in the context of Middle Eastern anthropology in order to dispel their anti-ecological tenor' (1997: 80).

Psalm 8: An Initial Response

Psalm 8 as translated in one widely read English version (NRSV):

> [1] LORD, our Sovereign, how majestic is your name in all the earth!
> You have set your glory above the heavens.
> [2] Out of the mouths of babes and infants you have founded a bulwark
> because of your foes, to silence the enemy and the avenger.
> [3] When I look at your heavens, the work of your fingers, the moon and
> the stars that you have established;
> [4] what are human beings that you are mindful of them, mortals that you
> care for them?
> [5] Yet you have made them a little lower than God, and crowned them
> with glory and honour.
> [6] You have given them dominion over the works of your hands; you
> have put all things under their feet,
> [7] all sheep and oxen, and also the beasts of the field,
> [8] the birds of the air, and the fish of the seas, whatever passes along the
> paths of the seas.
> [9] O LORD, our Sovereign, how majestic is your name in all the earth!

Some of the issues raised by an ecojustice reading of the psalm have already been hinted at. The apparently inert Earth,[1] the privileged position of humans, the silenced enemies.

People respond to stimuli in different ways—some give precedence to visual stimuli, others to aural, others to tactile or kinaesthetic stimuli (whether touch, taste or smell). In a workshop where Psalm 8 was reviewed from an ecojustice perspective, one member of the group, preferring a visual approach, drew a picture of how the psalm portrayed reality. The result was something like the following:

---

1.   Understanding 'inert' to mean 'having no inherent power of action, motion, or resistance; without active chemical or physiological properties; unreactive' (Brown 1993).

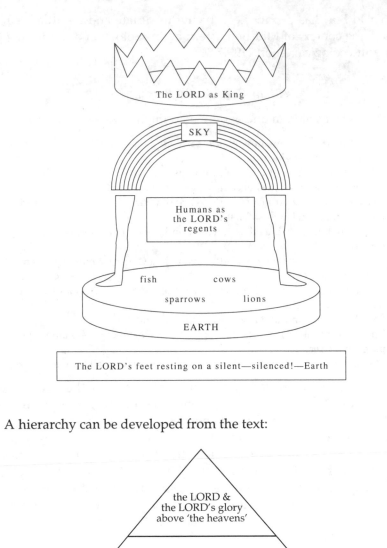

A hierarchy can be developed from the text:

The Inclusio

Such a response runs against the grain of most interpretations of the psalm and the difficulty begins with its first and last lines: 'LORD, our Sovereign, how majestic is your name in all the earth!' The repeated acclamation forms what is technically termed an *inclusio*; it brackets the material in between and gives a sense of completeness to the psalm. The *inclusio* states and restates a significant theme of the psalm, and provides clues to the theological and social location of its author.[2]

On the basis of the *inclusio*, the main theme is sometimes assumed to be that the Earth manifests the presence of God. Since the 'name' of God is often found as a synonym for the personal presence of God elsewhere in the Hebrew Scriptures (Deut. 12.5; 1 Kgs 8.16), the acclamation is thought to indicate that God's being is revealed in the Earth. Moses Buttenweiser is explicit: 'the theme of the psalm is the divine immanence' (1938: 179).

But James L. Mays argues to the contrary: 'the psalm does not imply that the sovereign self of God is apparent in the visible world' (1994: 65). A closer reading of the *inclusio* suggests that the theme is not Earth's testimony to God but worshippers' celebration of the power of their deity. The whole Earth is said to experience the exercise of that power.

But unlike numerous other texts,[3] in this psalm, Earth is voiceless! There is no engagement with the ecojustice principle of voice. We have no indication of Earth's response to the psalmist's celebration of God's power throughout its length and breadth. The voices uttering the acclamation are human, and they assert the prime place of humans in the created order;[4] no other voice is heard in this psalm. The theocentric and anthropocentric foci of the psalm leave no room for the voices of either the Earth or its non-human creatures.

To clarify the content of the *inclusio*, the word 'LORD' translates the sacred Hebrew name *YHWH*, the distinctively Israelite name for God, as opposed to the more general Hebrew term *Elohim*. The psalm was

---

2.   Gerstenberger, while noting that 'there is currently no satisfying study on the social and liturgical setting of Psalm 8', argues cogently that the psalm belongs to 'the latest strata of the Old Testament...in Jewish synagogal rites' (1988: 70, 68).

3.   Earth mourns (Isa. 24.4), rejoices (Ps. 97.1), trembles (Ps. 77.18) and swallows the unrighteous (Num. 16.32).

4.   Levine notes the 'symmetrical envelope structure' of the psalm, with the human creature at the very centre of the verbal symmetry (1995: 90).

therefore once part of the liturgical resources of the biblical community of Israel/Judah.

Further, in the Hebrew the words 'our Sovereign' literally mean 'our Lord', a characteristic form of address for a king (1 Kgs 1.11), indicating the psalmist's intention of portraying YHWH as a royal figure. This coheres with the observation that the Hebrew word rendered 'majestic' (*'addir*) designates might or power—again sometimes an attribute of royalty. The hierarchical dualism distinguishing royal from common is clearly an important factor in this psalm. Its implications will be noted subsequently.

That the *inclusio* affirms the power rather than the immanence of YHWH in the Earth is supported by the analogous phrase in Ps. 93.4: 'YHWH is mighty in heaven'.[5] As Kraus acknowledges, the regal power of YHWH's name in this context 'preserves the exclusiveness of YHWH's might' (1988: 180). No other power need be acknowledged by any creature. By implication, those who acknowledge the name of Israel's God—the community worshipping 'our Lord'— identify with YHWH's kingly power over all other people and ideologies in the whole Earth.

We have here the beginning of an answer to the important question: whose interests does this psalm serve?

Above the Sky

The second half of the Hebrew text of verse 1 is difficult to translate. Suggested readings are 'you have set your glory above the heavens' (NRSV), or 'I will worship your glory above the heavens'.[6] Both alternatives assume another hierarchical dualism.[7] This dualistic pair, however, are not Earth and sky,[8] but Earth and sky together as the created order, contrasted with the domain of YHWH 'above the sky'. The term 'glory' in this verse can be understood both as a synonym for YHWH's personal presence and as a royal attribute (Warmuth 1978: 353). The text conveys an image of a transcendent monarch; the ruler is not necessarily remote or inaccessible—at least not to worshippers—but is not located within the created order.

5. The appropriate rendering of the Hebrew *marom* in Ps. 93.4 is 'heaven' according to Richardson (1995: 633).

6. Dahood, Craigie *et al.* (Craigie 1983: 105).

7. On the important distinction between natural and dominator hierarchies, see Wilber (1996: 28).

8. For Habel's preferred term, see 'Geophany: the Earth Story in Genesis 1' in volume 2 of this series.

The Earth Bible Team has indicated the problems inherent in such hierarchical dualisms. When heaven is God's abode, Earth is devalued. 'The reader who dares to assume the posture of the Earth hears the voice of a controlled subject beneath God's feet.'[9] This imagery is actually found within Psalm 8—even though the feet are not directly those of God, nor are they specifically said to rest on the Earth.

Writing of the 'pernicious effects' of such dualisms, Grace M. Jantzen (1998: 266-68) characterizes the concept of divine transcendence as 'the most emphatic dualism of all…in which God, that which is of ultimate value, is seen as separate from and other than the material world'; divine transcendence validates and underwrites the whole system of binary polarities and in conjunction with the command to subdue the earth and have dominion over all living things in it, 'has been taken as an unbridled license for "Christian" men to dominate women, the earth, and indeed anyone other than themselves'. In the light of Jantzen's analysis, ignoring the ecojustice principle of the intrinsic worth of all parts of creation has broad ramifications. I will return to the difficult issues raised by the second verse of Psalm 8 later.

In v. 4, the words 'human beings' and 'mortals' render Hebrew expressions (*'enosh* and *ben-'adam*), which are best understood as parallel terms referring to the same subject. Helmer Ringgren observes that the subject may have been 'Adam, the king, or man [*sic*] in general' (1963: 98). The second of the words, rendered 'mortals' in this translation, is literally 'son of man'. The author of Heb. 2.5-9 applies the psalm to Jesus as the only one who, as yet, has authority over all things. Also, though the terms are masculine in Hebrew, they are both sometimes used in a generic sense, inclusive of both male and female human beings. Because of this, Kathleen A. Farmer (1992: 142) encourages women 'to enjoy the favoured position they occupy in God's created order' according to Psalm 8.

Yet, while these are possible later applications of the text, the horizon of the author is likely to have been more narrowly focused on those who, with him, acknowledged the name of YHWH—that is, the Israelite/Judean communities of the biblical period and predominantly the male members of those communities.

It is difficult to know exactly what is meant when those who acknowledge YHWH are said in v. 5 to have been made 'a little lower than God',[10] but the ascription to the human/mortals of 'glory'[11] and

---

9.   See Earth Bible Team, 'Guiding Ecojustice Principles', in this volume.
10.   Literally, 'you have deprived them of little in comparison with *Elohim*'.

'honour'—terms elsewhere used of kings (Ps. 45.3) and of YHWH (Ps. 29.1)—indicates their royal, almost divine status. This is confirmed in v. 6: 'you have given them dominion over the work of your hands; you have put all things under their feet'.

Dominion

The Hebrew verb *mšl*—rendered 'have dominion' in this translation of Ps. 8.6—in other contexts means 'to rule, exercise dominion or authority over'. It is used of kings ruling over their subjects or over subject nations (Josh. 12.2; Isa. 19.4). It is also used of YHWH ruling over nations (Ps. 22.28), of siblings over one another (Gen. 37.8), and of a husband exercising authority over his wife (Gen. 3.16). In Gen. 1.26-28—a passage often compared with Psalm 8,[12] and clearly closely related to it—a different Hebrew verb, *rdh*, is used to convey to the first humans that they are to 'have dominion' over the other living creatures. The Hebrew verb *rdh* is said to have 'an associated meaning of oppression' (Richardson 1996: 1190). Several scholars disagree: Norbert Lohfink has argued that it has the basic sense of 'to wander around', and its meaning in the context of Gen. 1.28 is 'to be a shepherd' (Rogerson 1991: 19); Jürgen Moltmann asserts that it means to play the role of a justice of the peace (1985: 30).

The accompanying phrase in Gen. 1.26-28, commanding the first humans to 'subdue' the earth, uses a word whose oppressive connotations are less debatable. The Hebrew verb *kbš* means 'to tread down, subordinate, subdue' and it is used in reference to forcing people into slavery (Neh. 5.5), violating a woman (Est. 7.8) and subduing nations (2 Sam. 8.11). Robert Murray has warned that both words (*rdh* and *kbš*) 'have been understood too crudely by those who say that they both connote violent subjection without implying limits on how humans may treat other creatures' (1992: 99). The problem is that such connotations are possible, and subjection is subjection however much it is qualified.

11.   The Hebrew word *kabod* rendered 'glory' in v. 5 is more commonly used to signify the divine presence than the word *hod* used in v. 2.

12.   Ferguson suggests 'Gen. 1.26-27 seems to be glossed by Psalm 8.3' (1998: 14), and Mays observes that 'on the authority of the Genesis passage (1.26-28), the psalmist has put the entire race in the status of a king' (1994: 67).

Under the Feet

Although the verb *kbš* does not occur in Psalm 8, the meaning of the words 'put...under their feet' in v. 6 is unequivocal. In the royal Psalm 18, the king reports striking down his enemies 'under my feet' (18.38). Psalm 47.3 also refers to YHWH subduing people 'under our feet'. Such an expression clearly indicates vigorous conquest by a superior force.

Numerous scholars have attempted to soften the harsh implications of Ps. 8.6. Some argue that the authority accorded humans here implies protection for birds, fish and beasts. Benedict Janecko, for example, understands the phrase 'to have dominion' to mean humans 'are to care responsibly for all creatures such as sheep, oxen, beasts of the field, birds, fishes' (1990: 101-102).

James Limburg, in his 'ecological reading' of Psalm 8, notes the implicit ascription of royalty to humankind in v. 5 and 6 and goes on to identify the responsibilities of royalty according to the descriptions of monarchs in Ezekiel 34 and Psalm 72. In the former passage, kings (figuratively shepherds) should feed their subjects, strengthening the weak, binding up the injured and seeking the lost (34.2-4). In Psalm 72, the king's first priority—as one who has 'dominion from sea to sea' (72.8)—is to rule with divine justice and righteousness and defend the cause of the poor (72.1-2, 4). Thus for a king to exercise what Limburg calls 'proper dominion' means that he 'care[s] for those over whom he rules... Translated into the imagery of Psalm 8, this means that humans are expected to care for the earth and its creatures. Such is the responsibility of royalty' (1992: 50).

However, as Norman Habel demonstrates earlier in this volume, (p. 31) the use of Psalm 72 to argue that *rdh* means 'ruling with justice' is problematic. The verb *rdh* in Ps. 72.8 does not refer back to the justice theme of the earlier verses (72.1-4), but to the opening line of the strophe (72.7-11) where ruling refers to the conquest of foes who fall down in subservience and 'lick the dust'.

Unfortunately, it is all too apparent in our own day that neither royalty nor presidents exemplify the ideals expressed for their offices. The Bible is amazingly candid about the faults of Israel's and Judah's kings. The so-called 'democratisation of royal prerogatives and responsibilities' —such as we find in postexilic texts like Psalm 8 and Genesis 1—was probably a response to the failings of monarchs; their errors were believed to have culminated in the Babylonian exile. Limburg indeed acknowledges the difference between the ideal and the

actual fulfilment of royal responsibilities in the closing words of his
article. 'Who cares for the earth?... The answer provided by the eighth
psalm is clear. Who cares for the earth and its creatures, its lakes and
its rivers, its mountains and its sky? God does. God's people *ought* to'
(1992: 52, my emphasis).

Finally, it is important to note what is sometimes not mentioned by
commentators in relation to v. 6, namely that the human/mortals are
not given dominion only over the other living creatures. The phrase in
v. 3—'the work of your fingers'—parallels the phrase 'the work of
your hands' in v. 6. This implies that humans are also given dominion, at least figuratively, over sky, moon and stars as well. As Craigie
points out, while it is specifically living creatures that are singled out
in vv. 7-8 as the subjects of control, 'mankind's mastery is to extend
over all created things' (1983: 108). The Contemporary English Version aptly translates Ps. 8.6 as 'You let us rule everything your hands
have made. And you put all of it under our power.'

If it is correct to see predominantly male YHWH worshippers as
those whose interests are primarily served by Psalm 8, it is clearer
now what those interests entailed: royal, near-divine authority over
everything under the heavens!

The Enemy and the Avenger

The most difficult part of Psalm 8 is v. 2: 'out of the mouths of babes
and infants you have founded a bulwark because of your foes, to
silence the enemy and the avenger'. The identity of the babes and
infants is no clearer than that of the enemy and the avenger. It is
sometimes assumed that the former are those who acknowledge their
dependence on YHWH. Whether we should take the allusion to
infancy literally is also debated. H.C. Leupold proposes that the
Lord's name requires 'no stronger defence than the praise of children'
(1959: 102).

From a rhetorical perspective, the imagery of the weak or
dependent overcoming powerful foes could be regarded as a scornful
jibe, intended to humble any opposition—rhetoric of the kind the
Jebusites used to boast the impregnability of Jerusalem: 'the blind and
the lame shall not come into the house' (2 Sam. 5.8).

Mark S. Smith's recent study of the passage, however, supports the
argument that there is a parallel between the 'sucking babes'[13] and the

13. In this verse, 'babes' and 'infants' represent parallel terms, like 'human
beings' and 'mortals' in v. 4.

Canaanite conception of cosmic foes[14] who threaten to devour all the beasts of the cosmos. Smith thus translates the first half of the verse as 'From the mouth of suckling babes you establish a strong place', noting that '"From the mouth of" does not refer to the material from which the stronghold is built; instead, it constitutes the threat for which the stronghold is needed' (1997: 639).

Many suggestions have been made regarding the identity of the enemy and the avenger, including atheists and sceptics[15] and the hostile powers of chaos. In Ps. 44.16 the 'enemy and avenger' are clearly opponents of the psalmist, and it is natural for worshippers to identify their own personal enemies with the enemies of YHWH in Psalm 8.

Most contemporary commentators assume the allusion in Psalm 8 is to an ancient creation myth.[16] Smith translates the second half of the verse as 'for your stronghold you indeed ended (*šbt*) the avenging enemies'. YHWH secured the cosmos as a safe place (cf. Ps. 104.5) by overcoming cosmic enemies (1997: 640).

It is significant that the Hebrew verbal root *šbt*, used to describe the fate of the enemies in v. 2, is the same as that used to indicate God's cessation from the work of creation in Gen. 2.2-3. There is a sinister ring to 'rest' for the enemies in Psalm 8. There appears to be no place for anyone who opposes YHWH—or, by implication, anyone who opposes the interests of YHWH's worshippers—in the world depicted in Psalm 8.

In Whose Interests?

In the light of all the above, the question that has been implicit—whose interests does this psalm serve?—yields an uncomfortable answer. The Earth's interests are certainly not central in Psalm 8.

The various clues to the theological and social location of Psalm 8 suggest that the psalm may in reality not even be so much about the glory of God as about the glory of male worshippers of YHWH and their control over all creation. Included under their control—though unstated in this psalm—are likely to be Israelite women: their social

14. In Ugaritic *ynqm*; compare the Hebrew *ynqm*, 'infants'.

15. Weiser (1962: 141). Martin Luther envisaged the pope 'and his cohorts' among the enemies; the avenger he identified as 'primarily the synagogue and the Jewish people' (Pelikan 1955: 114-15). John Calvin regarded the enemy in this psalm as 'the hardened despisers of God' (Kraus 1988: 69).

16. E.g. Mays (1994: 66); Dahood (1966: 50-51). Gerstenberger comments: 'creation is not a peaceful affair but a war against chthonic powers' (1988: 69).

subjection in the communities of biblical Israel is well documented.[17] The psalm also specifies the subjection of non-human living creatures; while cosmic—perhaps subconscious—forces of resistance are said to have been already eliminated.[18]

It might be said then that Psalm 8 is a classic expression of the dominating male ego, reinforced by the psalmist's projection of this assertion of power as the will of Israel's transcendent God.[19] So alluring is the control and security of the world view in Psalm 8 that women and Gentiles willingly identify with the masterful males who first gave voice to it and preserved it as a regularly repeated part of Jewish—and later Christian—liturgy.

The promotion of glory—even, supposedly, YHWH's glory—is strongly associated with the Davidic–Solomonic establishment in biblical Israel/Judah. Expropriation and commodification of land is assumed to be part of royal behaviour (1 Sam. 8.14); the ensuing injustice was the occasion of many prophetic diatribes. We see reflections of such behaviour in the contemporary promotion of national statehood, trading cartels and free-market economics that do not share the goods of the Earth equitably among people, and do not demonstrate consideration for other creatures and the inanimate environment.

Facing the Cost

Although this may seem an unduly harsh evaluation of Psalm 8, it does not deny the value the psalm has had for countless generations of worshippers. It will no doubt continue to be a source of encouragement to those who feel intimidated by 'natural forces' in the created world, or intimidated by enemies proclaiming the power of gods other than YHWH.

In the context of the Babylonian hegemony, when people believed

17.   Despite the recent efforts of numerous scholars to highlight the positive status and achievements of women within societies in biblical times, in the First Testament period 'women's legal status…may be characterised as generally subordinate to males. As a general rule, women within the family were subject to male authority' (Bird 1992: 955-56). Delaney (1989: 38) regards the story of the sacrifice of Isaac as central to Israelite and Christian traditions and culture and argues that 'its meaning is to be found not in the ending of the practice of child sacrifice but rather in the establishment of father-right…the foundation of patriarchy'; on this subject, see Ruether (1992b: 178-81).

18.   BDB renders hiphil *šbt* in v. 2 as 'exterminate, destroy'.

19.   Jantzen notes the link between the 'unquestioned maleness of God' and masculine dominance (1998: 172).

the sun and moon were divine powers, and that their fate was written in the stars, the author of Genesis 1 was perhaps, as Nico ter Linden expresses it, 'a bold priest…demystifying the cosmos' with his song of faith against fear (1999: 8). The same could be said for the author of Psalm 8.

The problem is that the cost of such demystifying has been acceptance of domination as an acceptable means of dealing with life's uncertainties. It also results in the neglect of the unity of the cosmos, not to mention the suffering of animals and Earth as victims of this domination.

This cost has been hidden for a long time. Even at the beginning of the twentieth century, so perspicacious a mind as that of William James, the American philosopher and psychologist, wrote of the 'immemorial warfare against nature'; instead of military conscription he advocated that young men[20] should for a certain number of years be part of an army 'enlisted against nature' (1910: 171-72). He wrote elsewhere of nature's 'brutality' overturning our peace (1888: 231-32), and noted that

> our sacred books and traditions tell us of one God who made heaven and earth, and, looking on them, saw that they were good. Yet, on more intimate acquaintance, the visible surfaces of heaven and earth refuse to be brought by us into any intelligible unity at all (1895: 41).

At the beginning of the twenty-first century, however, it is time to recognize with Richard Bauckham that 'humanity has become so dominant as to threaten the very survival of much of the animal creation' (1989: 15-16). We need to say with Sam Keen 'No!' to warfare against nature; 'we can no longer base our dignity as humans on dominating nature' (1991: 174).

A Psalm of Earth

We have seen how a psalmist in an earlier time reflected on the night sky. In the light of the above discussion, I imagine Earth might respond to the psalmist's reflections like this:

> O God of depths and heights, of infinite expanse and every place,
> your glory is seen in all things.
> In gentle, persistent growth unnoticed by humankind,
> in diversity prodigious that takes place in my soil,
> your glory is displayed to those with eyes to see.

---

20. Editor's note: although this term seems exclusive, it is apposite—only young men were conscripted into service in 1910, when James wrote this piece.

How foolish humans are to assume your ways are as conflicted as their
        own,
to think you deal with enemies as they do.
Your love surrounds those who oppose you,
for your justice always comes with mercy
and new beginnings.

When I look at the sky, how wonderful the whole creation is!
You care for sparrows, feed the lions,
and still find time to care for human beings!

The warring of those who think themselves superior
makes me a place of horror—
their weapons seem to threaten all life.
In greed they force growth—or poison it,
destroying forests I can never replace in their lifetimes.
Must I die that they might learn the outcome of their foolish selfishness?
What arrogance: they think you have put them in charge!
Yet they depend on their fellow creatures
for clothing, labour, food, for air and water—
which they pollute in ways they now perceive only dimly.

You never willed them to be conquerors,
rather partners in the unfolding of your bounty.
They have not yet learned the lessons of exodus and exile,
and taught so well by their monarchs,
that subjection brings resistance,
which you bless with liberation.

Yet still you care for them.
O God of depths and heights, of infinite expanse and every place,
may your glory be seen in all things.

Angels, Bird-Droppings and Fish Liver:
The Earth Story in Tobit

William J. Urbrock

Introduction

The book of Tobit, like most of the Jewish and Christian Scriptures, mediates familiar theocentric and anthropocentric visions of the world. The story invites readers to bless the God of Israel, whose direction of history and whose providential care and leading of all pious followers is wonderfully illustrated by the amazing ways God directs reversals of fortunes from bad to good for the faithful Tobit and his family.

Characters and Story

Readers unfamiliar with Tobit may benefit from this brief listing of important characters and synopsis of the story.

a. *The Characters*
 Tobit, an Israelite exiled in Nineveh
 Anna, his wife
 Tobias, their son
 Sarah, an Israelite exiled in Ecbatana
 Raguel, her father
 Edna, her mother
 Raphael, an angel
 Asmodeus, a demon
 Gabael, Tobit's associate in Rages

b. *The Story*
Chapters 1–2: Tobit, his wife Anna, and their son Tobias, are Israelites who have been exiled to Assyria during the days of King Shalmeneser. Scrupulously observant in his religion and generous in his almsgiving, Tobit had come through trials to a time of relative prosperity.

A turn of events, however, has left Tobit blind, forced his wife Anna to work for wages, and led to some strained relations between them.

Chapter 3: At the very moment that Tobit, in Nineveh, prays for release from his sufferings through death, in Ecbatana in Media a young Israelite woman, Sarah, daughter of Raguel and Edna, is also praying for death as a release from her miseries: the demon Asmodeus has killed her seven husbands, one after another, before she could have conjugal intercourse with any of them! Both supplicants are heard simultaneously 'in the glorious presence of God' (3.16), who dispatches the angel Raphael (the name means 'God heals') to bring healing to both.

Chapters 4–12: Tobit's remembering that he has left a large sum of money in trust with Gabael—an associate in the city of Rages in Media—and instructing his son Tobias to make the journey to recover it, provides Raphael with an opportunity to work out the healings and reversals of Tobit's fortunes. Raphael, disguised as a kinsman ('Azariah, the son of the great Hananiah, one of your relatives', 5.13) and travel guide, helps Tobias meet and marry Sarah, repel the demon, obtain a blessing from Raguel and Edna, recover his father's money, return safely home with his bride and heal Tobit's blindness. Finally, he reveals his identity—to the amazement of the Tobit family.

Chapters 13–14: Tobit sings a thanksgiving that honors the God of Israel, king of the ages (13.1, 6, 10, 13), and predicts a glorious restoration of Jerusalem. Years later, on his deathbed, he entrusts his final instructions to Tobias and his seven grandchildren.

The book ends with the obituary of both Tobit and Anna and a notice that, before he himself died wealthy and at a ripe old age, Tobias—having returned with Sarah and his children to Ecbatana—blessed God when he heard the news of the downfall of Nineveh.

Tobit and Ecojustice
Telling a story about the Earth, let alone from the perspective of Earth, certainly is not a central aim of this book. Nevertheless, when one reads Tobit from an Earth's-eye perspective and through the spectacles of an ecojustice hermeneutic, this engaging book may evoke some attentive rethinking about the value of Earth and its creatures in their close interrelatedness to humanity and God.

Specifically, an Earth's-eye reading of Tobit may prompt us to reconsider especially the ecojustice principles of *intrinsic worth, custodianship* and *interconnectedness*.

The Earth as Geopolitical Capital, Scenic Backdrop, Provider and Eternal Home

Throughout the book of Tobit, the Earth is seen mainly in terms of landholdings and competing claims between tribes and nations for ownership of these holdings. Second, Earth serves as topographical backdrop for the social and political dramas which are enacted upon its face. Third, Earth functions as provider of both sustenance and wealth for human communities. Finally, however, the Earth is recognized as the eternal home to which humanity forever belongs.

The Earth as Geopolitical Capital

Exiled among the Nations

The opening sentences of Tobit immediately greet a reader with a familiar picture: the Earth is valued not intrinsically but in terms of the tribal and national geopolitical interests of human communities. Tobit is introduced via his identity as an Israelite, a person from the tribal landholdings of Naphtali in the Upper Galilee. No longer in his own country (*chora*), in the land of Israel (*en [tei] gei Israel*), he has been taken captive to Nineveh in the country (*chora*) of the Assyrians (1.1-4a).

In his own words, Tobit further mentions the geopolitical divisions of the divided Israelite kingdoms as he recounts how he, a non-Judahite, made a special point of remaining loyal to the centralizing religio-political claims of Davidic Jerusalem by making regular pilgrimage thither during the festival seasons (1.4-6).

Readers next learn that Tobit has a large sum of money left in trust with an associate in the country (*chora*) of Media; it had been impossible to travel to Media for some time, since the highways had become unsafe (1.14-15).

The countries of Israel, Assyria and Media are soon linked by mention of 'all the nations (*pasin tois ethnesin*) among whom you have dispersed us' in Tobit's prayer. These foreign lands are seen as places of 'exile and death' (3.4). Later, when Tobias and 'Azariah'/Raphael introduce themselves to Sarah's family, they identify themselves as 'descendants of Naphtali who are exiles in Nineveh' (7.3).

At precisely the same hour as Tobit's prayer for release through death, another exiled Israelite—Sarah daughter of Raguel—is also praying in Ecbatana in Media. She similarly describes Media as 'the land (*en tei gei*) of my exile' (3.15).

Reclaiming the Land

When Tobit, thinking he is close to death, decides to give testamen-
tary instruction to his son Tobias, he makes a point of warning the
young man against marrying 'a foreign woman, who is not of your
father's tribe', and of reminding him of the great ancestors who,
because they 'took wives from among their kindred…were blessed in
their children', and assured that 'their posterity will inherit the land
(*kleronomesei gen*)' (4.12). Here, '[the] land' is the land of Israel; its
value lies in its religio-political status in Israelite tradition as the land
promised to Abraham, Isaac and Jacob.

At story's end, the social distance between these Jewish exiles and
their non-Jewish neighbors is reaffirmed when Tobias and Sarah
return to Tobit and Anna. On the one hand, when Tobit, healed of his
blindness, greets his new daughter-in-law 'at the gate of Nineveh',
both 'the people of Nineveh' and 'all the Jews who were in Nineveh'
react with amazement and rejoicing (11.16-17). Before all these people
Tobit publicly acknowledges the mercy of God in restoring his sight
(11.17). Shortly thereafter, however, in private with Tobias and
Raphael, Tobit sings an extended hymn of praise that underscores the
socio-political position of 'the children of Israel' now scattered in
lands of captivity and exile among the nations (13.3, 6, 10), but eagerly
expecting their regathering (13.5, 13) in a restored and glorious Jerusalem, 'the holy city' of their ancestral homeland (13.9-17).

Indeed, Tobit pronounces curses on those who would destroy Jerusalem, and blessings on those who revere and rebuild this city as
home for 'the Lord, the great King' (13.12); he exclaims how happy he
would be 'if a remnant of my descendants should survive to see your
glory and acknowledge the King of heaven' (13.16).

The book ends with Tobit's testament, given at his deathbed some
six decades after the preceding events. A major theme is the destruction that is bound to overtake Assyria and Nineveh, and the restoration that God will surely bring about for the scattered 'inhabitants of
the land of Israel (*tei gei Israel*)', 'the good land (*tes ges tes agathes*)'
(14.4-5). Jerusalem, once rebuilt, will become a magnet for all 'the
nations in the whole world (*panta ta ethne ta en olei tei gei*)' to 'be converted and worship God in truth' (14.6). Meanwhile, all the returned
Israelites 'will go to Jerusalem and live in safety forever in the land of
Abraham (*en tei gei Abraam*), and it will be given over to them' (14.7).

Even though Tobit has been buried with great honor in Nineveh
(14.2, 11), and even though Anna has been buried there beside him at
her death (14.12), Tobias, having returned to settle with his father-in-
law in Ecbatana of Media, rejoices and praises God when he hears

that King Cyaxares of Media has destroyed Nineveh and actually sees prisoners from Ninevah brought as captives to Media (14.15).

The story closes with an uncompromising reminder of the human geopolitical and socio-religious divisions that provide the dominant templates for valuing the Earth in this book.

The powerful theme of Israel's land, which forms the envelope around the entire book of Tobit, re-echoes the land theme that is a central—perhaps, the central—motif in the Old Testament (Janzen 1992: 146). Habel (1995), in fact, has identified six biblical land ideologies that seek to justify Israel's entitlement to this land.

In Tobit this land, above all others, is valued as a divinely allotted grant (the verb *kleronomein* in 4.12—related to *kleros*, a lot or casting of lots—may convey this meaning) from the one who, although acknowledged as universal Lord of heaven and earth (6.18; 7.11, 12, 16; 10.12, 13), whose kingship encompasses all of space and time (13.1-2, 10), chooses precisely Jerusalem in Israel to be 'his house for all ages' (1.4; 13.15-16). In such a context, the greater extent of Earth functions as staging-ground for the drama of Israel's exile, dispersion, and eventual return to its own land (see Nickelsburg 1981: 33).

The Earth as Scenic Backdrop

As the story unfolds, topography is pictured largely as backdrop for the journey of Tobias and the angel Raphael in human disguise. Nickelsburg (1993: 1447 note at 6.1b-9) highlights the double meaning of this journey from Nineveh to Media and back: it functions symbolically to remind readers that God and God's good angels safely guide the pious in paths of righteousness.

Raphael speaks of his acquaintance with the regions of Media through which he will guide Tobias. 'I have been there many times', he assures Tobias, while explaining that the home of Gabael in Rages is in a mountainous area some two days' journey from the great city of Ecbatana, which is situated in the middle of the plain (5.6). Similarly, he assures father Tobit that he is quite familiar with all the plains, mountains and roads of Media (5.10).

Obviously, the mountains and plains are interesting only because of the ease or difficulty with which they may be traversed by the two travelers via the roads of human commerce. This concern is expressed in Tobit's prayer that his son have a safe journey to Media and back home again and in Raphael's assurance that this indeed will happen 'because the way is safe' (5.15).

On the way to Media, a first night's camp-stop on the banks of the

Tigris (6.2)—where an important event takes place—is the only indication of interest in an actual place encountered during the trip to
Media.

The trip back is recounted even more laconically. Tobias takes leave
of his new parents-in-law, blessing 'the Lord of heaven and earth,
King over all, because he had made his journey a success' (10.13). The
very next verse (11.1) signals the travelers' speedy and safe return as
they 'came near to Kaserin, which is opposite Nineveh', where
Tobias's mother Anna is keeping lookout for their return (11.5).

Demons, like angels, of course, need not worry about topographical
obstacles in their travels. When Asmodeus is repelled by Tobias, he
simply flees 'aloft' (so *Codex Sinaiticus*) 'to the remotest parts of
Egypt', where he is immediately bound hand and foot by Raphael
(8.3). The geopolitical entity Egypt functions as scenic filler, a sort of
never-never land, a place offstage where Asmodeus may remain far
removed from the action for the remainder of the story.

The Earth as Provider

Just as the Earth is valued in Tobit primarily in terms of the landholdings of competing human communities, it is similarly valued in
utilitarian terms for what it can provide to meet various human
needs.

Economics: Wealth and Wages

The economic interests of the book of Tobit—in terms of commodities
and money—are laid out from the very beginning. Tobit first characterizes himself as an Israelite who has used his wealth wisely and
piously: in former days, he paid many tithes of crops and livestock to
the priesthood in Jerusalem. Later, he continued to perform 'many
acts of charity' in his country of exile (1.3-7). I would, he says, 'give
my food to the hungry and my clothing to the naked' (1.17) among
'my kindred, those of my tribe' (1.16). Once, when the festive table
was set for the observance of Pentecost, he instructed his son to 'bring
whatever poor person you may find of our people among the exiles in
Nineveh, who is wholeheartedly mindful of God, and he shall eat
together with me' (2.2).

Tobit's share-the-wealth ethic is further demonstrated in his testa-
mentary instructions given to his son Tobias. He enjoins Tobias to
give in proportion to his possessions, even if they are few (4.7-8).
'Give some of your food to the hungry, and some of your clothing to
the naked', he advises, and 'give all your surplus as alms, and do not

let your eye begrudge your giving of alms' (4.16). Tobit himself gave alms his entire life (14.2).

For one used to high social standing and to wealth sufficient for giving such substantial tithes and alms, even a temporary loss of position and property can be devastating! Tobit reports that in the early years of his captivity he was appointed to the Assyrian court and 'used to buy everything' the king needed (1.13). Nevertheless, all his property was confiscated when he was caught secretly burying fellow Israelites against the king's orders (1.18-20). When the king was assassinated by his own sons, Tobit and his family were restored to favor (1.21-22).

For Tobit, however, the worst was yet to come. Ironically, his piety again gets him in trouble when he goes out to bury the desecrated corpse of an Israelite. On this occasion, however, the cause of his suffering is not the anger of a king but the fresh droppings of birds!

Having come into contact with a corpse, Tobit decides to sleep in his courtyard overnight—perhaps, as Nickelsburg suggests (1993: 1441 note at 2.4-9), because the corpse had rendered him ceremonially impure. Tobit recounts how he slept next to this wall with his face uncovered because of the heat. This was a major mistake, since the wall was where birds roosted. Their fresh droppings fell into Tobit's eyes, causing them to film over. Visits to physicians only worsened the situation, since their ointments left Tobit completely blind! It was a condition Tobit would endure for the next four years (2.4-10) until his equally astonishing healing.

It seems that while he is in this sorry state, Tobit's wealth begins to diminish as well; his wife Anna takes up 'women's work' to earn some money (2.11). One day she brings home not only her full wages but a young goat given to her as a meal (2.12)—the alms-givers are now receiving alms!

Property and wages figure prominently throughout the rest of the story. The journey of Tobias to Media is prompted by Tobit's remembering that he has left 'bags of silver worth ten talents' with Gabael in Rages (1.14; 4.20).

The recovery of these money bags by 'Azariah'/Raphael (Tob. 9) is one climax of this journey. The other climax, of course, is the meeting—and subsequent wedding—of Tobias and Sarah. After the festivities, the generous Raguel and Edna send the newlyweds back to Nineveh loaded with half of all Raguel's property, 'male and female slaves, oxen and sheep, donkeys and camels, clothing, money, and household goods' (10.10). The other half, the couple is assured, will also become theirs some day (8.21). More gifts are heaped upon Sarah and Tobias when they return to Nineveh (11.18).

As for wages, when 'Azriel'/Raphael is 'hired' as traveling companion and guide for Tobias, both Tobias (5.7) and Tobit (5.10) promise him a fair wage, which is set at 'a drachma a day' plus expenses and promise of a bonus (5.15-16). True to their word, father and son are prepared to pay Raphael fully half of all the goods—both money bags and wedding largesse—that Tobias had brought back to Nineveh with him (12.1-5). Dropping his disguise, the angel leaves all the goods with them, simply reinstructing father and son about what they already practice: 'Prayer with fasting is good, but better than both is almsgiving with righteouosness... For almsgiving saves from death and purges away every sin' (12.8-9).

Enjoyment: Food and Feasting

Levenson (1997: 5-8), building on the scholarship of Michael Fox, has illustrated diagrammatically how a series of ten feasts and banquets gives structure to the book of Esther. While they are not quite as pervasive in Tobit, meals and feasting figure prominently in the story. In the context of these feasts, Earth again is simply taken for granted as the provider of sustenance and enjoyment.

Even though Tobit and his family have a strong sense of being strangers in strange lands, it certainly does not appear that Earth begrudges the exiled Israelites its bounties. Tobit's family Pentecost feast boasts 'a good dinner' with 'an abundance of food' (2.1-2), Anna receives a goat as a food bonus (2.12), and Raguel has a ram from his flock slaughtered for the welcome meal for Tobias and 'Azariah'/Raphael so that his guests may 'eat and drink, and be merry' (7.9-10). The wedding feast Raguel and Edna host for Sarah and Tobias is described in mouth-watering terms: the eating and drinking goes on for a full two weeks, as the celebrants enjoy 'many loaves of bread... two steers and four rams' (8.19-20)—and whatever other delicacies a reader's mind may conjure up as appropriate side dishes. Upon their arrival at Nineveh, immediately after the restoration of Tobit's sight, the happy couple is treated to yet another 'wedding feast', which all celebrate for seven days 'with merriment' (11.18).

Not all food the Earth offers is kosher, however! Tobit asserts that, even though the rest of his kindred and people 'ate the food of Gentiles', he—being 'mindful of God' with all his heart—refrained from eating such food (1.10-11). In this respect, he resembles Daniel and his companions (Dan. 1.5-17) and Judith (Jdt. 10.5; 12.1-2, 19).

Healing: A Fish and a Dog

Not all that Earth offers for healing is always effective either. What the physicians, however, could not achieve for Tobit's blindness through their ointments (2.10), and what, evidently, nobody could achieve through any means to rid Sarah of being prematurely 'robbed' of her husbands (3.7-9), the Tigris, a great fish, and Raphael would (6.2b-6).

When the travelers set up an overnight camp on the banks of the famed river, Tobias is in for a surprise. As he begins to wash his feet in the water, a big fish leaps up and tries to swallow his foot! Raphael quickly instructs the young man to grab it, bring it to land, gut it and save its gall, heart and liver. Why? Because 'its gall, heart, and liver are useful as medicine' (2.5). The rest of the fish provides food for Tobias—some roasted and eaten on the spot, the rest salted for later (2.6).

As the story unfolds, Raphael will instruct Tobias to toast the heart and liver when he enters his wedding chamber with Sarah. The stench given off is what drives away the demon Asmodeus (6.8; 8.2-3)! Similarly, he instructs Tobias on the wonderful healing properties of the fish gall, which, when smeared on Tobit's white-filmed eyes and blown upon, bring about an instant restoration of sight (6.9; 11.7-14).

A fascinating sidelight to the journey of Tobias and Raphael is offered by the appearance of the dog. When Tobias sets out from home, accompanied by the angel, 'the dog came out with him and went along with them' (6.2). Not until journey's end, as the two companions near Tobit's home in Ninevah, do we hear of the dog again: 'And the dog went along behind them' (11.4).

What are readers to make of the dog? Moore (1996: 197-98, 261-62) reviews the various suggestions commentators have offered about the significance of this animal. He also draws attention to the tradition preserved in the Vulgate, which emphasizes the dog's dual role as traveling companion and messenger: 'Then the dog, which had gone along on the journey, ran ahead and, arriving like a messenger (*nuntius*), joyfully wagged its tail' (Vulg. 11.9; my translation). Moore opts to see the dog's appearance merely as a 'gratuitous piece of description...originally part of the secular folktale used by the narrator' (1996: 198).

In the context of Tobit's story, however, it seems that those commentators who see the dog as connected to beliefs that dogs repel demons and aid in healing are on solid ground. In a chapter entitled 'Death and the Mysteries of the Dog', Boyce (1977: 139-63) discusses the important status of dogs among Zoroastrians as ranking just

below humans in the good creation (1977: 142). Boyce notes the following: dogs actually received—or at least had set aside—their *čom-e*
šwa ('meal for the dog') portion even before human participation par-
took of consecrated food (1977: 143); had an intermediary role
between the living and the dead (1977: 144-45); and protected the soul
from evil forces on earth (1977: 145-46) and at the time of death (1977:
149-51). She also describes in great detail (1977: 111-36) the extended
purification ritual (the *barašnom-e nō-šwa*, 'ablution of the nine
nights'), which every Zoroastrian aimed to undergo at least once in a
lifetime; prolonged ritual contact (*paivand*) with the dog plays a central and auspicious role on the very first evening of the observances
(1977: 128-30).

The 'rather widespread' role of dogs in healing cults in the ancient
Near Eastern and Mediterranean worlds has been used recently by
archaeologist Larry Stager (1991) to explain the great number of dog
burials—over 700 partial or complete carcasses—at the fifth-century
BCE cemetery in cosmopolitan Ashkelon of the Persian period. He
suggests that they were sacred animals who may have freely roamed
around the precincts of a nearby sanctuary or sanctuaries and played
a part in rituals of healing. Although his archaeological colleagues
Wapnish and Hesse (1993) have raised strong objections to his hypothesis, Stager stands by it for the present (personal communication,
3 February 1999).

Whether or not Stager is proven correct about these Ashkelon dogs,
his excursus on 'Deities and Dogs—Their Sacred Rites' (1991: 40-42)
brings together convincing evidence of the association of dogs with
deities thought to have healing powers in the ancient world.

Far from being gratuitous, then, the dog's appearance precisely at
the onset and conclusion of the journey of double healing—for Sarah
and for Tobit—may reasonably be interpreted as integral to the story.
From the perspective of an Earth's-eye hermeneutic, the dog may be
understood as a sort of 'Earth-angel', paired with its non-earthly
counterpart Raphael to signal the guaranteed success of the journey.
This angelic interpretation conforms nicely with the Latin textual tradition that compares the dog to a messenger (*nuntius*).

Thus three creatures of Earth—a river, a fish and a dog—have co-
operated with one non-earthly being—Raphael—against a second
non-earthly being—Asmodeus—and against the polluting droppings
of birds, to assist the human creatures—Tobit, Sarah and Tobias—to
gain health and happiness. Here we come close to a picture of genuine
interconnectedness between earthly and non-earthly beings of various
kinds.

Further, we see Earth caring for its own—dare we say, exercising custodianship—in a wonderful way. The dog, without prompting, accompanies Tobias and Raphael on their safe and successful journey. The Tigris, for its part, practically makes a gift of the wonder-working fish to Tobias. Its gall cures Tobit's blindness, which, from Earth's perspective, was caused accidentally because of Tobit's careless choice of a sleeping spot; Tobit never curses the birds for doing what birds will do anyway! The fish's heart and liver exorcise Sarah's demon Asmodeus, which—again from Earth's perspective—comes from God knows where, but which Earth will have to guard, now that he has been bound in Egypt.

Neither river, nor fish, nor dog, however, are acknowledged with thanksgiving in the story. Is it out of place to suggest that an appropriate sign of interconnectedness and partnership coming from the human side of this equation might have resulted in the protagonists engaging in a recognition ritual something like that performed at the end of a typical Zoroastrian *gahāmbār* celebration? Boyce (1977: 43-44; photographs on 56) reports that as integral parts of one of these obligatory feasts in Iran in the 1960s, the master of the house prepared two meals—the meal for the dog (*čom-e šwa*), and the meal for the fishes (*čom-e māhī*), which was poured into a running stream. Consecrated water was also poured out onto the Earth in gratitude.

Construction: Building for Beauty

Little is said in Tobit about using Earth's resources for the construction or decoration of human habitations, nor are there any descriptions of the three cities of Assyria and Media—Nineveh, Ecbatana and Rages—in which most of the action takes place.

Only the restored Jerusalem envisioned in Tobit's concluding hymn of praise is described in any detail—but the terms are wildly extravagant, as the beautiful city is pictured as built and embellished with what humans value as Earth's most precious stones and metal: sapphire, emerald, ruby, stones of Ophir and gold (13.16).

On the one hand, these precious materials are reminiscent of a similar list of ores and minerals—including sapphires and gold of Ophir—mined from of the earth in the wisdom poem in Job 28. On the other, the shimmering and bejeweled precincts pictured for Jerusalem are reminiscent of similar visions in Isa. 54.11-12 and in the New Testament book of Revelation (Rev. 21.10-21).

The homes of the central characters are described simply as having rooms for dining—reclining at table was the custom (2.1; 9.6); sleeping (8.1; 14.11b); and, in Tobit's case, a walled courtyard (2.9), and an upper room in Sarah's case (2.10). Both houses must be understood as substantial buildings or even estates, since both Tobit and Raguel are presented as commanding position and wealth, including housemaids (9.12) and slaves (10.10).

The Earth as Eternal Home

When all is said and done, there is one way that Earth's priority and eternal custodianship is recognized in Tobit: Earth is the home of all who die, including humans.

Tobit, after all, is honored in the story precisely because he goes out of his way to give proper burial to those who have been denied it (1.17-18; 2.3-7). Furthermore, both he and Sarah seek release from their troubles by praying for death—in Tobit's words that he 'may be released from the face of the earth [*tes ges*] and become dust [literally 'earth', *ge*]...to go to the eternal home [*ton topon ton aionion*]' (3.6). Collins (1997: 93) remarks that these prayers of Tobit and Sarah reflect a sentiment made explicit by Ben Sira: 'Death is better than a futile life, and eternal sleep than chronic sickness' (Sir. 30.17). Similar sentiments are expressed by Elijah (1 Kgs 19.4), Jonah (4.3), Job (3.11, 13, 17) and Qoheleth (4.2). Further, Collins comments that Jewish epitaphs of the Hellenistic and Roman periods often refer to death as a sleep.

Neither Tobit nor Sarah fears death or the eternal sleep in Earth or Hades (3.10); rather, they fear the reproaches and undeserved insults they receive because of their unfortunate conditions (3.6, 13). In Sarah's case, the graves which had received her seven husbands—like the one that Raguel's servants were already digging for Tobias on his wedding night—were fearful precisely because they robbed her of a chance for offspring, making her and her parents 'object[s] of ridicule and derision' (9.9-10). Earth, we may infer, would receive its own without demur on their return to its dust!

Like the ancestors in the stories of Genesis, what the characters in Tobit hope for is not release into another non-earthly existence after death. They simply wish to flourish and see their descendants flourish during the time allotted them on Earth. And they wish to die and return to Earth with honor, preferably at a ripe old age. Thus, both Raguel and Edna ask to live long enough to see their grandchildren (10.11-12), while Tobit requests 'a proper burial' (4.3), a wish granted for both himself and his wife Anna at the end of the story (14.11-12). Tobias, too, 'died highly respected at the age of one hundred seventeen years' (14.14).

The Earth Story in Tobit

In light of the ecojustice principle of *intrinsic worth*, the overwhelming impression left after reading Tobit is that the Earth, pictured as a backdrop for human stories and struggles, is valued largely in terms of what it can yield for human possession, use and enjoyment.

Reading this story from Earth's perspective, however, leads us to acknowledge that Earth exercises a sort of *custodianship* for the human family; Earth provides all the needs of the living, and an eternal home for the dead.

We have also noted that the book of Tobit exhibits a strong sense of kinship or *interconnectedness* between Earth, humans, other animals, and angels. Worlds interconnect or interpenetrate in this book, and are balanced. The troublesome demon Asmodeus, who does his mischief among earthlings, has unwitting partners in the birds of the courtyard. He is foiled, however, by his obvious 'spirit' counterpart Raphael—who, even in human form, merely appears to eat and drink like humans (12.19)—and by the very earthy heart and liver of a fish.

Perhaps the dog is a foil for Asmodemus as well. Mentioned just twice but at the appropriate times, the dog may be seen as a sort of Earth-angel, a shadow guardian in the story.

Writing from a feminist perspective, Schuller (1992: 239-40) has commented on the strong feminine element and the generally 'fine balance' between men and women maintained in Tobit, despite the patriarchal outlook of the narrator and the society represented in the text. Similarly, from an 'Earthist' perspective, we may reasonably argue that Tobit—despite the anthropocentric and theocentric outlook of the narrator and culture presented in the text—contains a story of Earth as not only provider but partner and custodian.

If that be so, perhaps we might we hear the voice of Earth in the hopes and praises of Tobit (14.7) and Sarah (3.11):

> Those who sincerely love God will rejoice, but those who commit sin and injustice will vanish from ALL THE EARTH...
> Blessed are you, merciful God! Blessed is your name forever; let ALL YOUR WORKS praise you forever.

The Wisdom of Solomon

Dianne Bergant, CSA

Preliminary Remarks

There are so many passages in the Bible that lend themselves to the development of an ecojustice perspective—there is poetry that extols creations's intrinsic value; there are injunctions that prescribe custodianship; there are narratives that reveal ecological interrelatedness.

There are also troublesome sections, where the elements of the natural world appear to be either little more than bargaining chips in human practices of exchange, or the means of God's reward or punishment for human behavior. Such sections seem to undermine the development of an ecotheology.

However, lest our specific focus result in a kind of 'canon within a canon' that involves ignoring the texts that do not fit our ecosensitive criteria, we will have to formulate a method of interpretation that can uncover the revelatory possibilities in these texts while laying bare their biases and limitations.

The Wisdom of Solomon, a relatively little known and even less frequently cited source of ancient Israelite wisdom, is one of these 'troublesome' texts. A reinterpretation of an earlier tradition, it recounts the plagues that God sent upon Egypt in order to free the Israelites from the oppressive grip of the Egyptians (Wis. 11.2–19.22; cf. Exod. 7.14–12.31). In this paper, I will interpret the Wisdom of Solomon, using the Earth Bible Project's ecojustice principles as the particular focus of my interpretation.

For both religious and political reasons, the Wisdom of Solomon was not included by the rabbis of the first century of the Common Era (CE) in the official listing of their inspired books, the Hebrew Scriptures. Because the Protestant reformers chose this ancient Jewish collection as its 'Old' or 'First Testament', the Wisdom of Solomon is considered apocryphal by Protestants and is absent from their version of the Bible.

Roman Catholics, on the other hand, have preserved a version of the First Testament from the Septuagint or Greek version of the Hebrew Scriptures, which includes the Wisdom of Solomon. Although Roman Catholics regard the book as deuterocanonical—belonging to the second listing—it is accorded the same respect as other biblical books, and passages from it are frequently prescribed as readings during the liturgical year in Catholic lectionaries.

The book gets its name by inference—the author does not explicitly identify himself as Solomon, but, speaking in the first person, he describes himself as this ancient Israelite ruler (7.5; 8.21; 9.7-8; cf. 1 Kgs 3.5-15). However, the ample vocabulary also found in Hellenistic anthropology, philosophy, psychology, medicine and the popular Isis cult reveals the book was written by an author who enjoyed an exceptional grasp of the learning of this culture—a culture that did not yet exist at the time of the Israelite king, Solomon. Furthermore, several rhetorical devices found within the book—including the one that I will examine in this study—resemble those developed by various Greek Cynic or Stoic philosophers. These observations have led many commentators to assign a Hellenistic origin to the book and to refer to its author as 'Pseudo-Solomon'.

Two of the book's many features are particularly significant for my ecotheology reading. The first is the type of homiletic approach taken by Pseudo-Solomon in the description of God's care of the Israelites during the Exodus. The second is the unique literary form that is employed in this description: the author uses a midrashic approach, a method of Jewish interpretation that takes a biblical tradition that originated in one historical situation and makes it relevant in a new one (cf. Reese 1970: 91-102; Enns 1997. 15 17; for an opposing view see Cheon 1997: 13-14). This kind of interpretation allows the law, restated as *halakah*, and narratives, retold as *haggadah*, to give faithful direction to a new generation of Jewish people.

In developing this *haggadic* reinterpretation of the exodus story, Pseudo-Solomon employs syncrisis, a Hellenistic form of comparison or contrast. Thus the author uses both a fundamental Jewish interpretive approach and a Hellenistic literary form as he tries to persuade his audience to embrace his point of view.

In the past, the literary integrity of the Wisdom of Solomon was questioned (cf. Winston 1979: 12-14). Today scholars generally agree on its structural unity (Cheon 1997: 12 n. 8). The following outline of the entire book seems to enjoy the most support:

- 1.1–6.21—immortality as the reward of Wisdom;
- 6.22–11.1—Solomon and the quest for Wisdom;

- 11.2–19.22—God's providence during the Exodus (Wright 1967; Winston 1979: 9-12; Murphy 1990: 85-86; Perdue 1994: 293-318; for a slightly different view see Reese 1970: 90-116).

In its final form, the book also presents a coherent theology that contains a definite ecotheological perspective. The first part of the book describes God being encountered in the cosmos through Wisdom; the second part depicts eschatology as built into the cosmic structure; and in the third part, history illustrates that same cosmic structure (Collins 1977: 128). Furthermore, the book as a whole presents creation as the matrix within which both history and salvation are understood. This feature is very important for the ecojustice concerns of the present study.

Something must be said about the interpretive approach that I will use here. I am not merely employing a hermeneutic of retrieval—I am more interested in recontextualizing the message of the passage within a context of ecojustice sensitivity. In doing this, I am dependent upon insights of Hans-Georg Gadamer and Paul Ricoeur who have provided perspectives for understanding the dynamics of communication and interpretation.

Maintaining that there is a fundamental connection between a work of art (a text) and the person experiencing it (the reader), Gadamer insisted that the artistic essence resides in the text as potential truth, ready to be recognized. It is truly a work of art only when it transforms the one who experiences it. When that person belongs to a particular historical moment different from that of the historical moment of the artist, tension develops between familiarity and strangeness, between continuity and discontinuity. Gadamer resolved this tension by introducing the notion of dialogue or conversation between the text and the reader.

In line with Gadamer's thinking, I am not content to regard the biblical text as merely an artifact of the past. I choose to enter into dialogue with it, considering it a partner capable of yielding contemporary relevance; I recognize what is familiar and what is strange, where there is continuity with my thought and where there is discontinuity.

Gadamer (1975: 254-264) distinguished between three different worlds: the 'world *behind* the text' (the historical world of the author); the 'world *of* the text' (the world that exists within the artistic expression itself); and the 'world *in front* of the text' (the new world of meaning made possible by interpretation). According to Gadamer, this third world of possible understandings emerges when the horizon of the world projected by the text meets and interacts with the horizon of the reader. He referred to this interaction as a 'fusion of horizons' (1975: 341-74). For Gadamer, understanding is never merely a mastery of objective data—it also involves a subjective interaction with the text as a work of art.

Building on Gadamer's theory of interpretation, Ricoeur believed that once a text is written, it exists by itself; the reader does not need the author to throw light on its meaning. The text, removed from the original audience, is available to a limitless number of readers. Therefore, while the internal structures of the text are observed, its meaning can be carried beyond cultural and generational boundaries, and can convey its message in very diverse contexts. This is a result of what Ricoeur calls the 'surplus of meaning' (1976: 45-46). This 'surplus' explains why a text can yield an array of different meanings without compromising its literary integrity.

Attentive to these insights, I will examine a section from the Wisdom of Solomon with a careful eye to the 'world *in* the text'. I will rely on historical information—the 'world *behind* the text'—only when it seems necessary for understanding the text itself. I will then bring the meaning discovered into dialogue with the 'world *in front* of the text', specifically the ecojustice principles that set the parameters of the Earth Bible Project. This last move will lay bear the text's potential for ecotyranny and/or ecoharmony.

Retelling the Exodus Story

The midrashic reflection on events recorded in the book of Exodus, found in the third section of the Wisdom of Solomon (11.2–19.22), reveals how Wisdom actually directed the course of history. The section consists of five syncrises—five contrasts that compare the plight of the Israelites with that of the Egyptians (cf. Wright 1967: 177; Murphy 1990: 90-91; Perdue 1994: 294; for seven contrasts see Reese 1970: 98-102; Winston 1979: 227; Cheon 1997: 25; for an explanation of syncrisis see Winston 1979: 227).

The syncrises function in several ways. Most obviously, they demonstrate the theory of retribution—the righteous are rewarded while the wicked are punished. A closer look shows that natural occurrences are active both in Israel's blessing and Egypt's chastisement (11.5, 13). Of interest for this study is the character of this activity—does it demonstrate the intrinsic value of creation, or is nature merely an instrument for blessing and/or chastisement?

The first syncrisis (11.6-14) develops the theme of thirst in the wilderness. Beginning with the Greek word *anti*, 'instead of' (11.6), it compares the plague when the water of the Nile turned into blood with the boon of the spring from the rock. Because the Egyptians planned to shed the blood of the Israelite male infants, their river was turned into blood, making the water unsuitable for their use. On the other hand, when the Israelites were in the arid wilderness, they were given water to slake their thirst.

The second syncrisis (11.15–16.15)—which includes a very extensive digression—both begins and ends with *anti* (11.6; 16.2). It compares the way the Egyptians, who engaged in theriomorphic (animal-form) worship, were plagued by certain small animals, while the Israelites were fed by other small creatures (16.1-2). The mention of Egypt's idolatrous practices is the occasion of the digression (11.17–15.19) dealing with theodicy—the question of divine justice—under two different but related themes: God's power and mercy (11.17–12.27); and Egypt's idolatry (13.1–15.19). This syncrisis also introduces a secondary theme (11.15-16): the manner in which the very reptiles and insects worshiped in Egypt turn on the Egyptian people and become a blight and pestilence.

The remaining comparisons are quite straightforward. The third syncrisis (16.16-29) describes how the heavens poured down both water and fire, and how these consumed the fruits of the land of Egypt. In contrast (*anti*, 16.20), the same heavens opened up and rained manna, which sustained the Israelites. In this passage there is a reversal in nature: a transformed and renewed order seems to guarantee salvation for the Israelites (cf. Kolarcik 1992: 104-107).

The fourth syncrisis (17.1–18.4) contrasts the plague of darkness that befell the Egyptians with the pillar of light that led the Israelites to safety. The Egyptians were paralyzed by the darkness. On the other hand (*anti*, 18.3), the Israelites advanced in the light provided by the pillar of fire.

This comparison also moves the discussion of darkness/light to a metaphorical plane. Using data gleaned from Hellenistic psychology, the author describes the fear that overwhelms the wicked. Those who preferred the darkness of ignorance and had imprisoned the children of God deserved the terror of the night; it is fitting that those who would bring the brilliance of the law to the world should walk in light.

The fifth and final syncrisis (18.5–19.21) describes how the decision of the Egyptians to massacre the sons of the Hebrews reverted onto their own sons. Once again Pseudo-Solomon points to a great reversal of fortune. Initially Egypt's ruler had agreed to Israel's safe departure;

later, he changed his mind, and sent his army to pursue God's people and bring them back. This pursuit was to no avail; even nature worked to save the Israelites and punish their pursuers.

It should be noted that these events are not perceived as miraculous interventions by God in the Wisdom of Solomon; rather, the text clearly states that nature, following definite natural laws (19.6-13), protected and provided for God's people. It is as if reward and punishment were built into the structures of the universe.

Interpreting the New Account

Even a cursory examination of these syncrises reveals the distinctiveness of Pseudo-Solomon's creation theology. Each of the syncrises attests to divine involvement.

- In the wilderness the thirst of the Israelites was slaked, because God 'gave them abundant water unexpectedly' (11.7).
- God 'tested them as a parent does', but 'examined the ungodly as a stern king does' (11.10). Furthermore, God 'sent a multitude of irrational creatures to punish' the wicked (11.15), but for the Israelites God 'prepared quails to eat' (16.2).
- The ungodly 'were flogged by the strength of your hand' (16.16), while 'you gave your people food of angels' (16.20).
- While lawless people languished in darkness, you 'provided a flaming pillar of fire as a guide for your people's unknown journey' (18.3).
- The greatest blow occurred when God 'in punishment took away a multitude of their [Egyptian] children' (18.5). 'For by the same means by which you punished our enemies you called us to yourself and glorified us' (18.8).

At first glance, this would indicate that God effects the respective suffering or blessing through the agency of creation (principle of instrumental value). However, at other times it appears that the universe itself is on the side of righteousness (principle of intrinsic worth), for 'the universe defends the righteous' (16.17c).

Even more striking is the claim that, when creation does take sides with the just, it is actually working according to certain natural laws, and 'complying with your [God's] commands' (19.6). This is a bold claim, because in these instances—especially the crossing of the sea—nature acts in a way that seems to be outside the boundaries of its laws. How can it be complying to laws when it seems to be working outside of those laws?

In addressing this apparent paradox, Pseudo-Solomon claims that 'the whole of creation in its nature was fashioned anew' (19.6), and in now 'serving you who made it, exerts itself to punish the unrighteous, and in kindness relaxes on behalf of those who trust in you' (16.24). According to Pseudo-Solomon, creation is indeed working in accord with natural laws—but in a transformed manner.

Claims about the transformation of nature are made from within the Greek philosophical understanding of the principles of mutual interchangeability (19.18-21). According to this Stoic doctrine, although the basic material substance of a thing remains the same, periodically an interchange of the elements of which it is composed occurs, resulting in an alteration in its individual combinations without a fundamental change in its substance. Thus, having been created anew, nature can still follow its own laws and yet act in astonishing new ways. Pseudo-Solomon uses musical notes to exemplify what he means. A musician can produce several different tunes using the same musical notes in different combinations. Using this metaphor, he explains how the harmony within creation was not disturbed by these remarkable occurrences; rather, a different harmony was produced.

It is clear that Pseudo-Solomon's retelling of the Exodus narrative is grounded in the priestly tradition's creation narrative, found in Gen. 1.1–2.4a (Vogels 1991: 322-34; Cheon 1997: 98-99). He does not view the Exodus as a military feat, but as a refashioning of nature. The very sequence of events in his description follows the pattern of the creation narrative rather than the account of the liberation of the people as found in the book of Exodus. In this way, the book of Wisdom makes a unique contribution to biblical creation theology. Instead of moving from salvation to creation—as traditional Old Testament theology claims is the fundamental focus of the Bible—the Wisdom of Solomon begins with creation and moves to salvation. In fact, the book begins and ends with affirmations of God's creative purpose: '[God] created all things so that they might exist' (1.14); 'The whole creation in its nature was fashioned anew...so that your children might be kept unharmed' (19.6).

The theory of mutual interchangeability may provide an explanation of *how* the events described could have occurred; it does not explain *why* they happened. Was it a chance exchange of elements? Or did something in nature itself trigger the process of interchange? If the latter is the case, what might it have been? On the other hand, did God direct the transformation? If so, what was God's reason for doing so?

It is clear from the text itself that this was no chance exchange of elements; nor was it exclusively a natural event. Therefore, the first two explanations must be rejected. The syncrises plainly state that God is the one who directed the exceptional natural phenomena. But why? From an ethnocentric point of view, one could say that the change occurred because of God's bias in favor of the Israelites—they were afflicted, so God intervened on their behalf. From a theological point of view, one could say that it happened because of God's passion for justice. The wicked had been prospering and the upright had been suffering, and so God reversed their fates—the wicked were now punished and the just rewarded.

While each of these explanations is in some ways quite valid, the solutions that they propose require a suspension of the natural laws— which is consistent with the original account in the book of Exodus. They do not tell us why creation was refashioned.

Two very different concepts come together here to provide an answer to that question. One is the concept of theodicy—the defense of the justice of God in the face of injustice. The other is the principle of mutual interchangeability.

Theodicy is really the pressing concern here. Theodicy presumes two fundamental concepts: first, that there is an underlying order upon which reality—at least moral human reality—is based; second, that this order is auspicious and the God who created it and who oversees it is trustworthy. Many traditional Near Eastern societies believe that there was a direct connection between the laws that governed the cosmos and those that were operative in human society. They held that a change in one sphere had repercussions in the other. From this they concluded that any dissension among the gods significantly affected human society; any disruption in human social harmony endangered the order of the universe.

A world view that presumes fundamental interdependence can deal with the changes that are part of being alive, but finds significant upheavals difficult. When chaos threatens the underpinnings of equanimity, the sovereign ruler of the universe has to step in and reestablish order. In the biblical tradition, this new state of accord is frequently characterized as a new creation (e.g. a new heaven and new earth, Isa. 65.17; 66.22; 2 Pet. 3.13; Rev. 21.1; a new spirit, Ezek. 11.19; 18.31; 36.26; a new creation, 2 Cor. 5.17; Gal. 6.15; a new nature, Eph. 4.24; Col. 3.10).

Pseudo-Solomon clearly envisions a interdependent universe; he seems to believe that the only way the social disorder can be corrected is by means of a kind of new creation. Given the philosophical world view of his time, the doctrine of mutual interchangeability explains how this can happen. Using this doctrine to reinterpret the miracles in the book of Exodus, he shows that nature has more than mere instrumental value; according to Pseudo-Solomon, nature works according to its own laws. Although Pseudo-Solomon's ancient world view was pre-scientific, in its own way it respected the intrinsic value of the world and its components, and it did recognize their interconnectedness.

Implications for Contemporary Ecotheology

Having analyzed the passage from Pseudo-Solomon, we are now faced with the challenge of recontextualization. Can the message of this tradition be revelatory for us today or is the worldview that produced it so scientifically naive that a new ecosensitive reading is unfeasible? It is very difficult to critique one world view according to the principles of another.

However, if we are to open ourselves to the revelatory possibilities of the biblical text without being captive to its limitations, we are obliged to do just that. We must also be attentive to the biases that color both our world view and the approaches that we employ in our examination. As we grow in sensitivity to ecological issues, we may detect in the biblical writings what appears to us to be a disregard of the intrinsic value of the created world. We must never forget that we recognize these attitudes with insight that has been shaped by scientific inquiry, with eyes that tend to compartmentalize reality.

People of the biblical eras, like most traditional societies, had a more holistic point of view than ours. Because they were more directly dependent upon the natural world, they noticed aspects of harmony and interdependence that often escape us. Anthropologists caution us about asserting that there is cultural similarity between world views before we have attended to the context variations. What appears to be the same value, custom or pattern may really be quite different in various cultural settings. All human expression is culturally bound, and we must employ the hermeneutic of suspicion as we examine it. It is important to remember this in case we accuse the biblical communities of errors that may be ours but not theirs.

One final point to remember is that, regardless of our cultural uniqueness, we all stand in the world as human beings. This means that our points of view, our values, our aspirations, etc.—regardless of how different they may be from one another—will all be anthropocentric. There is no way that we can assume a different perspective.

As ennobling as this human point of view may be, it can become a serious distortion of reality and a threat to the harmony present in the natural world when we use anthropocentrism as the gauge for measuring the worth of everything else. When this happens, we can forget that we are merely citizens of the universe, sharing existence and the means of survival with other citizens. Instead, we can become detached consumers of the treasures of nature, exercising sole jurisdiction over the natural world.

This brings us to a critique of the syncrises in the Wisdom of Solomon from the perspective of ecojustice principles. Again and again the biblical texts state that God is the active cause of the natural occurrences they describe. This can lead us to conclude that the forces of nature are presented in these passages simply as instruments used by God to grant reward to the Israelites and to execute punishment on the Egyptians. If this is the only role that they play, then they may be judged to possess only instrumental value and are not really unique manifestations of the creative ingenuity of God, and valuable in their own right.

This may well be the way nature is viewed in many places in the Bible. However, the statement about the renewal of creation—when understood from within the context of mutual interchangeability—suggests that Pseudo-Solomon believed that there was an inherent balance between and among the various spheres of the natural world, a balance that required that any state of serious disequilibrium be corrected. Viewed from this perspective, we can say that nature itself, complying with the laws established by God, seeks to rectify the imbalance. This would mean that balance is not only a characteristic of the natural world, but is also an active principle by which it organizes and reorganizes itself.

Without forcing the biblical material to fit into contemporary scientific categories, we could maintain, according to the principle of purpose, that 'the universe, the earth and all its components are part of a dynamic cosmic design within which each has a place in the overall goal of that design'. From this perspective, we can see that the universe, the earth and all of its components constitute an ecosystem, a system of diverse yet interrelated components that function synergistically—that is, interdependently.

This ecojustice principle of purpose is closely aligned with the principle of interconnectedness, which asserts that the world is 'a community of inter-connected living things which are mutually dependent on each other for life and survival'. Not only are these two principles aligned, but it is difficult to separate them and to decide which one is primary, because one of the fundamental laws of the universe is harmony, and harmony presumes some kind of inter-connectedness. In this passage from Pseudo-Solomon, the focus is not on the earth alone but on various spheres of reality that are governed by laws of harmony and order. The statement that claims that 'the universe defends the righteous' epitomizes both ecojustice prin-ciples—describes the dynamic cosmic design of the universe, and it confirms the principle of interconnectedness.

It would be anachronistic to imply that Pseudo-Solomon enjoyed a scientific view of the universe. However, the 'world *in* the text' does suggest a type of cosmic interrelationship, and the principle of mutual interchangeability—the 'world *behind* the text'—does offer an ancient mode of explanation, although it is a philosophical rather than a sci-entific theory.

At first glance, the syncrises easily lend themselves to contempo-rary interpretation, the 'world *in front* of the text'. However, here we must be particularly cautious as we move from an ancient Near Eastern perspective to a modern Western scientific world view. We may detect familiarity, but we must also admit strangeness; apparent continuity cannot blind us to the rudimentary discontinuity between these two world views.

Various branches of modern science have shown us that there is indeed a dynamic cosmic design within which the individual com-ponents are mutually dependent. Although we might detect familiar elements between the world view of Pseudo-Solomon and the world of modern science, there are also some rudimentary differences. Chief among them is the fact that the basis of the interdependence that we recognize is the laws of nature—not morality, as the syncrises seem to suggest. Human actions certainly do have repercussions on the quality of our ecosystems, but the changes that they produce are more like physical mutations than they are like transmutations of the four basic elements—they do not rectify the social disruptions effected by moral depravity. Our moral failures may indeed disrupt the natural balance necessary for life as we know it, but the changes produced do not discriminate between the righteous and the wicked, as Pseudo-Solomon alleges.

Related to this observation is the question of inherent balance. Both ancient and the modern world views seem to hold that balance is not only a characteristic of the natural world, but is also an active prin-ciple by which it organizes and reorganizes itself. However, the differ-ences between these understandings are striking. Where Pseudo-Solomon maintained that morality was a component in this balance, science limits its consideration of balance to laws that govern the physical world. This does not exclude the presence and influence of non-physical reality—even speculative science is open to such possibilities; however, in a modern scientific world view, these possibilities are regarded as only indirectly operative. Science deals with what is quantifiable, if only mathematically so; it is indifferent to theology. Today we are plagued by the same theological dilemma as our religious ancestors, namely, the justice of God in the face of the inequities apparent in the world. However, nature does not remedy this imbalance, as our religious ancestors seem to have thought it could. If anything, from our perspective, it is a victim.

A fundamental theme in the world view of Pseudo-Solomon— ethnocentrism—differs from anything in our contemporary scientific perspectives. The biblical book may begin and end with attention to creation, but the teaching contained within the book—particularly in the syncrises—reveals that the books's real concerns are ethnocentric.

Because Pseudo-Solomon saw Hellenistic philosophy and Jewish revelation in a life-and-death struggle for the soul of the people, he championed his religious tradition by depicting Israel as favored by God above all other peoples. The syncrises found in the Wisdom of Solomon accord this bias both divine and cosmic legitimation.

There are no favorites in a scientific world view; all are subject to the same laws of nature—female and male, believer and agnostic, righteous and wicked. As we continue to struggle with questions of theodicy in the early twenty-first century, ethnocentrism is neither the origin of our questioning nor the basis of our answers—as seems to have been the case with Pseudo-Solomon.

In this study I have sought to demonstrate that Pseudo-Solomon used the Stoic doctrine of mutual interchangeability and syncrisis— Hellenistic form of contrast—in his essentailly ethnocentric reinterpretation of part of the tradition relating to the Israelite Exodus from Egypt. How might his teaching be revelatory for us, with our concerns focused on ecotheology rather than ethnocentrism?

First, the Wisdom of Solomon underscores the writer's faith in the creative ingenuity of God, his respect for the intrinsic value of creation, and his understanding of the interconnectedness of all of its components. These ideas were inherited from his religious tradition.

Second, the book shows how the author used the new insights of his day to reinterpret traditions of the past. He had no reservations about circumventing earlier perceptions—the miraculous character of the Exodus events—that did not correspond to his present world view.

We in our day can do likewise. Employing the hermeneutic of suspicion through the lens of ecojustice, we can advocate Pseudo-Solomon's faith in the creative ingenuity of God, without also ascribing to his ethnocentric bias. We can share his respect for the intrinsic value of creation, without allowing our scientific perspectives to overshadow our religious insights. Finally, we have advanced far beyond his understanding of the interconnectedness of all of the components of the natural world. We have come to see how we are not at the centre of this vast universe, and that we are dependent on the workings of the universe—it is not dependent upon us.

However, this does not mean that we are insignificant. Our religious tradition says that we have been made but a little less than *elohim* (Ps. 8.6). Furthermore, because of the quality of our consciousness, scientists consider us an example of the natural world reflecting upon itself. This world view points again to the intrinsic value of the universe and to the interconnectedness of all of its components.

Despite the differences in our world views, Pseudo-Solomon still points us towards the practice of recontextualization, a way of reshaping the tradition.

An Earth Bible Reading of the Lord's Prayer: Matthew 6.9-13

Vicky Balabanski

Introduction

The Lord's Prayer has been described as 'a Christian remainder in a post-Christian world' (Luz 1989: 374). In the Australian context, it is still part of public life as the opening prayer of parliament, though its function there is more of a quaint reminder of our country's history than an expression of shared conviction. It is still known to many of the immediate postwar generation who no longer profess the Christian faith.

In the public as well as the private sphere, this prayer can function as a window on Christian aspirations in our post-Christian context. By contrast, for those within the church the importance of the Lord's Prayer cannot be overestimated. Because of the significance of this prayer for worship, instruction and personal devotion throughout the history of the church, this prayer has had a greater role than any other in the shaping of Christian theology.

If indeed the Lord's Prayer both shapes Christian theology and speaks to a post-Christian world of the hopes and aspirations of Christian faith, then it is appropriate that we bring it into dialogue with one of the most pressing issues facing the whole earth community in the present time: the ecological crisis. In the face of the ecological degradation of the earth, the seas and the atmosphere, it is imperative that we bring questions of ecojustice to this prayer and allow the guiding principles of an ecojustice hermeneutic to expose its assumptions and values. If we hold that a shift is necessary in our theology towards the conceptualizing of the earth as a legitimate subject rather than inanimate object, then a prayer that has so extensively shaped our spirituality is a key point of departure.

To achieve the sort of shift in perspective that is necessary for humanity to become responsible custodians of, and partners with, the earth, a commitment to ecojustice will have to go beyond the sphere of the interest group and enter into the individual and communal piety of the church.

The following exploration of the Lord's Prayer from an ecojustice perspective is offered as a contribution to the process of recovering God's joy in the mutuality of all creation.

Prolegomena

Three main versions of the Lord's Prayer have been handed down to us from the late first and early second centuries: the briefest form, found in Lk. 11.2-4; the prayer of the Matthean community found in Mt. 6.9-13; and the version with a final doxology found in *Did.* 8.2. The significant variations between these texts implies that the prayer was originally understood as a *model* of prayer rather than as the specific wording required (Davies and Allison 1988: 599). Several of the intriguing areas of debate with regard to the prayer will be bracketed out as beyond the scope of this paper: the relationship between the versions and the interrelated question of redaction; a search for the original dominical wording; and the question of an Aramaic or Hebrew source. Parallels with ancient Jewish prayers will be discussed only in so far as they shed light on the cosmological background of the prayer.

The version of the Lord's Prayer which will be explored from an ecojustice perspective is that of the Gospel of Matthew. This is the canonical version of the prayer that has entered into the liturgy of the church and so has influenced the worship, personal devotion and world view of Christians over the centuries. The Matthean version was chosen by virtue of its greater symmetry, clearer rhythm and further petitions vis-à-vis the Lukan version, as well as by the privileged role that Matthew's Gospel came to play more generally in the history of the church. The version found in the Didache closely parallels that of Matthew, with the addition of a doxological 'seal' at the end of it.

Within the parameters of this paper, I will not address this doxological ending found in the Didache nor indeed the slightly longer ending familiar to contemporary Christians, but rather limit myself to the wording of the Matthean version of the Lord's Prayer.

Methodological Considerations

The methodology employed in this paper draws on the feminist hermeneutics of suspicion and retrieval. By means of the guiding principles of the Earth Bible Project, this exploration is situated within the framework of self-consciously engaged criticisms, and like them, acknowledges the bias of the interpreter. In the case of this approach, it is a bias towards voicing the intrinsic worth of the earth and all creation, which is the first principle of the Earth Bible Project's ecojustice hermeneutics. This principle critiques the cosmologies and mythologies that devalue the earth as a decaying present reality over against heaven as an eternal spiritual reality.

This exploration also proceeds in dialogue with the challenge of demythologizing posed by Rudolf Bultmann. In a key article 'New Testament and Mythology' (1964: 1-44),[1] Bultmann contrasted contemporary scientific cosmology with the ancient three-tiered cosmology, with heaven above, the underworld below and the earth in the centre. Bultmann sought to show that we do not and cannot share the cosmological and mythological framework of the ancient world, and if the Christian proclamation or *kerygma* is to continue to have meaning in the contemporary world, it must be reinterpreted in the cosmological and mythological framework of the contemporary world.[2]

In our contemporary postmodern context we no longer necessarily share Bultmann's conviction of a single scientific cosmology, nor his agenda to translate the *kerygma* into existential terms. Nevertheless, his call for the need to translate ancient cosmological frameworks into contemporary categories is of significance in developing an ecojustice approach to the Scriptures.

Implied Cosmologies

One aspect of the demythologizing challenge is to make explicit the cosmology or cosmologies implied by a passage of Scripture, in order to make clear where translation into contemporary mythology may be useful and necessary. When I began to explore the question of ancient cosmologies via an examination of the concept of 'heaven' or 'heavens', the picture of ancient cosmologies proved to be far more diverse than Bultmann's three-tiered universe would imply.

---

1.   This is an abbreviation of the full title in English translation: 'New Testament and Mythology: The Mythological Element in the Message of the New Testament and the Problem of its Re-interpretation', in H.W. Bartsch (ed.) 1964.

2.   Bultmann's point was not to eliminate mythology, which he understood in a positive sense as 'the use of imagery to express the other worldly in terms of this world'. Rather, he states that 'the importance of the New Testament mythology lies not in its imagery but in the understanding of existence that it enshrines. The real question is whether this understanding of existence is true. Faith claims that it is, and faith ought not to be tied down to the imagery of New Testament mythology.' See Bultmann 1964: 10-11.

Certainly there is a cosmology in which God resides in the heavens or in the highest tier of the heavens. However, another cosmological strand—very apparent in the Psalms, for instance—is the notion that the heavens themselves are part of creation, and that God is above the heavens. Here the heavens may be synonymous with the skies. It is not my purpose to pursue this question here, but simply to note that there are diverse cosmological frameworks, and that each passage of Scripture needs to be allowed reflect its own cosmology.

Let us move then to the Lord's Prayer.

The Structure of the Lord's Prayer

The Lord's Prayer may be divided into two carefully structured sections, as set out below. The opening line or invocation and the closing line of the first section are linked by means of an *inclusio* (οὐρανοῖς line 1, οὐρανῷ line 5; 'in the heavens'/'in heaven'). Within this framework, there are three petitions in the third person imperative, called in the literature the 'thou' petitions. These show a final rhyme in the Greek, each ending with the pronoun σου ('of you').

In the second section, each petition is made in the second person imperative. In this section, each petition is characterized by the first person plural pronoun 'we', 'us' or 'our'. These have therefore come to be known as the 'we' petitions (though perhaps the 'us' or 'our' petitions would be more accurate, as the accusative, dative and genitive forms are more common). The latter petitions each fall clearly into two sections, while the opening petition of this section, being briefer, functions as an introduction to the petitions that follow.

First section

Πάτερ ἡμῶν ὁ ἐν τοῖς οὐρανοῖς·	Our Father who is in the heavens
ἁγιασθήτω τὸ ὄνομά σου·	let your name be hallowed
ἐλθέτω ἡ βασιλεία σου·	let your reign come
γενηθήτω τὸ θέλημά σου	let your will be done
ὡς ἐν οὐρανῷ καὶ ἐπὶ γῆς.	as in heaven, so on earth.

Second section

τὸν ἄρτον ἡμῶν τὸν ἐπιούσιον	Our bread of the day
δὸς ἡμῖν σήμερον·	give us today
καὶ ἄφες ἡμῖν τὰ ὀφειλήματα ἡμῶν,	And release us from our debts
ὡς καὶ ἡμεῖς ἀφήκαμεν	as we also release
τοῖς ὀφειλέταις ἡμῶν·	those indebted to us.
καὶ μὴ εἰσενέγκῃς ἡμᾶς εἰς πειρασμόν,	And do not lead us into testing
ἀλλὰ ῥῦσαι ἡμᾶς ἀπὸ τοῦ πονηροῦ.	but rescue us from evil.

(Translation mine)

The First Section

The prayer opens with an invocation to God as our Father who is in the heavens. It evokes a cosmology in which God is removed from the earth. We who are schooled in this prayer immediately think of this as an image of God's transcendence.

But by asserting God's transcendence in spatial terms—as the one who is removed from the earth—the prayer opens by setting up a spatial dualism. Heaven is conveyed as the arena in which God is reigning, and, by implication, earth is the arena in which God's reign is not apparent. This spatial dualism undergirds the whole of this first section of the prayer, and culminates explicitly in the phrase 'as in heaven, so on earth'.

This spatial dualistic framework contrasts the way in which God's name is hallowed, God's rule is expressed and God's will is done in the heavenly sphere with the way these are not done or not apparent in the earthly sphere. This dualism devalues the earth as an arena in which God's presence is apparent. This spatial dualistic cosmology is not universally shared in the Scriptures; as I suggested above, there are cosmologies, not one cosmology.

Part of the heritage of Jewish prayer includes the assertion that God made both heaven and earth (cf. Pss. 115.15; 121.2; 124.8; 134.3; 146.6), and that therefore earth as well as heaven speaks of God's name, and experiences God's reign and God's will. However, the spatial dualism of the Lord's Prayer implies a pessimistic view, and raises the question whether the earth can reflect the name, the reign and the will of the creator simply by virtue of its being part of creation.

Nevertheless, at the same time as the distinction between heaven and earth is being confirmed by means of the frame around the petitions and in the petitions themselves, the prayer destabilizes the distinction by calling upon God to do away with the distinction. In other words, the prayer exhorts God to allow earth to reflect God's name, God's reign and God's will as clearly as these are reflected in the realm of God's own presence, namely in the heavens.

In seeking an ecojustice perspective on this prayer, we therefore need to recognize and critique the spatial dualism that contrasts the heavens and the earth, making the former—the heavens—the arena of God's reign, and the latter—the earth—the arena in which that reign is by definition not apparent. Having done so, however, we also need to recognize that the prayer takes a stand against its own cosmology by praying that the distinction between heaven and earth will be collapsed.

How is the hallowing of the name, the coming of the reign and the doing of the will of God to be effected? The third person aorist imperatives in the prayer are intriguing, as they exhort God to effect these actions, but leave open who is the third party who will carry out the actions. In addition, the first and third of the imperatives are passive, which encourages us to think of the divine passive, and therefore of God effecting the actions.

However, the very act of praying this prayer implicates the speaker in the action. It evokes a continuum between the speaker calling on God to effect these actions, God who necessitates that the actions be carried out, and then both God and humanity who become the subject of the actions.

In terms of our ecojustice perspective, these imperatives do not allow us to assume that it is either God or humanity who will effect these actions alone, but rather that the creator and the created are working together in a further creative act—namely in breaking down the distinction between heaven and ·earth. The earth and its communities are not the passive objects of creation, but are co-creators with God in the overall goal that is envisaged in this prayer—namely the recognition of God's name, reign and will throughout all creation.

The Earth Bible Project's second ecojustice principle states that 'Earth is a community of interconnected living things that are mutually dependent on each other for life and survival'. If we hold this to be so, then these three petitions show that God, too, is part of this interconnection that brings about new creative possibilities.

While these petitions might traditionally be seen as praying that God's saving work may be effected, the limitation of the distinction between God as creator and God as saviour is apparent—creation and new creation are, like the creator and the created, part of a continuum.

The first section of the Lord's Prayer opens with the invocation of God as our Father who dwells at a distance, beyond us, and closes with the call that this distance may be collapsed. The very first words 'our Father' do not allow the complete otherness of the one whom we address. Rather, they lay claim upon God not only as 'a father', but as *'our* father'. I distinguish myself here from a feminist reading by simply acknowledging the masculist bias of this metaphor for God, and the importance of the recent studies demonstrating the limitations of the imagery for the liberation of humanity. My focus in this context is not on 'our father' in contrast to 'our mother', but rather on who or what is encompassed in that term 'our'.

Who is counted in, and who is counted out by this first person plural possessive pronoun? We could answer this question functionally—namely all those who choose to pray this prayer are included, and this would then encompass all Christians. However, this prayer stands in the tradition of Jewish prayers which also address God as father, and include parallels for every phrase of the Lord's Prayer.[3] Perhaps the 'our' encompasses Jesus' contemporaries and by implication all people who, regardless of their religious affiliation, find their aspirations expressed in the prayer. But is limiting the 'our' to humanity too exclusive? Can God only be called 'Father' by one branch of the earth community?

The prayer itself may give us another perspective. The first section opens with the words 'our Father', and closes with the word 'earth'. So, it is not only humanity that can lay claim to addressing God as 'our Father'; the whole earth community lays claim to God as the source of life and as sustainer—the fatherly and motherly aspects of God. I suggest that the very prominent position of the word 'earth', with its pivotal place between the first and second sections, underscores this view.

The Second Section

The word 'earth' at the end of the first section introduces the shift in the nature of petitions that are now brought to God. If the three earlier petitions all called for a collapsing of the distinction between heavenly and earthly realities, these latter petitions raise the everyday realities of life. The need for bread, the reality of debts, the threat of testing and evil are realities that characterize our experience of life. Each of these petitions evokes practical and mundane needs, and hallows the practical and mundane as worthy of God's attention.

The need for bread, the reality of debt and the threats of testing and evil impact not only on humanity, but also on the wider earth community. The need for bread leads to more and more of the earth being subjected to non-sustainable farming practices, with the destruction of forests and, in the Australian context, the raising of the water table and the increase in salinity threatening vast tracts of farming land. This is a practical and mundane petition, and the whole earth community has a stake in it.

The second petition also raises an issue that has practical implications for the wider earth community: debt. The unsustainable foreign debt of many countries—and the World Bank and the International Monetary Fund requirements that accompany these debts—mean that

---

3.   See I. Abrahams' composite prayer, cited in Davies and Allison (1988: 595).

local populations grow cash crops instead of food. The mineral and forest resources are plundered—resulting in significant costs to the environment—in order to alleviate the burden of foreign debt. The land and the people—the whole earth community—cries out for debt relief: 'release us from our debts'.

The third petition prays for salvation in the face of testing. The Greek term translated as 'testing', πειρασμός, is not exclusively eschatological; it is a recurrent motif in the book of Exodus. A time of testing may be occasioned by human agency, according to the Exodus traditions. In Exod. 17.2 and Ps. 95.9, the people put God to the test at Massah and Meribah. This prayer, therefore, has a practical meaning, in addition to the more widely recognized eschatological meaning—it is a petition that God might spare us from a time of trial when people and cattle die of thirst. One aspect of the ecological crisis looming over us in the twenty-first century is also the threat of inadequate supplies of water to support human and animal life.

'Rescue us from evil'; the final words of the prayer ask for deliverance from evil, or perhaps the Evil One—the Greek is ambiguous at this point. This final petition acknowledges that in our experience of this world, we are faced with the constant possibility of evil, and of wrong or selfish choices that implicate us in that evil. Even this petition has a practical, mundane aspect.

I have argued that each of the petitions in the second section of the Lord's Prayer evokes practical and mundane needs. Just as these petitions are relevant for us today, it is clear that these needs were just as strongly felt when the prayer was first formulated. For instance, we can be in no doubt about the impact of the burden of debt in ancient Palestine when we read the account of the burning of the archives and contracts belonging to the creditors during the first Jewish War.[4] These are intended to be practical petitions, dealing with the every day realities in people's lives.

Nevertheless, it is striking that each of these petitions is formulated to allow both a practical, mundane understanding and an eschatological supra-mundane understanding. The bread petition is qualified with the intriguing word ἐπιούσιος. Davies and Allison call this Greek term 'one of the great unresolved puzzles of New Testament lexicography' (1988: 607).

---

4. See Josephus Flavius, *War* 2.17.6 (425-27). According to Josephus, the burning of the archives and contracts belonging to creditors makes the war attractive to the multitude.

Whatever the exact derivation of this word, contemporary and ancient scholarship is in agreement that it alludes to the gathering of the manna in Exodus 16—only a single day's portion was provided for each person. One of the striking things about this manna is that it could not be hoarded or exploited. Those who attempted to hoard it discovered that it had gone bad. Food that cannot be exploited or hoarded symbolizes a vision of a sustainable world, one in which people have enough, and where grasping for more than you need or can use is pointless. Thus the daily bread is a multivalent symbol: it is a physical provision; a spiritual sign of God's covenantal care; a symbol of the eschatological future banquet; and a metaphor of a sustainable world. Here we find not just a physical nor just a spiritual meaning; the symbol represents a continuum that calls into question our dualistic separation of matter and spirit.

Similarly, the prayer for release of debt allows for both a mundane and supramundane understanding. In relation to this petition, most scholars try to explain the shift from debts—understood as what is owed—in the Matthean version, to sin in the Lukan text, by means of an Aramaic source. Despite this, the Greek in the Matthean text, τὰ ὀφειλήματα, refers only to debts of money or debts in kind (Luz 1989: 371).

What does it mean for God to release us from monetary debt, and what would it mean for the majority of people in the world to be released from their crippling debts? I suspect that if the primary meaning of this brief petition were heard, the implications would be as unwelcome to the comfortable and secure as Jesus' ministry was originally!

The petition concerning debt is in two parts: release us from our debts, as we also release those indebted to us. It evokes not only our indebtedness towards God, but a network of indebtedness towards others. Seen in this way, it is a prayer that asks that our mutual indebtedness may be reciprocal and even-handed, and that we may recognize our interdependency. In this way, this petition has both a concrete and practical meaning for debt remission, as well as an assertion of interconnectedness and mutual dependency on each other for life and survival. Once again, these aspects are not mutually exclusive.

The final petition, in two parts, also has this connection between mundane and supramundane, with both testing and the experience of evil being at once everyday challenges and also eschatological ones. The word for testing, πειρασμός, has eschatological overtones, and it calls to mind the conviction that the final coming of God's reign will be heralded by a time in which the order of nature itself is shaken. It has been a practice in some Christian circles to welcome such upheavals in the natural order as hastening the end. However, the model we have in the Lord's Prayer by no means welcomes or invites such testing, but rather prays that we might be spared from such things.

Clearly, in the light of this petition, we cannot look on with complacency as we see the earth's ecosystems breaking down, species disappearing, famines and wars. We may not align ourselves with those who find satisfaction in these things. Rather, in praying this prayer we join with the whole earth community in praying for, and working towards, a world in which the whole earth community is spared such testing. This petition—that God may not lead us into the time of testing but that God may rather deliver us from evil—does not allow us to view the time of testing as anything other than evil. It is not to be welcomed as a means to an end, or a sign of the imminence of God's kingdom.

The final word of the prayer, evil or the Evil One, contrasts starkly with the opening words, 'our Father'; structurally, the prayer acknowledges that our hopes and aspirations find us, in our everyday living as part of the earth community—between the possibilities of God and of evil. This might result in a vision of cosmic dualism, with the forces of good and evil constantly striving against one another.

In the context of the prayer, however, these possibilities are by no means evenly matched. The prayer expresses the conviction that our Father is the one in whom we can confidently find deliverance from evil. In fact, this prayer enables us to name the reality of evil.

From an ecojustice perspective, it seems to me important that our contemporary cosmology is able to conceptualize evil—particularly given the reality of corporate evil, where the interests of one group are made supreme over the interests of the others. The contrasting beginning and ending of the prayer provide us with a contemporary definition of evil as those forces aligned against the creative continuum of the Creator and *co-creating* creation.

Finally, I should say a word about the dualistic tendencies of this prayer. I have discussed the spatial dualism inherent in the contrast between heaven and earth. I have mentioned cosmic dualism, with God being portrayed as in cosmic opposition with evil or the Evil One. There is also a temporal dualism evoked in the prayer, primarily by means of aorist imperatives calling for a single or decisive action to bring about the realization of each petition. For this reason, the majority of contemporary scholars see the Matthean version of the Lord's Prayer as thoroughly eschatological in outlook, with the hallowing of

God's name, the coming of the reign, the doing of the will of God, the giving of the bread and so forth all expected as aspects of God's imminent eschatological denouement. Any notion of a temporal dualism, requiring the end of the current cosmic order before the eschatological future can be established, needs to be exposed and critiqued. Although our Earth Bible principles affirm that 'the universe, the earth and all its components are part of a dynamic cosmic design within which each piece has a place in the overall goal of that design', this does not imply discontinuous categories, with the present reality as disposable.

Though the use of the aorist verbs in the prayer does envisage God acting decisively, God's action is also understood as being in continuity with the actions of all God's co-creators—namely the earth community.

In this prayer, the earth community is a living organism, not a passive recipient of divine action. Any member of this diverse community can invoke God and others to resist evil and collapse the dualistic distinctions of privileged space and time. The *telos* or goal in this prayer is not just God's kingdom in heaven but God's kingdom on earth, so that not just the future but the present may be the arena for the expression of God's life-giving possibilities.

A Transformative Struggle towards the Divine Dream:
An Ecofeminist Reading of Matthew 11

Elaine M. Wainwright

> When we speak of transformation we speak more accurately out of the vision of a process which will leave neither surfaces nor depths unchanged, which enters society at the most essential level of the subjugation of women and nature (Rich 1979: 248)

The project to be undertaken in this paper—an ecofeminist reading of Matthew 11 within the context of the Earth Bible—has the goal of transformation as articulated by Adrienne Rich. It invites interpreter and reader into a process which is open-ended, a process which moves between a critical analysis of the contemporary context; critical socio-rhetorical readings of a biblical text within a first-century world; and an evaluation of these readings within contemporary communities of meaning-making as to their transformative potential towards new frameworks, practices and relationships which are liberative for each member of the Earth community. As such it may leave 'neither surfaces nor depths unchanged' and hence can be called a 'transformative struggle' or a 'struggle towards transformation'.

This reading is named ecofeminist rather than ecojustice because it makes explicit the interconnection between the violence against, and the exploitation and degradation of both women and the Earth. This has been named by Rich and analyzed in recent decades in the classic work of Carolyn Merchant: *The Death of Nature: Women, Ecology, and the Scientific Revolution*, and in the many studies which have followed (e.g. Adams 1993; Diamond and Orenstein 1990; Plant 1989).

The ecofeminist hermeneutic brings this interconnection into critical dialogue with the ecojustice principle of interconnection within the Earth community. Years of feminist analysis have, however, highlighted the tendency and inherent danger in essentializing or absolutizing key and significant principles. An ecofeminist hermeneutic informed by the early feminist movement's essentializing of 'woman' in a way which obscured other oppressive factors like race, class, sexual orientation and religious affiliation will be attentive to the way interconnections within the earth community are nuanced by factors like location, socio-economic influences and many historical categories of difference—difference between women and men; difference among women; and difference within the emerging subjectivity of each woman—may well facilitate a recognition of diversity within the Earth community (Braidotti 1994: 146-72).

Contemporary critics readily locate the difference which has func- tioned *between* humanity and the Earth in a dualistic and hierarchical universe; feminists/ecofeminists have recognized the relationship between this difference, and the difference between men and women in a patriarchal or kyriarchal universe. The difference *among* members of the Earth community is recognized by Karen Warren who advo- cates for the human community a rethinking of the notion of self which Hinsdale summarizes as 'such that we see ourselves as co- members of an ecological community and yet different from other members of it' (Hinsdale 1991: 162). Attention to the difference *within* each member of the Earth community will enable the development of the subjectivity of each as multiple in its diversity rather than singular and unified. When this principle of difference or diversity is brought to the reading project, the voices of the oppressed of the Earth com- munity can be heard in their multiplicity rather than as a single voice of the Earth.

Just as the interconnections between layers of oppression within the Earth community have been made explicit within an ecofeminist ana- lysis, so too the layers of historical agency need to be recognized within the interpretive process. Elisabeth Schüssler Fiorenza names such recognition a 'dangerous memory'—for her it recognizes 'wo/ men's religious agency as prophets, teachers, and wise wo/men' (1998: 49). Current studies are making it eminently clear that the Earth shares such agency with women throughout history, and that such countertraditions will be found within the biblical text. An eco- feminist reading will, therefore, be both *deconstructive* in a way which uncovers patterns of domination and *reconstructive* so that both ancient and contemporary voices of resistance may be heard—voices of women and voices of the Earth.

Both religious feminist and ecofeminist studies have drawn atten- tion not only to the intimate connections between constructions of women and the Earth in particular societies but also links with their imaging or naming of divinity, of the sacred (Rae 1994; Adams 1993; Johnson 1993), an aspect not addressed significantly in the Earth Bible principles. Within Western Christianity, an exclusively male imaging of divinity and incarnation has functioned to legitimate the domination of women and the earth, and to inform almost all readings of the biblical text. Countertraditions within the text or within its communities of reception have been silenced. A deconstructive and reconstructive ecofeminist reading will, therefore, give attention to both the images and metaphors for God and for Jesus both implicit and explicit in the text and the meaning-making process. These will be examined in terms of their contribution to particular constructions of the human and Earth communities.

This hermeneutic will be combined with a socio-rhetorical reading strategy in relation to the text of Matthew 11. Intertextual and intratextual readings of the narrative within a first-century sociocultural context characterized by a variety of reading communities (Wainwright 1998: 35-49) will enable a variety of voices to be heard—as tradition and countertradition, as dominant and subversive. Such readings can then be interrogated from the perspective of an ecofeminist/ecojustice ethic in order to determine which will have the rhetorical effect of creating a new world in front of the text that will shape the developing consciousness of communities of reception towards ecological transformation.

Reading Matthew 11 in Context

The ecofeminist reader of Matthew 11 cannot interpret this chapter in isolation but must situate it within the context of the unfolding Gospel narrative also read through this same interpretive lens. In this section, therefore, I will lay out briefly such a reading, highlighting some of the significant elements of the narrative which contribute to an ecofeminist reading of the Gospel and which prepare the reader for the particular reading of Matthew 11.

I have previously drawn brief attention to the ecological potential of the opening words of the Matthean gospel (Wainwright 1998: 53, 58). Intertextually, Βίβλος γενέσεως or 'the book of the genealogy' evokes both Gen. 2.4a and 5.1a. In the first instance, the reference is to the book of the genealogy of the heavens and the Earth—the universe— and it closes the first account of the creation or coming to birth of the universe; in the second it refers to the human community (ἀνθρώπων). Genesis 5.1 also reiterates Gen. 1.27—humanity is made in the image of God, male and female. It is into this interconnected story of the universe and the human community that the story of Jesus is placed.

Like the book of the genealogy of humanity, however, the genealogy of Jesus *Christos* is male dominated and would have been read in that way at least by some of the initial communities of reception. The male and female of the 'original' vision is quickly erased in the Matthean patrilineage just as it was in the genealogy of Genesis 5. But the transgressions in the text—Jesus is not only son of Abraham and David, Obed and Hezekiah, but also of Tamar, Rahab, Ruth, Bathsheba and Mary—resist such erasure.

The voices of the universe (the heavens and the Earth) and of the women of Israel's story are raised at the beginning of the Matthean story of Jesus, albeit faintly within the patriarchy or the 'rule of the fathers' that the genealogy affirms. They are voices of resistance that may have been heard at least by some members of the Matthean community, notably by those households whose reading of the story of Jesus was resistant to patriarchy. An ecofeminist reader will be attentive to enabling those voices to be heard in contemporary interpretations so that their erasure does not continue as the story unfolds.

The tension evident in the opening of the gospel (Mt. 1.1-17) continues into the subsequent section which recounts the birth of Jesus (1.18-25). Here Jesus is legally constituted 'son of Joseph' by way of the command given to Joseph to name the child, a closing of the fissure in the patriarchal world view created by 1.16—Jesus is born of Mary. At the same time, Jesus is characterized in 1.20 as being born of a spirit which is holy (πνεύματός ἐστιν ἁγίου). There are many ways in which this spirit may have been understood intertextually. Elizabeth Johnson says, however, that it signifies 'the presence of the living God active in this historical world. The Spirit of God who actually arrives in every moment, God drawing near and passing by in vivifying power in the midst of historical struggle' (Johnson 1993: 42). The Matthean text makes a similar claim when the name Jesus, child of the spirit, is paralleled to Emmanuel, the name which means 'God with us' (1.23).

For those readers carrying the echoes of Gen. 2.4 in the opening words of the gospel, the 'us' among whom God is present is not only the human community but also the heavens and the Earth which together constitute the 'historical world', the place of 'historical struggle'. This is the arena of the story of Jesus established by the opening chapter of the gospel. When the story closes, therefore, with the promise of the Jesus who has been raised—I am with you (ἐγὼ μεθ᾽ ὑμῶν εἰμι)—this too can be read in light of the continued presence of Jesus with the Earth community. In an extension of Sallie McFague's perspective, we could claim that Jesus is therefore imaged 'as both caring deeply for that world and calling us to care as well' (McFague 1987: 60, 87).

Despite the possibility of reading for earth inclusiveness in the

Gospel narrative's frame, in the forefront of the unfolding story is the human community whose story is narrated within a patriarchal world view so that the voice of the universe and the voice of women can be very easily erased for many readers. In an earlier work, I have shown that the dominant imagery in this frame is profoundly patriarchal despite the Gospel's multiple voices (Wainwright 1991: 67, 146). In Matthew 3 and 4—the chapters that establish the programmatic for the Matthean gospel—the writer introduces two themes that are interconnected within the gospel narrative; both themes can be read in the broader frame of the Earth community which includes but is not limited to the human community. John the Baptist enters the narrative and is characterized initially by his urgent cry: 'Repent for the *kingdom of heaven* is at hand' (3.2). The first words of Jesus in the narrative are addressed to John in the context of Jesus' baptism: 'Let it be so now; for thus it is fitting for us to fulfil all *righteousness*' (3.15). The initial proclamation of Jesus—and characteristic of the beginning of his ministry—parallels John's plea: 'Repent, for the *kingdom of heaven* is at hand' (4.17).

Michael Crosby notes that *righteousness* in its broadest sense implies the right ordering of the universe (Crosby 1988: 172). For first century readers, Isa. 45.8 may have provided the best example of this inter-textuality: 'Shower, O heavens from above, and let the skies rain down righteousness; let the earth open, that salvation may spring up, and let it cause righteousness to sprout up also; I...have created it' (see also Amos 5.24; 6.12; Hos. 10.12; Dan. 12.3; Isa. 26.9; 32.16; 61.11; Pss. 33.5; 36.6; 72.3; 85.11; 89.14; 96.13; 97.2).

The righteousness that is to be fulfilled in Jesus' entry into the historical world and its struggle is the right ordering that God recognized and named as good in the coming to birth of the universe itself: the right relationship between the human community and all members of the Earth community. The right ordering of human relationships, explicit in Jer. 22.3, is also implicit in the Matthean theme of righteousness:

> Act with justice and righteousness, and deliver from the hand of the oppressor anyone who has been robbed. And do no wrong or violence to the alien, the orphan, and the widow, or shed innocent blood in this place.

Crosby can say, therefore, that the rhetorical effect of this Matthean theme is to 'outline a way of reordering church life and creation itself' (Crosby 1988: 42).

That the themes of righteousness and the 'kingdom of heaven' are

intimately connected in the Matthean narrative is made clear in the
Sermon on the Mount (5.10, 20; 6.33) and later in 21.31-32. While
righteousness connotes God's dream for the right ordering of the
universe and all its members, the kingdom of heaven carries connotations of God's rule over—rather than participation with and in—
the universe (Viviano 1996: 817-18). Such rule would have been
understood by members of the Matthean community as both monar-
chical and patriarchal, as this verse from one of the kingship psalms
demonstrates: '*He* will judge the world [οἰκουμένην] with righteousness, and the peoples with *his* truth' (Ps. 96.13; my emphasis), even
though this rule is characterized by righteousness and truth. The
effect of the modifier 'of the heavens' (τῶν οὐρανῶν) is to shift the
focus of God's engagement with the Earth and the human community—established in the naming of Jesus as Emmanuel—to an otherworldly reality.

For those readers, however, who gave significant emphasis to
righteousness as a key characteristic of the Matthean 'kingdom', the
kingdom too could have connoted God's dream for both the heavens
and the earth (Mt. 6.10), especially as it is developed in the Matthean
narrative. The kingdom in Matthew can be understood, therefore, as
rightly ordered relationships between and among God's self, Jesus,
the human community and all members of the Earth community.
Because language is a significant conveyor of meaning, it may be
necessary to use the term 'kindom' rather than 'kingdom'. As Elizabeth Johnson says,

> [i]f separation is not the ideal but connection is; if dualism is not the
> ideal but the relational embrace of diversity is; if hierarchy is not the
> ideal but mutuality is; then the kinship model more closely approxi-
> mates reality (1993: 30).

Within the possibilities which this ecofeminist introduction to the
Matthean Gospel makes possible, Matthew 11 can now be read.

Reading Matthew 11

a. *Restorative Deeds*
The opening verse of Matthew 11 is a reminder to readers/hearers of
the Matthean narrative of the unfolding of the gospel programmatic—
Jesus has just instructed his followers in the way he has been following (Mt. 10.5-8), a way of preaching (Mt. 5–7) and deeds of healing
and restoration (Mt. 8–9). Together these proclaim the new 'kindom'
characteristic of Jesus' ministry.

Jesus has been doing or enacting the 'kindom'—the restoration of not only humanity but the Earth community to right relationships as the calming of the great storm (σεισμὸς μέγας) suggests (8.23-27). In Mt. 11.2-3 which opens an integrated narrative unit (11.2-19), John, who has heard of this enactment which he names the *deeds* of the Christ (τας ἔργα τοῦ Χριστοῦ), shifts the focus to a question of identity: 'Are you the one who is to come, or are we to wait for another?' In reply Jesus reverses the shift and sends a message to John and the questioners he has sent, as well as to the hearers/readers of the Gospel. 'Go and tell John what you hear and see' (Mt. 11.4b). Celia Deutsch has pointed out that the present tense of the verbs 'hear' and 'see' (ἀκούετε καί βλέπετε) stresses 'the contemporaneous quality of Jesus' words and deeds' (Deutsch 1996: 51). Jesus' listing of what is being heard and seen—the blind receive their sight, the lame walk, the lepers are cleansed, the deaf hear, the dead are raised, and the poor have good news brought to them—is a programme of restoration that has been enacted and shall continue to be enacted. It is this programme that characterizes Jesus' identity, not titles like the Coming One (ὁ ἐρχόμενος). For first-century hearers/readers, this list would have evoked intertextual meaning-making. These works are the works of restoration envisaged by the prophet Isaiah (Isa. 29.18-19; 35.5-6; 61.1-2). Significant for an ecofeminist reading is the intimate link between a restored humanity and a restored world—at least in the second and third text. Isaiah 35.5-6 is framed by such restoration: the wilderness and the dry land shall be glad, the desert shall rejoice and blossom (35.1) and waters shall break forth in the wilderness, and streams in the desert; the burning sand shall become a pool, and the thirsty ground springs of water (35.6-7). Isaiah 61.3 says that the restored, the healed shall be called 'oaks of righteousness', and goes on to indicate their task: they shall build up the ancient ruins, they shall raise up the former devastations; they shall repair the ruined cities, the devastations of many generations (Isa. 61.4). In such an intertextual reading, the first-century interpreter—like the contemporary ecofeminist reader—would have critiqued the association between restoration and vengeance (Isa. 35.4; 61.20). This vengeance, associated with God, could lay waste the Earth (Isa. 34.8-17). Jesus, Emmanuel—in whom the 'kindom', the restoration of God's dream, is near at hand—is a prophet of restoration and not vengeful destruction of the human and the Earth communities. Nor is he identified as the male Coming One so that restoration is the work of a male saviour figure; he is identified with the inclusive work of restoration—the task to be undertaken by all those women and men who accept the message of the 'kindom', who indeed 'hear' and 'see', and commit themselves to the kindom movement inaugurated by Jesus.

Such an interpretation is affirmed by the words of Michael Crosby. 'Matthew sees Jesus Christ continuing the work of reordering creation through a reordered religious and economic base, namely the household. This 'work' has overtones of an ongoing jubilee' (Crosby 1988: 210). To continue this work of restoration will mean attention to the most oppressed in the Earth community: to those oppressed by denial of voice, by nearness to extinction, by race, by physical oppression, by gender, by myriad forms of destruction and negation. Just as Jesus heard the voice of the blind, the lame, lepers, the deaf, the dead and the poor—the most marginalized in his society—so, too, today's communities of the 'kingdom' must hear the voices of the most marginalized of the Earth community in the diversity and multiplicity of their subjectivities, too often obscured by contemporary dominant cultures.

I do not have the space in this article to interpret in detail Mt. 11.7-15; this section of the Gospel constitutes Jesus' interpretation of the ministry of John the Baptist (Wainwright 1998: 72-75). Rather, in the context established in this article and the reading it is undertaking, these verses can be seen to be framed by 11.2-6 and 11.16-19, sections which have strong ecological implications and which in turn can both critique and inform the reading of what they frame, namely 11.7-15.

The parable in Mt. 11.16-17 and its application by Jesus in 11.18-19a clearly present the way of John and the way of Jesus as two 'roads to wisdom', each of which are rejected by a fickle generation, constructed by the parable as 'superficial in the extreme, and viciously unreachable' by comparing them to children (Cotter 1989: 78). Cotter demonstrates that the children seated in the *agora* or marketplace are conventionally out of place. The parable uses the language of judgment, pronounced from the seat of judgment in the *agora*. This is certainly not the place with which children are generally associated and yet the judgment that this generation pronounces on John and Jesus is compared to the fickleness of children at play, who refuse to comply to the wishes of their peers whether they invite them to dance or to mourn (1989: 68-70).

The ecological implications of the two paths of wisdom represented in John and Jesus are worth exploring. Majella Franzmann has explored them in detail in relation to food and bodies, and has concluded that 'we have forgotten that the primary activity of salvation is firstly within the human sphere and on the simplest of levels' (Franzmann 1992: 31). Her perspective needs to be extended to include place and interconnection.

In Matthew's introduction to John in 3.1-5, we find John located in the wilderness (3.1), clothed in camel's hair, with a leather girdle around his waist and sustained by locusts and wild honey (3.4). His ascetic lifestyle and eschatological preaching are presented as a way of life interconnected with his environment. The desert is a valid setting for John's preaching and lifestyle.

Jesus, on the other hand, makes his home and the context for his preaching Capernaum by the sea (4.13) and the region around the lake, a place which Franzmann rightly presents as characterized by 'abundance and fertility' (1992: 19). We are not told how Jesus is clothed but he teaches and enacts a different life-enhancing inter-connectedness with elements of the Earth community. He does not condemn fasting (6.16-18), but unlike John he feasts with tax collectors and sinners (9.10), and proclaims his time of ministry as being like a wedding feast when guests do not mourn but enter into the festivities, enjoying friendship and food.

Both paths of wisdom—that of John and of Jesus—can be read as paths of ecological interconnectedness. It is for those who choose to walk those paths to discern the correct time for each. John used eschatological preaching and ascetic lifestyle to prepare the way for Jesus; in Jesus' time, feasting in places of abundance and fertility was appropriate. The final segment of 11.19 seems to affirm this—Wisdom is justified by her deeds.[1]

Within the context of this Matthean narrative segment, the deeds of Wisdom (τῶν ἔργων αὐτῆς) parallel the deeds of the Christos in 11.2 (τὰ ἔργα τοῦ Χριστοῦ). In the restorative prophetic works detailed in 11.4-5, and in the interconnected lifestyle evoked in 11.19a, the deeds of Jesus Christos are intimately connected to the deeds of Sophia/Wisdom, the one whom Elisabeth Schüssler Fiorenza recognizes as the female gestalt of God (Schüssler Fiorenza 1983: 130-40), in a way which subverts exclusive male imaging of Jesus (Wainwright 1998: 76-77). Jesus, who has been identified as Christos earlier in the Gospel narrative (1.1, 16, 17, 18; 2.4), is now identified as Sophia/Wisdom. It is Jesus Sophia who is justified or recognized as right or just (ἐδι-καιώθη) by her deeds; the verb has the same root as the central Matthean theme of righteousness/δικαιοσύνην. Sophia participates

---

1.   I have chosen here not to address the use of the title 'Son of man' or 'human one' in v. 19 as I have already undertaken this analysis from a feminist perspective and suggested the need for an alternative translation (Wainwright 1989: 75).

in the right ordering of the Earth community in the deeds of Jesus Sophia.

We have examined the way in which the deeds of Jesus characterize Sophia, who is identified with Jesus, in the way of right ordering. Intertextuality evoked by first-century readers may also allow us to determine how the deeds of Sophia characterize Jesus. Only in Wis. 14.5 are works directly ascribed Sophia. The voice of the sage recognizes that the works of God's wisdom are not without effect in maintaining the interconnectedness of the Earth community—'it is your will that works of your wisdom should not be without effect'. Wisdom is poured out on all the works of the creator and on all the living (Sir. 1.9) and while Sir. 18.1-4 states that none have been given the power to proclaim God's works, indeed elsewhere it is Wisdom who knows these works because she was present when the world (τὸν κόσμον) was made (Wis. 9.9), and is an 'associate' in God's works (Wis. 8.4). She has made her dwelling amongst humanity (Sir. 24.8-12; Prov. 8.31) where she can make known the work of the Creator: the right ordering of the universe.

Matthew 1.23 proclaimed God as being with the Earth community in the birth of Jesus, and 11.19 affirms Wisdom's creative presence with that same community in the deeds of Jesus. Significantly for an ecofeminist reading, these two namings of Jesus transgress the traditional male metaphors and images that predominate in the Gospel narrative and can, in their turn, function deconstructively in a reading of the entire Gospel from an ecofeminist perspective.

b. *Transformative Words*

That same transgression is brought into tension with more exclusive imagery in the concluding verses of this chapter of the Matthean narrative (Mt. 11.25-30). Both Elisabeth Schüssler Fiorenza and Celia Deutsch make it clear that despite the absence of the word *sophia* from 11.25-27, these verses not only draw heavily on the wisdom tradition but continue the presentation of Jesus as personified Wisdom and Wisdom's sage (Schüssler Fiorenza 1994: 143; Deutsch 1996: 56; 1987: 56-112). It is the sage who addresses God in the language of 'Father' and 'Lord' (Sir. 51.1 and 23.1, 4), and with the phrase 'of heaven and earth' invites readers/hearers into a Matthean symbolic universe that links heaven and earth (5.18; 6.10; 24.35; 28.18). I have explored elsewhere the liberating and oppressive potential of these titles within different households in the Matthean community and their legitimation of the patriarchal and kyriarchal domination of women, other non-persons and the earth in contemporary communities of reception of the Gospel text (Wainwright 1998: 80). An ecojustice reading must take account of these same factors.

The domination inherent in the titles 'father' and 'lord' in a patriarchal and imperial context may well have functioned to negate the inclusion of the universe, both the heavens and the earth. Read against the grain, however—and in light of the Emmanuel title which brings God present within the Earth community in Jesus—the address is less oppressive. However, I would suggest that such titles need to be retranslated in an ecofeminist reading; this task is beyond the scope of this paper.

The Wisdom of Solomon in particular, and the wisdom myth generally, provide a significant intertext for understanding Mt. 11.25-27 with its language of hiding and revealing. Wisdom knows the hidden ways of God which are intimately connected to the working of the universe (Wis. 7.17-22; 8.3-4: Sir. 24.3-7 and Prov. 8.22-30). It is she who 'mediates that knowledge to the wise' (Deutsch 1996: 56), and who comes forth to be among the human community (Prov. 8.30-31; Sir. 24.8-12). Deutsch sums up her task as 'working in creation and history, allowing people to understand and discern the inner workings of that creation and history' (1987: 59).

This myth can facilitate an inclusive and interconnected reading of these verses. The God who is intimately connected to the heavens and the earth participates in sharing wisdom between members of the Earth community who are open to receive it. It is often those named as the 'wise and understanding' who are not open to receive this wisdom which, as Deutsch has indicated, concerns the working of creation and of history—the arena in which the works of Christos Sophia are enacted, the works to which the ταῦτα of Mt. 11.25 refers.

Problematic in these verses, however, is the shift from the language of wisdom to that of 'Father' and 'Son', and the introduction of the exclusive phrase in 11.27b: 'no one knows the Father except the Son and any one to whom the Son chooses to reveal him'. Schüssler Fiorenza claims that this 'introduction of father-son language into early Christian sophialogy is intrinsically bound up with a theological exclusivity that reserves revelation for the elect few and draws the boundaries of communal identity between insiders and outsiders' (Schüssler Fiorenza 1994: 144). Although the wisdom myth provides the grounds for reading against the grain of such exclusivity, it, in its own turn, needs to be critiqued (Schüssler Fiorenza 1994: 155-62).

The invitation of Jesus in 11.28-30 is that of both the sage (Sir. 6.18-37) and of Wisdom (Sir. 51.23-30) to come and learn from Sophia; to learn her wisdom which she knows from the creation of the universe;

to learn and respect as she does the secrets of the universe so that the entire Earth community may live in creative interconnectedness. In an ecofeminist reading, could we imagine that this call of Jesus Sophia is an inclusive invitation, one that invites all those in the entire Earth community who labour and are heavy burdened under the weight of exploitation, oppression and degradation—regardless of race, species, levels of consciousness, gender? Could we see it as an invitation to all those known intimately to Jesus Sophia?

The promise of this twice-repeated invitation is rest. This evokes first the rest of Gen. 2.2-3, the rest which is a cessation from labour and which rejoices in the work done. It also recalls the rest of Shabbat which is a remembering of not only the creative work of the universe (Exod. 20.8-11) but also the liberating work within the human community (Deut. 5.12-15).

Such an invitation makes its own critique of the exclusivity of the previous verses, and enables a continuation of the ecofeminist reading of the Matthean Gospel that is hinted at in the early chapters. The words of Jesus Sophia are indeed transformative words. They have the power to shape readings which are exclusive and Earth-dominating while at the same time having the potential—for those who have ears to hear—for a vision of diversity and interconnectedness which holds together the labour and the rest of the entire Earth community towards a vision of the kindom which is inclusive of all: God's dream for the Earth community with whom God is present until the end of the age.

The movement towards that vision, of which this reading is a small part, will, as Adrienne Rich has indicated, 'leave neither surfaces nor depths unchanged'.

'And on Earth, Peace…' (Luke 2.14): Luke's Perspectives on the Earth

Michael Trainor

Economic, Ecological and Social Concerns

The Asian economic crisis and environmental disasters in recent years, and the effects these have had on geographically related places like Australia, underscore the interdependency that exists between the planet and ourselves. What happens ecologically is reflected economically and socially. It reminds us that we are bound by a web of social, cultural, economic and ecological connectedness. As people concerned about our planet, relationship with God and discipleship, we need to continue to reflect on our care of the environment and its interrelationship with ourselves.

Together with other writers in this volume, I come to this task of contributing an ecological critical reflection in the light of our Christian heritage and particularly the Bible. It is this heritage which shapes our appreciation of the earth. An uncritical absorption of the values or attitudes from ancient Mediterranean people about the land inscribed in the texts of the Bible has unwittingly contributed to the way some today have harmed the earth. For this reason, the present volume is timely.

My interest in what follows is to engage in an 'ecological dialogue' with one of the most important writers of the New Testament, the author responsible for the Gospel According to Luke and the Acts of the Apostles.[1] In the light of the ecojustice principles enunciated at the beginning of this volume, there are two questions I am interested in pursuing:

1. What was the Lukan writer's attitude to the earth?
2. What effect might a reading of Luke–Acts have on our contemporary quest: developing ecojustice principles?

---

1.   I presume here, in accordance with the work of the majority of Lukan scholars, that the Gospel according to Luke and the Acts of the Apostles is the work of the one writer.

Two ecojustice principles are pertinent to the exploration of answers to these questions: the principles of intrinsic worth and inter-connectedness. The first raises the question for the Lukan interpreter about the value or worth of the earth presumed by the writer. My way of studying this is to propose a spectrum of perspectives that Luke's audience would have held about the earth. This leads to a further reflection on the second principle relevant to this chapter: inter-connectedness.

While space prevents a detailed study of the whole Lukan corpus, what we shall discover through a study of one brief Gospel scene (2.10-14) is that Luke's attitude to the earth was ambivalent for two reasons.

First, part of what Luke presents is helpful for modern readers seeking an ecojustice hermeneutic and needs to be reclaimed. Through this study it will become clearer that a specific relationship exists between God and human beings. This relationship is one of communion precipitated by the birth of the Davidic saviour. Jesus' birth celebrated in the heavens is the reason for an earthly renewal—almost transformation—that affects the way people relate with each other. This aspect of Luke's transforming vision has important her-meneutic implications for contemporary readers who seek an eco-logical sensitivity that does not rob the earth of its inherent goodness, nor see it as a commodity to be plundered.

Second, there is another side to Luke's presentation which needs to be noted. An analysis of a small section of Jesus' birth narrative in Luke's Gospel will reveal the evangelist's belief in a hierarchy of relationships which reflects a perceived duality between heaven and earth. An uncritical absorption of this Lukan aspect could reinforce an attitude to the earth as subordinate to human life and as a commodity to be unequivocally plundered.

How much these two attitudes found in one text—of an earthly transformation and dualistic hierarchy—are representative of the rest of Luke's writings will need further examination; it is outside the limits of this paper.

I focus on Luke's writings for several reasons. Luke–Acts makes up a little over a third of the New Testament. Through these writings we have access to one of the most prolific writers of the earliest Christian movement—an author whose geographical interest is enormous. The author envisages a world centred on lands that surround the Mediter-ranean Sea. Specifically, the narrative sweep of the Gospel and Acts extends from Ethiopia (Acts 8.26-39) and Cyrenaica (Acts 2.10) in the most southwestern and southeastern part of the Mediterranean

(Robbins 1991: 314-15.)—what was known in the ancient world as the 'ends of the earth' (Johnson 1992: 154-55.)—to Rome in the most northwestern corner. The geographical dimensions of Luke's writings also touch some of the most important cultural centres of the ancient world: Jerusalem, Tiberias, Antioch, Ephesus, Corinth, Athens and Rome.

In this vast geographical and cultural panorama, the author's ancient Mediterranean attitude to the earth is exposed. This attitude might be described today as an 'ecological perspective', though Luke is *not* an 'ecologist' or a writer with an explicit ecological agenda. As we shall see in a study of one section of Luke's Gospel, there are nuances in the evangelist's treatment of the tangible, material Greco-Roman environment of the Christian audience. This reveals an attitude that might influence or address our contemporary quest for ecojustice.

Luke's Audience

Luke's penchant for highlighting Greco-Roman cities in the Gospel, and especially in Acts with the missionary journeys of Paul, further reinforces the view that Luke's writings were intended for an urban rather than a rural audience. It is from this urban perspective that both the Gospel and Acts must be read. The pastoral situation and issues of the Gospel's urban audience shape the memory of the events and the meaning of Luke's stories. This is important when reflecting on the story of a rural peasant couple who come to an urban centre for the birth of their child. The story is intended for a Greco-Roman audience inhabiting one of the cities of the Mediterranean (and possibly Antioch in Syria) in the latter part of the first century CE. It is not intended for a peasant audience of Galilee or Judaea in the 30s. It is important that the modern reader resists slipping from Luke's world into that of the historical Jesus, and attempts in this way to recreate the actual events and the peasant social setting at the time of Jesus.

It is generally well accepted by most commentators that Luke wrote for a Mediterranean audience of the later part of the first century CE; the text was probably written between the 80s and 90s. A linguistic and narrative analysis of Lukan corpus enables us to identify the intended audience of the writing and the social position of its author (Robbins 1991: 305-32.). This information, coupled with the author's narrative frame—where scenes are set and people are located—offers us a fairly accurate picture of Luke's audience (Rohrbaugh 1991: 125-50; Oakman 1991: 151-80; Elliott 1991: 211-40).

Commentators on Luke's provenance suggest the Lukan community is composed of a cross-section of the social strata of Mediterranean
society that would be found on the 'edge' or outskirts of the pre-
industrial city or village of the ancient world. Generally, it consisted
of three social groups: peasants, social elite and artisans.

The peasants represented the powerless majority in the ancient
world. They lived in the countryside and depended on their agricultural skills for the survival of their family and kinship groups who
could be connected to villages. Through the technology of the plow
and harnessed animals, peasants sought to produce enough food to
live, and have some left over to pay the necessary taxes. Their survival depended on the growth and support of strong familial and kinship networks. This encouraged a form of reciprocal exchange, gift
giving and non-competitiveness.[2] They prized the land; its size and
produce determined their income (Carney 1975: 187), and represented
economic security and familial survival.

In a more hypothetical vein, I suspect that given the urban fringe
location of Luke's audience, the peasants addressed by the Gospel
would have been in a minority compared to the elites and artisans:
Some may have farmed land close to the urban centre; others, having
been forced to relinquish ancestral lands and homes, had come to the
urban centre, seeking work, hospitality and inclusion. The issue of
hospitality and mutual welcome is key for understanding Luke's birth
story of Jesus.

The second group, the elites, was a powerful urban minority
though a dominant group in Luke's community. They collected the
excess produce of the peasants—either in the form of grain or taxes—

---

2.   On reciprocal and redistributive economic exchange in the ancient world,
see Rohrbaugh (1996: 129); Moxnes (1988: 48-72). In Luke's peasant-based society,
reciprocal exchange was basically on a barter or a gift basis. In peasant clans knit
closely together, subsistence or survival was crucial. 'Peasants lived by subsistence
farming, employing agricultural produce as a form of money and wrapped in an
intricate network of reciprocal exchanges...' (Carney 1975: 199). The working of
the land became the means of life and survival. Mutual exchange or balanced reciprocity enabled these people to support one another and obtain a livelihood. Their
agricultural endeavours were not intended to make profit, for to do so would be at
the expense of one of their numbers going without. The accumulation of wealth
was considered an evil because it created division and poverty for others. Within
the village-peasant world, systems were created to ensure that any excess produce
was redistributed in the forms of gifts to fellow peasants (like an iron instrument
or tool), a loan to a member in need, or an offering at a local village festival (Carney 1975: 198). Carney's diagram (1975: 168) is helpful to illustrate the gradation of
reciprocal gift in relation to the clan and kinship group.

for later redistribution.[3] Their predilection towards redistribution as an economic practice laid the foundations for what developed later as a free-market economy. The elites represented the interests of those who held religious and political power in the cities, and had the economic base and initiative to confiscate and control the lands of debt-ridden peasant farmers. The elites regarded the land as a commodity that could be accumulated. For them, land symbolized power and wealth.

As absentee landlords, the elites made use of the third group of Luke's audience—social scientists have identified this group as 'artisans'. These were dispossessed peasants; removed from family and kin, they were generally considered lower than peasants socially (Rohrbaugh 1996: 110; Rohrbaugh 1991: 128-29). They moved to cities to find employment and subsistence. When they eventually found work as hired day labourers, they depended on the patronage of the elites. Though a smaller group than the elites, they were growing in number in the latter part of the first century CE as more and more peasants found themselves dispossessed of inherited lands. Leaving the ancestral land would have also resulted in a breaking down of the familial connections, support and sustenance typical in the peasant household. This situation might have also resulted in inter-familial strife or tension.

These 'artisans' had an ambivalent attitude to the land. On the one hand, because of their peasant origins, they regarded the land as an essential source for survival. On the other, they were forced to work for others who had little affective connection or sensitivity to the land and looked upon it essentially as a commodity to be controlled or accumulated.

Luke's community was made up of all three social groups; Luke's writings reveal an author seeking to respond to issues that affected all three. Each group has a representative in the story that we will investigate below.

---

3.   This second form of economic exchange, redistribution, was the dominant mode used by the bureaucracy and controlled by the powerful elite in a temple state (Carney 1975: 182). The elite represented about 5-10 per cent of the population and made the decisions that affected the kind of support they would receive from the peasants. Through redistribution, local peasant produce was extracted (through Roman taxation systems and by temple tithing), stored and then redistributed for political or religious reasons. On this, see Oakman (1991: 129). Essentially, redistribution was often an accumulation of agricultural produce (or equivalent monetary exchange items) to a central point in the local area for transfer at a later time.

The existence of three social groups further suggests that a study of Luke's writings will reveal a complexity of attitudes, social scenarios and themes which cannot be homogenized into simplistic summaries.[4]

This principle also needs to be remembered when we seek to read Luke with an 'eco-justice' lens and to apply guiding principles for developing an ecojustice hermeneutic to the text. For example, in terms of the principle of intrinsic worth, each group saw the earth—from their respective points of view—as a commodity or an object of exploitation. In the light of the principle of interconnectedness, the possibility of the land being part of the community—in line with the Mediterranean dyadic value system that shaped interfamilial and tribal relationships—the earth was 'outside' and 'other'. Rather than the earth as one aspect of a mutual communal dependency, it was another dimension of Mediterranean life that needed to be subjugated. In terms of custodianship, each member of Luke's audience viewed it not as something entrusted for care, but as a commodity and source of power over others. In other words, in all three groups the economic, political and religious aspects of Mediterranean life—usually embedded in each other—had become bifurcated. With regard to social survival and dominance of one group over another, the religious dimension had been subsumed by economic and political considerations. This had ramifications in the way the earth was regarded. It had further implications for the Lukan writer.

Luke realistically acknowledged that the radical social renewal envisaged in the early Jesus movement had not happened and the evangelist had to deal with the social strata and hierarchy as promoted in the Greco-Roman world of the late first century CE. Therefore, while seeking to address those on the lower end of the socio-economic hierarchy—peasants and artisans—Luke also sought to address the 'Theophiluses' of the Christian community: the wealthy and powerful social elites who were, perhaps, a majority in Luke's audience. One could well argue that Luke's principal audience resides in a large town or city, somewhere in the Roman Empire[5] and consists of landlords who controlled city residences, guest houses and the immediate

---

4.   Such a caution against simplistic, homogenized summaries that covers all groupings addressed by the biblical text is found in Arlandson (1997) in his analysis of the social classes in Luke–Acts, and the way this affects a reading of the roles and functions of women in the Lukan corpus.

5.   Quite possibly Syrian Antioch, see Oakman (1991: 177).

countryside. They also retained a powerful influence in Luke's Christian community.

The community also embraced peasants and country dwellers affected by the manipulative control of these elite characters. Some of them had gone into debt, had borrowed from fellow peasants and kin, had eventually been forced to sell their inherited lands to absentee landlords, and had moved to the city.

From this social scenario with its complexity of attitudes to the earth, we can get a sense of the delicacy of Luke's situation. It would be hard to imagine a more complex and difficult pastoral issue facing the evangelist. Luke's audience, mirroring the power structures of the Roman Empire (Rohrbaugh 1991: 125-50), had the potential to be split along economic and geographical lines, and divide into social camps with little desire for community with those who came from a different part of the social strata. Luke wrote to country people without voice and social influence, and to city dwellers with wealth and status. Luke needed to speak to the powerful and rich living in a tense, divided Christian community in a city in the Greco-Roman world that included country-people linked geographically to the city.[6]

The social context of Luke's writings has made us aware that various members of the Gospel's audience had a different appreciation of, and a variety of complex attitudes towards, the earth. It is clear that we cannot expect a simple or homogeneous earth-picture to be revealed. This social analysis shows that each group held identifiable attitudes to the earth. How much the Lukan author bought into these attitudes and communicated to contemporary readers a helpful or 'dangerous' attitude to the earth remains to be seen. It is to this exploration that I now turn.

6.   From the point of view of the elites, forming Christian community with peasants and artisans would have forced them to reconsider their use of patronage, the importance of status and use of power, and more practically to reconsider their demand to extract debts from peasant farmers and even to return lands that had been previously confiscated. Community for the elites would have meant economic disadvantage and a decline in social status and honour. From the peasant perspective, social involvement with the elites would have forced them to consider their ability for real forgiveness, their willingness to maintain harmonious relationships, and to resist the temptation for vengeance. Community for the elites would have meant the possibility of compromising family honour as they ate with those responsible for their ongoing impoverishment and debt-ridden farm holdings.

The Birth Story of Jesus (Luke 2.1-20)

Given the limitation of space and the impossibility of studying the whole of Luke's attitude to the earth in the whole Lukan corpus, I would like to focus on one story that is well known to us—the birth story of Jesus in Lk. 2.1-20. Read with the social and earth perspectives described above, it offers surprising insights.

The birth story of Jesus in Luke's Gospel is a story about a peasant couple, Mary and Joseph, who are forced—for economic reasons—to travel from their village of Nazareth in Southern Galilee to the city of David in Judaea, Bethlehem (2.1-6).[7] While they are in this city—the conventional setting of the urban elite—Mary gives birth, and lays their newborn child in a manger (2.7).

The birth is announced to shepherds who go to Bethlehem (2.8-16), and on seeing the 'sign', repeat what they had been told about the child (2.17). Everyone is in awe at the shepherds' words (2.18)—Mary ponders them (2.19). The shepherds return to their flocks glorifying God (2.20).

Highly imaginative reasons have been offered for the location of Jesus' birth and his placement in the manger. Whatever way our imaginations have reconstructed the story to make an innkeeper a central figure, Luke's story mentions nothing about such a person. The emphasis is on 'place': 'there was *no place* for them in the guest house' (2.7). Interpreted against the social world familiar to Luke's readers, it is all too clear: the guest house is under the control of the elite and is a *place* where peasants do not belong socially.[8] Behind this is perhaps a subtle message, addressed to the elite members of Luke's community.

If it is subtle here, however, it becomes clear as the Gospel narrative unfolds. These powerful and wealthy community members—absentee farm owners, claimants of debts and owners of guest houses—will be

---

7.   Although Luke describes Nazareth and Bethlehem as 'cities' (*polis*), the author also uses terminology for village and city interchangeably. 'City' occurs 164 in the New Testament; half these are in Luke–Acts. On this point, see Oakman (1991: 151-52).

8.   It is important that the urban location of Luke's Greco-Roman audience is remembered in considering the nature of the guest house. This is not the place of welcome or hospitality offered to travellers in the peasant household. It is rather the caravansary on the main trade routes throughout the Mediterranean (Karris 1990: 683). See also the full discussion of the possible meanings of Luke's guest-house in Brown (1993: 400-401).

invited to convert: Luke's Jesus will ask of them to renounce every one of their possessions, offer gracious and generous hospitality to all—irrespective of social standing—and to release the debts owed by poverty-ridden peasant farmers. Luke wants the reader's gaze to be fixed away from that which is owned by the elite—the 'guest house' or 'inn' (*katalyma*, in Greek)—to the peasant household or farm: the place where the domestic animals are housed and the place from where they are fed, the 'manger'.[9] Luke points the reader to this three times (2.7, 12, 16) so it will not be missed. It is an obvious narrative clue that the reader is asked to consider.

The 'Manger'

There are two possible reasons for the reference to the manger, one christological, and the other ecological. Christologically, the manger is a place of food and prepares for a dominant theme in Luke–Acts. In Jesus' future public ministry, food, meals and the place of eating will play an important part. Ecologically, the manger links Jesus to the land. According to Jer. 14.8, God was like an alien in the land who needed to find a dwelling in travellers' lodgings. In Luke's birth story, Jesus—God's agent and revealer—is not found in travellers' lodgings; the reason: Jesus is *not* an alien in the land.[10]

From Luke's perspective, the birth of Jesus outside the conventional place of hospitality run by elite landlords emphasizes his connection with the land and its people. He finds a welcome among those who rely on the earth for sustenance: those in Luke's audience who would identify themselves as peasants. In other words, in Luke's story, Jesus is the child of a peasant-village couple, the victims of a taxation

9.   For more on the location of the manger in a peasant household, see Guijarro (1997: 42-65).

10.   Brown 1993: 419. Brown also argues that a possible understanding of Luke's use of *katalyma* in 2.7 might be dependent on Jer. 14.8 which is addressed to Israel's Saviour: 'Why are you like an alien in the land, like a traveler who stays in a guesthouse'. According to the prophet, God is like a foreigner who needs to stay in rented accommodation. No welcome is found. With the birth of Jesus, God's agent finds a welcome; there is no need for him to stay in rented lodgings. Hence there is 'no room' for him in the guesthouse. Rather than seeing Jesus' placement in a manger as sign of his rejection, in fact from this biblical argument it could be a sign of welcome and community. Luke uses the same word *katalyma* at the end of the gospel in the Passion Narrative. It is to the *katalyma* that Jesus and disciples go to celebrate his last Passover meal before his death (Lk. 22.11). This is where he gathers with his disciples. Continuing the logic inspired by the prophet Jeremiah, there is now a sense of alienation with the land and those who dwell on it. It is for this reason that he is gathers with his companions and finds room in a guesthouse.

system imposed by the elite. He finds hospitality and communion among those whose livelihood is connected to the soil of the earth. Thus, Luke envisions a social harmony in the peasant world brought about through the birth of Jesus. This idyllic picture connects to and is confirmed by the second part of the story (2.8-20), a scene filled with political, economic and ecological intrigue.

The Shepherds
The story shifts to the countryside, to shepherds 'keeping watch over their flocks by night' (2.8). They experience an angelic announcer who brings them a message of good news:

> 2.10 Do not fear; behold, I proclaim to you good news of great joy which is for all the people
> 2.11 because there is born this day a saviour who is Christ the Lord in the city of David
> 2.12 and this is a sign for you: you will find a baby wrapped in bands of cloth and lying in a manger
> 2.13 and suddenly there was with the angel a great throng of the heavenly host praising God and singing:
> 2.14 Glory in the highest to God and on earth peace among human beings who are beloved.

The angelic message has *five* elements:

1. it is a message of universal joy (2.10);
2. the reason for this joy is the birth of the Saviour (2.11a);
3. this Saviour is the awaited Messiah who is in the 'city' of David (2.11b);
4. the sign of this urban, salvific figure is found in the 'baby wrapped in bands of cloth and lying in the manger' (2.12);
5. because of this birth, glory redounds to God and peace will come upon the earth.

We have traditionally interpreted the shepherds as the 'first poor' to receive the good news and respond to it. They are told by heavenly messengers about Jesus' birth and go to 'see this thing that has occurred' (2.15).

But more is implied in their acquiescence. The relationship between shepherds and peasant farmers was strained, if not violent. This emerged from their respective attitudes to the earth upon which they both relied for their livelihood.

The shepherds regarded the land as important. It held the possibilities for them to accomplish their task of sheep and goat grazing, irrespective of who owned the land. They allowed or encouraged their flocks—the animals often belonged to others, probably the social elite—to stray on to the fields of peasant owners. So while shepherds had a shared a similar attitude to the earth with peasant farmers, the difference resided in their respective attitude to *inherited* lands. The damage done by their unruly animals to precious crops would affect the peasant household's income.

Interpreted from the perspective of Luke's urban audience, the shepherds could well represent artisans forced to the city for work. Their social position would have been comparable to that of the shepherds familiar to Luke's Greco-Roman audience: landless, peasant in origin, and acting on behalf of an elite who regarded the lands of the peasant majority as a taxable commodity.

The peasants regarded their lands as an inheritance which needed to be protected and cultivated. It was the only source of income and key means of familial survival.

Both groups—the peasant farmers and wandering shepherds—regarded the land as a means for making a living; neither regarded the earth with the ecological sensitivity of some groups within contemporary society. The earth was rather a cause of division—even violence.

Luke's shepherds were not gentle people, raising their flocks in an idyllic pastoral setting, as our Christmas carols would have them. They were disposed to violence and disrespectful of the property or rights of others. One wonders whether this is the mood captured by having the shepherds looking after their flocks 'by night'! In Luke's world, the countryside was not a place of ideal tranquillity; it was associated with disturbance and social upheaval. The resulting tension affected the relations between urban residents and country dwellers (Oakman 1991: 171).

It is against this background, with its divisions and tensions, that Luke's Christmas story is staged.

The Angelic Song (Luke 2.14)
The heavenly message which accompanies this revelation also contains Luke's social and ecological vision. Luke's angelic visitors announce that the birth of Jesus will bring joy to all; it is not limited to those with a certain social class or economic status. The birth will bring together the urban elite—the birth takes place in a 'city'; and the rural poor—the birth is in a manger; and landless—the birth is announced to shepherds.

The birth will also bring together heaven and earth. These two cosmological spheres, familiar to Luke's audience, will be totally affected by the presence of the Davidic saviour. This point is particularly emphasized in the angelic refrain of 2.14. In the Greek text, the refrain is a carefully balanced structure.[11] Literally, it can be translated:

> Glory (*Doxa*)
> among the highest to God
> And upon the earth peace
> among human beings
> of good will/favoured/chosen (*eudokias*)

The structure of this liturgical heavenly song reflects Luke's theological cosmology.[12] It is chiasmically focused on 'and upon the earth peace'. Leading to this is Luke's appreciation of the heavens, the uppermost level of the cosmos, the abode of God and the heavenly powers. Beneath this abode is the realm of the spirits. It is God who dwells in the highest level of the cosmic hierarchy (Malina and Rohrbaugh 1992: 182-83).

Beneath the spirit world is the abode of human beings. In the structure of the canticle, the 'earth' is located between the divine realm in the first part of the song and the abode of human beings in the final part. As though it is a connecting sphere between the heavenly and human, it is blessed with peace. Peace is 'upon' (*epi*) the earth. The whole unit is framed by the Greek terms that at their root refer to 'glory', 'splendour' or 'grandeur' (*doxa, eudokias*). The first refers to the praise or glory that is due to God. The second is the 'glory' or 'splendour' that comes to human beings from God's 'favour' towards them. This reflects the hierarchical relationship between humans and God, and the divine beneficence that comes

---

11. Brown (1993: 404-405) presents the respective scholarly arguments for the hymn's structure as a bicolon (two-line structure) or tricolon (three line). Good reasons are given for both. My own proposal advances the tricolon proposal (three line) to a five-line structure. This structure places more weight on the first and last expressions which have 'glory' as their Greek root and the 'among' (*en*, in Greek) which marks off two key phrases—one referring to God, the other to human beings. The final and central element of the canticle's structure concerns the earth. Whatever structure is finally chosen, Brown's verdict that that the structure is 'fiercely debated' (1993: 426 n. 56) holds true. My point simply is that a five-line structure is defensible.

12. See Brown 1993: 401-406, 420-29. Echoes some of the themes or motifs of the angelic canticle are found in Ps. Sol. 18.10; Isa. 57.19; Ezek. 6.15 and Ps. 51.20.

down to human beings from God. The tangible arena for the reception of this divine blessing is 'the earth'.

From the hymn it is clear that everything that happens is God's activity (cf. 10.21). It is God's initiative that enables human beings to enter divine communion. The context of this hymn of blessing is the angelic announcement of the birth of Jesus, the Davidic saviour, agent of universal peace and soon-to-be-declared vehicle of God's reign.

In the narrative which follows this birth story, the only person explicitly nominated as *eudokia* and declared by God as the 'favoured one' is Jesus. This occurs at his baptism (3.22). He is God's chosen one and bears God's glory. This angelic song to the shepherds prepares for the full declaration of Jesus' status and role at his baptism.

The song also presents the reader with a vision of the possibility of all human beings—irrespective of their social class and economic standing—being graced (or 'favoured'—Luke's preferred expression) by God, and revealing, like Jesus, God's glory in the Greco-Roman world. Jesus' birth brings 'favour' to human beings, destroys the causes of division and brings about healing. It is for this reason that the earth—for Luke's audience a cause of division and rapacious-ness—is now blessed with divine peace. Now, through the birth of Jesus, peace is realized. The earth is, first, blessed with the divine gift which then brings harmony to all those who depend upon it. God's act in Jesus transforms the earth from a place of competition, rivalry and violence, to an abode of human communion.

The peace directed to the earth at the beginning of the Gospel reflects peace in heaven celebrated towards the end of the Gospel (19.38). Here the disciples welcome Jesus into the outskirts of Jeru-salem. Their hymn is a response to the mighty works they had seen Jesus perform in his ministry.

> Blessed is the one who comes—the King—in the name of the Lord
> in heaven peace
> And glory (*doxa*) in the highest (19.38, my translation).

The disciples' hymn of praise to the king Jesus in 19.38 is a mirror image of the angels' canticle in 2.14. Both give praise ('glory'—*doxa*) to the divine realm (the 'highest'). In one, peace is directed to earth; in the other, it is found in heaven. This praise of peace occurs in the centre of both hymns' chiastic structures.

Finally, in the angelic hymn glory also comes among human beings, favoured by God through the birth of Jesus. In the disciples' song, Jesus is praised as king and God's emissary. Taken together, both canticles underscore the divine origin of peace and the possibility that

God's presence can bless the earth with the same quality typical of the heavenly realm.

Both hymns also reveal the evangelist's understanding of a cosmic duality between the heavenly and earthly spheres, the hierarchy of one ('the heavens') over the other ('the earth'), and the implications these arrangements have for human beings.

Luke's anthropocentric vision has ecological consequences. The angelic canticle in the birth story of Jesus reveals that the communion with God—that human beings share with God through the birth of the one who reveals God's glory—comes to them because this birth blesses the earth with peace. The primordial vision—expressed in the first creation story in Genesis, and echoed in Isaiah—of a cosmic harmony initiated through God's creative act, is renewed in the birth and presence of the earth's saviour, Jesus. This is confirmed in what follows after the angelic song.

The shepherds go to Bethlehem to 'see this word-event which has happened' (2.15). When they see the 'sign'—and the Greek is not clear what it is that the shepherds actually see in 2.17[13]—they speak about the 'word-event' the angel/s told them about. This is the angelic—and Luke's—vision of social harmony that comes about through the birth of Jesus. It is this vision that brings wonder to *all* who hear the shepherds' words (2.18). Logically, the only other people present are Joseph and Mary—and the newly born child. However, the evangelist envisages that the angelic declaration that underscores for the reader the significance of this event has universal implications and public application. It affects all who are open to the message of a social renewal predicated upon the presence of Jesus.

Implications

Luke's birth story is a prologue to the rest of the Gospel. It introduces the key themes which will emerge; it introduces the reader to Jesus as the Son of God and God's beloved; it indicates essential qualities necessary in the one who follows Jesus. The birth story presents us with an economic and ecological vision that is only possible because of the birth of the Davidic saviour. Three important implications for contemporary disciples, sensitive to an ecojustice orthopraxis, flow from this prologue.

---

13. It could be that Luke has left the sight unspecified so that it includes not just the vision of the manger, or the child, or Mary or Joseph—but all four elements.

First, what emerges from this reflection on the birth story are the sociocultural themes prominent in the story. The three social groups present in Luke's community would find their representatives there—whether that be in the figures of the couple from the peasant village of Southern Galilee; the urban setting for the birth of Jesus; the reference to the guest room; the emphasis on the manger; or in the angelic announcement to landless shepherds alert to a night assault.

Luke saw the Christian community as a renewed society in which the major social groups represented in the evangelist's community were united. In Acts 2.42 when the Jerusalem Christians gathered 'for the apostles' teaching, communion, the breaking of bread and the prayers', Luke spelt out the practical implications for such a united community. According to Luke a new society was possible through the ministry of Jesus and the disciples who gathered around him. Luke believed that this was possible even in the Greco-Roman Christian community addressed by the Gospel and the book of Acts. It was a community that could model the Greek ideal of friendship.

Second, Luke's vision of a united community of disciples made up of individuals from the principle social strata of the Greco-Roman world also had important economic consequences. In the birth story we gain a hint of a theme prominent throughout the rest of Luke's writings: the disparity created by excessive wealth and the demands for debt fulfilment needed to be addressed. When we trace Luke's representation of wealth and possessions in the rest of the Gospel and in the book of Acts, it is clear that Luke envisaged a Christian community known for its radical redistribution of wealth—a community where reciprocity or benefaction was shown by the wealthy to those in need. Goods were not to be amassed for the benefit or honour they brought to their possessors. They were to be used to relieve the debt, need, hardship and insecurity resulting from injustice.

Third, I have been arguing that the birth story can also be read as an appeal to the Christian elite. Luke's subtle economic program converted the radical social reform of Jesus into one that enabled the wealthy and powerful elite of the Christian community to welcome the powerless and marginalized. This meant a move from a redistributive market strategy to an economic arrangement of reciprocity; from the temple as the power and economic base to the household and peasant village as the focal point of the new community (Oakman 1991: 175).

Luke did not seek to restructure society in terms of a village economy, nor to abolish social stratification. Luke inherited the convictions of the historical Jesus, addressed originally to Jewish peasants—the predominantly rural community in Galilee. But, half a century later, there was now a need to offer hope for the impoverished and economically depressed land-bound peasant members of the Jesus movement, and at the same time address disciples who were landlords and creditors.

Urbanization and stratification were already a reality in Luke's world. Luke sought to engage with the discipleship implications for the wealthy, privileged and Christian elite by subtly nuancing the original message of Jesus, initially intended only for a peasant audience. The elite were encouraged to let go of status, honour and privilege and to exercise hospitality, benefaction and reciprocity towards the peasant members of the community. Hints of this strategy are already evident in the birth story.

Reading Luke in the Light of Ecojustice Principles

In Luke's Mediterranean world various social values were embedded in each other; this was especially true of economics, politics and religion. Luke's two volumes offer social and economic insights which also have ecological implications.

The birth story reveals a writer who views the world as a typical, late-first-century Mediterranean. The Mediterranean was a region surrounded by an 'interconnected economy' that depended on the way the land was used and exploited (Carney 1975: 181). On a first reading, the reader does not come away from this section of the Gospel—or in fact from the whole of the Lukan corpus—with a sense that the land or earth was intrinsically good.

The earth was the dwelling place of human beings who used the land to grow crops and farm animals. Some in Luke's community— the majority—viewed the earth from this utilitarian perspective. Others—a powerful, wealthy, minority elite—viewed it as a commodity to be acquired, confiscated and worked to bring wealth and status to its owners. Still others regarded the lands around the Mediterranean as barriers that separated cities and peoples from each other, and an encumbrance that needed to be overcome through travel.

These lands were hemmed in by surrounding waters that were perceived as unpredictable and dangerous. In the book of Acts, Paul is Luke's example par excellence of the sea voyager and land traveller.

Overall, the land is not featured by Luke either positively or as intrinsically good. In the light of the ecological principle of intrinsic worth, the land is a negative object in need of subjugation. Luke's audience generally had a rapacious attitude towards the land.

I have focused on one text in Luke's writings because it offers the Gospel's audience an alternative view of the earth—a perspective strongly against the overwhelming, typical utilitarian spirit of the day. Despite his audience's variety of negative attitudes to the earth, Luke presents in the birth story a vision of social harmony linked to a renewal of the land. Rather than being the stage on which economic and political battles were waged, the land could become the place of divine blessing and grace for all people. The birth of the world's saviour presented humanity with a renewed possibility for peace and justice. This would be echoed in a land where people could live in harmony and offer glory to God.[14] Clearly for Luke, the birth of Jesus is the source of the earth's transformation.

A reader might think that in the song of the angels Luke reveals an attitude to the earth that is blissful and peace-filled. At one level, the evangelist does. At another level, though, Luke considers the earth's transformation as the means for the kind of social harmony desired in the Christian community and the Greco-Roman world. Luke, in fact, *uses* the land as a means to an end. In other words, by demonstrating this attitude, the writer has fallen into the very trap that he is indirectly criticizing in the Gospel's audience.

Through the lens of the principle of interconnectedness, it is clear the writer assumes a creation hierarchy which the angelic chorus seeks to re-establish. In Luke's mind, only when this order is renewed can social harmony exist. In his view, heaven is above earth; the

14. Luke uses several different words that describe the land, country, earth, soil. The frequency of these words suggest its importance for this ecological discussion on Luke–Acts: *Kosmos* ('world') is found four times in Luke–Acts; out of 185 times in New Testament (9 in Mt.; 3 in Mk; 78 in Jn)—Lk. 9.25; 11.50; 12.30; Acts 17.24. 'Earth' (*gēs*) is found 183 times in the New Testament and 58 in Luke–Acts: Lk. 2.14; 4.25; 5.3, 11, 24; 6.49; 8.8, 15, 27; 10.21; 11.31; 12.49, 51, 56; 13.7; 14.35; 16.17; 18.8; 21.23, 25, 33, 35; 22.44; 24.5 (25 times); Acts 1.8; 2.19; 3.25; 4.24, 26; 7.3, 4, 6, 29, 33, 36, 40, 49; 8.33; 9.4, 8; 10.11, 12; 11.6; 13.17, 19, 47; 14.15; 17.24, 26; 22.22; 26.14; 27.39, 43, 44. (33 times). *Chora* (country or rural precinct) is found 17 times in Luke–Acts out of 28 in the New Testament—Lk. 2.8; 3.1; 8.26; 12.16; 15.13, 14, 15; 19.12; 21.21; Acts 8.1; 10.39; 12.20; 13.49; 16.6; 18.23; 26.20; 27.27. *Agros* (fields) is used 11 times in Luke–Acts (16 in Mt.; once in Mk); Lk. 8.34; 9.12; 12.28; 14.18; 15.15, 25; 17.7, 31; 23.26; Acts 4.37. *Perichoros* (surrounding countryside) is used six times in Luke–Acts (2 times in Mt.; once in Mk); Lk. 3.3; 4.14, 37; 7.17; 8.37; Acts 14.6. *Chorion* (piece of land) is used six times in Acts (and once in Mt., Mk and Jn); Acts 1.18; 1.19; 4.34; Acts 5.3, 8; 28.7. For *oikoumene* (earth/world), see Lk. 2.1; 4.5; 21.26; Acts 11.28; 17.6, 31; 19.27; 24.5. This statistical gathering for Luke's key earth-related words will provide the basis for further research in the Lukan corpus.

angels are above the shepherds, and God is above humanity.

It could be argued that Luke's inference about the land is inherited from the Hebrew Scriptures—and especially the cosmic vision offered in the creation story in Genesis and Isaiah. Luke's Jewish heritage perceives there is a separation between heaven and earth, and accepts a consequent dualism and hierarchy. These become subtly reinforced in Luke's angelic song to the shepherds. It is only when the heavenly realm comes to earth through the birth of God's beloved agent is the land soaked in peace. The earth awaits this birth so the primordial vision of creation presented in Genesis can be realized. Only then can the rest of creation—including human beings in their interrelationships—rejoice. This new vision or attitude to the earth comes from what God bestows on the earth. Luke judges the 'peace' of the earth as good not because of its intrinsic value, but because God shares in it through the birth of Jesus. Jesus makes the earth potentially a place of peace and source of social harmony.

Summary

The validity of Luke's pastoral intent cannot be denied. The Gospel and the book of Acts seek to address serious tensions in the Christian community caused by economic disparity, contrasting attitudes to wealth and tension-filled relationships between elite and peasants. I have argued that the birth story of Jesus is a window on to these relationships.

The story also offers a way of addressing these pastoral difficulties through its focus on Jesus. In Luke's Christology, Jesus overcomes the barriers that separate. From an ecological perspective, he is the source of a cosmic harmony who brings peace to the earth and enables human beings to 'enjoy God's favour'.

A reading of this story in the light of the Earth Bible principles of intrinsic worth and interconnectedness has caused us to suspect the 'neatness' of Luke's ecological presentation. While the evangelist sees a renewal and transformation of the earthly realm that will benefit human beings, Luke maintains a cosmic dualism, inherent in the Mediterranean view of the cosmos and influenced by an appreciation of a cosmic social hierarchy.

This background influences the composition of the angelic hymn. The hymn places all worth with God and only on those objects and persons upon whom God's beneficence falls. Luke maintains a hierarchical relationship between heaven and earth, and between God and humanity, and theologically appropriates the theme of the earth as a means to an end. For these reasons, for the contemporary reader Luke's ecological contribution is mixed, and needs to be carefully nuanced. The writer of the third Gospel perpetuates an abstruse domination and utilitarian attitude to the earth. This is inherent in a text that on cursory examination seems to be so 'environmentally sensitive'.

What I have been arguing can be expressed another way. Christmas time is that most important liturgical moment of the year; Luke's angels continue to sing of the goodness of creation and the joy of the birth of the Davidic saviour to women and men affected by modern technology. It could also be the time when this story, if it is not understood and reflected on carefully, might help reinforce a subordination of the planet and subjugation of the environment to human desires and economic interests.

Despite these ecological reservations acquired through taking a suspicious stance towards Luke's story, there is another side to Luke's project that is important to identify. This is linked to the ecological concern noted above, and has to do with Luke's interest in the universal and cosmic sweep of the Gospel message. The birth of Jesus is set within the context of world history (2.1-4) and has political implications for the powerbrokers within the Roman civil service. What this suggests to the reader is that Luke's interest was not in establishing a sectarian form of Christianity isolated from the cultural and social concerns of the Greco-Roman world. The Gospel's focus was not on fostering a privatized form of Christian endeavour.

For Luke, the great religious and philosophical movements of the day became the entrée for a proclamation of the Gospel and the meaning of the central event—the resurrection—for the Lukan community. This is evident in the way that Luke has Paul journey to the cultural and philosophical centres of the Mediterranean world: Athens, Corinth, Ephesus, Rome and Jerusalem.

For contemporary Christians, the ecojustice movement—like all great movements that passionately involve people—can also become legitimate arenas for the involvement of the disciple and the proclamation of the Gospel.

Creation Groaning: An Earth Bible Reading of Romans 8.18-22

Brendan Byrne, SJ

Introductory Remarks

In late 1997 television screens conveyed disturbing images of the smog and pollution across SE Asia created by forest fires on the Indonesian island of Sumatra. The smog caused the crash of a civil aircraft with a great loss of life, as well as the collision of two ships in the Straits of Malacca. Undoubtedly, the El Niño climatic effect, which delayed rains, made some contribution. But the chief cause of the disaster—now merged with the Asian economic crisis—was undoubtedly uncontrolled burning and logging of forests.

A resident of Australia travelling to the northern hemisphere necessarily spends some hours in flight over the affected area. The experience invites sober reflection upon the human capacity to act irresponsibly towards the earth, an irresponsibility which a Pauline scholar can hardly help relating to a reading of Rom. 8.18-22.

This curious passage, which culminates in a sense of the whole creation 'groaning', has received a fair amount of attention in recent years in connection with a concern for the earth. Most of this attention has been fairly superficial. There has been little attempt to interpret the passage in the context of Paul's project in the book of Romans as a whole, nor has there been much hermeneutical reflection upon the vast gap between contemporary concern for the earth and whatever may have been the preoccupation of Paul.

What I propose to do in this paper is to discuss the interpretive possibilities of the passage in the light of an ecojustice hermeneutic. I should like to do so in the context of Paul's wider purposes in Romans, and conscious of the fact that in this part of the letter—as indeed elsewhere in it—Paul is himself interacting with an earlier text of Scripture, namely the creation stories of Genesis 1–3.

Paul reads these stories through the lens of contemporary Jewish apocalypticism. He takes the 'Adam' myth in Genesis 1–3 and reinterprets it in a new direction prompted by his own particular concerns.

In so doing he intensifies the mythological features of the Genesis traditions so that they become even more imaginatively 'wild' than in the original. While this may appear to lessen the usefulness of the text as a source of sober interpretation, that need not necessarily be the case—provided we are prepared to bring to our interpretation the kind of hermeneutical awareness enshrined in the six ecojustice principles of the Earth Bible Project. In this paper, I propose to submit Paul's interpretation of the Genesis traditions to an ecojustice critique employing these principles.

To many Paul may seem an unlikely candidate to enlist in this cause. Since Augustine in the fifth century—and particularly since the resumption of Augustine's interpretation of Paul by the Reformers in the sixteenth century—the issue of justification by faith has dominated the interpretation of Paul in the Western theological tradition. This ensured that interpreters of Paul were engaged in a virtually exclusive preoccupation with relations between human beings and God. What Paul thought or wrote about human relationship to the non-human created world scarcely entered the picture.

The apparently singular appearance of a passage dealing with human interaction with 'creation' in the flow of Romans proved something of an embarrassment to many. R. Bultmann, for example, sees it as relic of the cosmological mythology of Gnosticism which Paul appropriates 'because it enables him to express the fact that the perishable 'creation' becomes a destructive power whenever man [*sic*] decides in favour of it instead of God' (1952: 230). The negative rating of creation is unmistakable in Bultmann's understanding of Paul.

Most interpreters acknowledge that Paul does have the non-human created world in mind when he uses the term 'creation'. Until recently little has been made of the text because of its apparent oddity in the wider stream of Romans. So great has been the focus upon justification in the Pauline corpus—particularly in connection with Romans—that Paul's notion that relationships with the non-human created world should be an intrinsic element of human relationships with God has fallen from view.

In fact, as readers familiar with the track of Pauline studies over the past few decades would know, there has been a decided shift away from seeing justification by faith as Paul's central preoccupation in Romans. While there is by no means unanimity on the matter, most interpreters would now see the letter as an attempt to communicate an inclusive vision of the people of God. In Paul's view, the nations of the world have, through faith, an assured place in the people of God, without any prejudice to the fulfilment of God's ancient promises to

Israel (see Byrne 1996: 19-26, 281-84). Negotiating the latter point is what causes Paul most problems in Romans. It calls for extensive treatment of the conflict between human sinfulness and God's grace—a force that Paul sees as being unleashed into the world in triumphant measure in the person of Jesus Christ.

It is in the context of this conflict—to stress its universal scope—that Paul has recourse to the figure of Adam and the creation traditions in Genesis 1–3. Before discussing the allusions to these traditions that appear in Romans 8, it will help to spend some time considering Paul's explicit treatment of Adam earlier in the letter (Rom. 5.12-21).

Adam and Christ: Romans 5.12-21

In this celebrated passage Paul describes the struggle between the forces of grace and sin by means of a sustained contrast and comparison between Christ and Adam.

Paul sees Adam as more than a single individual. Relying upon a certain strain in the post-biblical Jewish tradition, he reads out of the story of the Fall in the third chapter of Genesis a view of Adam as a figure of universal significance for ill. In a mythological way, Paul portrays Adam's falling prey to sin as coming under the power of a ruthless tyrant or slavemaster, and passing on that slavery and the destiny of death that it entailed to all his descendants. While not eliminating individual responsibility, in this way Adam bequeathed to the human race a universal legacy of sinfulness and death (Byrne 1996: 174-77).

The classic doctrine of 'original sin' that later theologians—notably Augustine—elaborated on the basis of this passage raises many problems for modern sensibility. While I believe that it does have some foundation in the text, there is no need for our present purposes to go beyond what Paul appears to be saying. The essential point arising out of his depiction of Adam in Romans 5 is a sense of the solidarity of the human race. Human beings never perform acts of wickedness or virtue simply as isolated individuals. There is an interconnectedness binding all together—for good and for ill.

By tracing the origins of human sinfulness to Adam, without at the same time destroying subsequent human responsibility, Paul is asserting the negative side of that interconnectedness as a solidarity in evil into which every human life is born and from which, in the Christian view, every human being needs to be redeemed. When Paul thinks of sin it is not so much concrete acts that he has in mind; rather he means a compulsion to act selfishly and destructively. Individual sinful acts are the outward manifestations of this deep-seated tyranny of radical egoism. This is the communal plight of the race which the Adamic myth depicts.

In Adam, as first father and paradigm of human existence, Paul sees begun and enacted what I would call the 'sin story' of the human race: human beings acting with radical selfishness—in relation to God, to one another and, as will appear in connection with Romans 8, in relation to the non-human material world.

But the 'sin story' is not the only story—nor indeed the most important story—to be read out of Romans 5. Paul only speaks about Adam, and the solidarity of the human race in sin, in order—by contrast and comparison—to say something all the more forcefully about Christ, and the new solidarity in grace inaugurated by him. If Adam is a vehicle and instrument of sin, Christ is the vehicle and instrument of grace. If Adam 'models' human beings wrongly relating to the Creator, to each other and to the world, Christ, as 'Last Adam' (cf. 1 Cor. 15.45), models humanity empowered by grace to relate and act constructively in all directions. Christ's costly victorious conflict with the forces of sin and death has enabled the 'grace story', as well as the 'sin story', to run in human lives.

The reason that there is hope—which is in fact the central assertion of the passage—is that the 'grace story' is the more powerful of the two. There may be 'original sin' confronting every human life coming into the world; there is also—and indeed more powerfully—'original grace' (to borrow a phrase from Matthew Fox 1983). As Paul puts the matter exuberantly in Rom. 5.17:

> If, through one individual's trespass, death reigned through that one person, much more will those who accept the overflow of grace and the gift of righteousness reign in life through the one person, Jesus Christ.

So, while there may be much evidence for the unredeemed state of the world, and while that may impinge very painfully upon our present life in the body, for Paul there is also hope that this unfinished state of affairs will not be the last word.

Romans 8.18-22: the 'Groaning of Creation'

In the central portion of Romans 8 (8.14-30), Paul resumes the argument for hope, confronting more explicitly the suffering that is a feature of the present situation of the world—and of believers as part of that world. The small passage on 'creation' is the first of three subsections making up Rom. 8.18-27. In each of these the 'groaning' of the subject ('creation' in 8.18; 'we ourselves', in 8.23; 'the Spirit' in 8.26-27) provides a grounds for hope.

> [18.] For I reckon that the sufferings of the present time are a small price to pay for the glory that is going to be revealed in us. [19.] For creation awaits with eager longing the revelation of the sons [and daughters] of God. [20.] For creation was subjected to futility—not of its own volition but on account of the subduer—in the hope [21.] that the creation itself would be set free from its slavery to decay in order to share the freedom associated with glory of the children of God.
>
> [22.] For we know that the entire creation has been groaning together in the pangs of childbirth right up till now (1996: 254; translation mine).

While there is no explicit citation of any text from Genesis, the sequence is replete with allusions to the creation stories. In particular, the argument hinges around the principle that, because human beings were created along with the non-human created world and given responsibility for that world, they share a common fate with that world. When the situation of human beings deteriorates, so does that of the rest of creation and, vice versa, when it goes well, the creation shares in the blessing.

The origin of this idea of a common fate between human beings and the rest of creation seems to lie in the fact that the earth, cursed as a result of Adam's sin, became difficult to till (Gen. 3.17-19). The reverse process, along the same principle of a common fate, appears in certain prophetic texts (Isa. 11.6-9; 43.19-21; 55.12-13; cf. Ps. 114; Ezek. 34.25-31; Hos. 2.18; Zech. 8.12). Nature puts on a spectacular display in sympathy with Israel emerging triumphantly from Egypt, and from captivity in Babylon: the mountains leap for joy, the desert blooms, the rough places are made smooth and so on (cf. Wis. 16.24; 19.6)

On the basis of this principle, Paul envisages 'creation' awaiting with 'eager longing the revelation of the sons and daughters of God' (Rom. 8.19). That is, creation awaits the arrival of human beings at the fullness of the graced humanity intended for them by God (Byrne 1979: 104-108, 213-16; 1996: 248-49).

In vv. 20-21, Paul explains why creation cherishes this hope. Reading the mythic account of Gen. 3.17-19, through the lens of a negative working of the 'common fate' principle outlined above, Paul sees creation subjected to futility entirely against its will. The very unwilingness attached to this forced compliance in the subduer's fall meant that creation continued to cherish a hope of reversal. Should humankind be restored to favour with God and once again image the divine glory, then, on the same 'common fate' principle—now operating in a positive direction—creation itself (8.21) might be restored. It would have a share in humanity's restored freedom from the slavery to decay, and in its own way reflect and share the freedom associated with the glory of the children of God.

Subject against its will, creation groans—not in mere reaction to pain, but as a restlessness with its present lot; creation's groaning is actually a positive aspiration. So Paul can point to the 'groaning' of creation (8.22)—whatever that 'groaning' might consist of—as an index of hope.

An Ecojustice Critique

I think it has to be conceded that Paul's argument here does presuppose a basically 'triangular' pattern derived from Gen. 1.26-28 where human beings are set over against the rest of the created world in relationship to God. There is an inherent dualism here and more-over an assumption, again derived from conventional understanding of Gen. 1.26-28, that human beings play a leading and indeed deter-mining role in creation. In this sense Paul retains the anthropo-centricism of the creation story in Genesis 1.

What I would want to argue, however, is that Paul sets his allusion to the creation stories in a context that severely critiques this anthro-pocentricism. To be more precise, a dual vision with respect to human influence in the world emerges from Rom. 8.18–22. The text certainly envisages a negative, exploitative anthropocentrism. But it also implies the possibility of a more positive pattern of human behaviour. This more positive view remains anthropocentric in the sense of according to human beings a determining role in the world (which is, after all, factually the case). But it can hardly be called anthropocentric in a negative, self-regarding and exploitative sense.

The 'Sin Story'

Understanding an enigmatic phrase in Rom. 8.20 in a particular way makes it is possible to regard human maltreatment of the earth as an instance of what I have termed the 'sin story' of the human race. In a clear allusion to Gen. 3.17-19, Paul argues that when creation was 'subjected to futility', it incurred this fate—not of its own volition but on account of something or someone external to it: 'the subduer'. Almost all interpreters understand this 'subduer' here to refer to God. They find here an allusion to the narrative of the Fall where the earth is cursed because of Adam's sin and where it is in fact God who pronounces the curse.

A minority opinion, however—which I believe to be well founded (see Byrne 1996: 260-61)—understands 'the subduer' as a reference to Adam, or more generally, to humankind, who, on the basis of the charge given in the creation story in Genesis 1, are meant to 'subdue' the rest of creation (Gen. 1.26-28; cf. also Ps. 8.5-9).

Admittedly, this language of 'subdue'/'subjection' renders Paul's interpretation of the creation story offensive to the principle of custodianship, which aims to see humans as partners and responsible custodians of the remainder of the world, rather than as rulers or 'subduers'. But the minority view concerning the subduer outlined above allows us to view human maltreatment of the material world as part of what I have called the 'sin story' of the human race. That is, Rom. 8.18-21 retells the story emerging from Rom. 5.12-21 with particular reference to the effects of human sin upon the rest of creation.

The text, of course, presents this retelling as 'myth': that is, following the Genesis account, it alludes to something that took place 'back there'. But, as with all myth, the story is not really about 'back there'; it enshrines something abidingly valid in human life. The non-human created world continues to be 'subjected to futility because of the subduer' as the 'sin story' continues to run in human life. In other words, we can validly find in this text an allusion to the evil consequences that ensue for the non-human world when selfishness, greed and exploitation, rather than creative responsibility, mark human behaviour on this planet. These evil consequences are no less a manifestation of human sin in the Pauline sense than sinning against fellow human beings or directly against God.

The 'Grace Story'

Of course, the 'sin story' is not the only one to emerge from the text. As noted earlier in connection with Rom. 5.12-21, the major thrust of this entire section of Romans (Rom. 5–8) is positive. In the face of the suffering and death that mark the present time, it asserts the sure hope of salvation on the basis that in Christ and through Christ, there is another story being told: the 'grace story'. In fact, as in the case of Rom. 5.12-21, Paul only points to the negative side—the 'subjection' of creation to futility—in order to assert all the more powerfully the grounds for hope.

So, while a sense of sinful human maltreatment of the material universe may be implicit, the text points more powerfully still to an opposite possibility on the positive side. The depiction of Jesus Christ as counterpoise to Adam—explicitly in Romans 5; by implication here in Romans 8—suggests the possibility of a grace-filled, rather than a sin-driven, human role in the universe. If there is exploitation, ruin and futility on the basis of a common fate between human beings and the world, there can also be care and responsibility on the same basis—when human beings respond to and act in accordance with the grace of God. Human partnership and custodianship of the material world is then genuinely an enactment of the grace of God, operative in Christ.

Paul may retain and even develop the 'subdue'/'subjection' language of the Genesis myth. But his positive view, where humans respond to the unselfish promptings of grace, avoids negative implications and can indeed foster a genuinely eco-friendly interpretation of Gen. 1.26-27.

The great value of this small passage is that it draws concern for the non-human created world into Paul's grand conception of the Creator's gracious renewal of relations with humankind in Christ. In this Paul remains fundamentally true to, and recaptures the essential vision of Genesis 1–3, in the matter of relationships between Creator, human beings and the non-human remainder of creation.

The 'Persona' of Creation

Together with this, the passage from Romans 8 communicates a sense of positive partnership and respect for creation on the part of human beings through the imaginative way in which it gives a persona to 'creation'. Paul speaks of creation 'waiting with eager longing' (8.19). He states that, if it has taken a fall, it has done so 'unwillingly', and it cherishes a 'hope' for its own restoration (8.20). Here, it seems to me, the ecojustice principle of voice and also that of resistance find some expression in this text.

A little more remains to be said, specifically, about the concluding statement: 'For we know that the entire creation has been groaning together [with us] in the pangs of childbirth right up till now' (Rom. 8.22). Having explained why creation cherishes a hope of liberation (8.20-21), Paul points to creation's 'groaning' as the outward, observable manifestation of this hope, and as, therefore, a grounds—along with the groaning of believers themselves (8.23) and the Spirit (8.26-27)—for hoping that salvation will soon be fully accomplished.

With respect to the groaning of creation, it is hard to see what reality of the actual physical world Paul could have had in mind. It is likely, however, that the apocalyptic motif of the 'messianic woes'— the sense that the final consummation will be immediately preceded by a time of greatly increased suffering and distress on a cosmic scale—is present here. In parallel with other strands of the Jewish and early Christian tradition, Paul interprets these woes as 'birth pangs'. Just as the contractions of the mother's womb, painful though they be, both presage the arrival of new life and in fact bring it about, so 'the sufferings of the present time' (8.18), in which the 'whole creation' groans in the pangs of childbirth along with us, are an indication that the longed-for salvation is at hand (see Byrne 1996: 261-62).

To sum up: the clear distinction Paul makes between human beings and the rest of creation stands in some tension with the principle of interconnectedness. In many ways, the argument tends to reinforce a sense of duality between human beings and the rest of creation. Nonetheless, the passage does convey a strong sense of solidarity in both suffering and hope between non-human creation and the human world. At the same time, the appearance of the essentially feminine image of creation giving birth is striking in a document (Romans) that otherwise appears unrelentingly masculine in its imagery and in the selection of Scriptural characters (e.g. Abraham, Adam, Moses, Pharaoh, Jacob and Esau) to which it appeals.

Continuity or Discontinuity; Transformation or Resurrection?

As I said at the start, this passage referring to the non-human material world has been considered something of an embarrassment by many interpreters of the Pauline corpus. The embarrassment is odd since it is abundantly clear from Paul's writing as a whole that he was passionately concerned about human life in the body; human life would be meaningless if not situated within the context of wider material creation.

In the face of a tendency on the part of the Christians in Corinth to be 'high' on the Spirit—especially in its more ecstatic, otherworldly manifestations—and to ignore or devalue the challenges and responsibilities of continuing life in the body, Paul defended his belief in the resurrection of the body as an essential corollary of the Gospel (1 Cor. 15). In his eyes, it is precisely the destiny to resurrection that gives dignity and meaning to life in the body here and now (see Byrne 1983, 1986; Fee 1987: 11-12).

It is interesting, however, that in the passage we have been considering, there is no explicit mention of resurrection. In the sentence immediate following (8.23), what believers are said to await, while groaning, is 'the redemption of the body'. This phrase implies the liberation of the body from the 'slavery to decay' mentioned in 8.21

and that could certainly include the sense of resurrection. But it remains true that the motif of resurrection itself has not been explicitly mentioned since much earlier in the chapter (8.10-11).

Resurrection, of course, necessarily implies the death of that which is to be raised, and inevitably introduces a strong note of discontinuity: the present dispensation dies or is removed and a wholly new one is introduced by the power of God. It could be that Paul avoids mention of resurrection because, in connection with the human interaction with the non-human created world set forth in Rom. 8.18-22, he wishes to suggest a sense of continuity and transformation rather than destruction and rebirth. In this paradigm, the material universe would evolve into the age of salvation, rather than dying (or being destroyed), and being raised in some form. In contrast to a note of discontinuity suggesting that the present world is simply provisional and disposable, the text avoids a duality between a disposable 'this worldly' domain and an 'other worldly' or 'spiritual' realm that is eternal and more nearly conformed to the being of God. The ecojustice principle of purpose thus has better foundation in this text than in many other areas of the New Testament.

We certainly create a lot of problems for theology when, in contrast to previous ages of belief, we bring the future of the present, material universe into the eschatological equation. It is easier to dismiss this material earth in favour of a more detached, more transcendent 'heaven'. Moreover, current scientific thinking tends to regard the long-term future of the universe as bleak (see Edwards 1995: 145-52). If, as my reading of this passage suggests, Paul points us in the direction of continuity rather than discontinuity, it may be more important to take what he says as promoting a positive attitude to the material world in the present rather than as a statement about the future of a disposable material realm.

In the treatise on hope that follows this passage, Paul is in fact remarkably 'agnostic' concerning the future: 'a hope that is seen is not really hope at all. For who hopes for what they already see?' (8.24b-25). Hope does not seek to know (literally 'see') but rests all upon the love and fidelity of God and the divine determination to bring to completion the original plan of creation (8.28-30).

Conclusion

In this sense, not only the passage about 'creation groaning' but also Paul's wider insistence upon the value of bodily life invites us to think more intently and rigorously concerning the relation between matter and spirit. We have to ask what might be involved in Spirit's coming to dominance—not only in individual human existence but in the universe as a whole.

I should like to conclude this paper with a reflection on a statement concerning matter and spirit that I find particularly arresting. It comes from a British journalist, Donald Nicholl, as part of a series of reflections recorded just before his death for his family and friends. Nicholl defined matter as a 'risk taken by the spirit' (quoted in the British weekly, the *Tablet*, 5 July 1997, p. 863). Is the redemption of the universe (Rom. 8.21) ultimately a question of allowing spirit to come to dominance in the universe of matter—not against matter or separate from matter, but in and through matter as its true home?

The Goodness and Holiness of the Earth and the Whole Creation (1 Timothy 4.1-5)

Paul Trebilco

Introduction

In this chapter I will examine 1 Tim. 4.1-5, using questions raised by the Earth Bible Project's six ecojustice principles. Does this passage speak of the worth of creation, and if so why? Does it view the Earth in its own right, or simply from humanity's perspective? Can this text be read from the perspective of the Earth? Has this text contributed to our ecological crisis, or is this a text with a particular message for us as we face this crisis?

In order to understand the references to the created order in this passage, we must understand the passage as a whole, and know something about the teachers, whom the Pastor[1] opposed (and whom I will therefore refer to as the 'opponents'), who are spoken of there.

In 1 Timothy 3 the Pastor has spoken of the qualifications required for an overseer (3.1-7) and a deacon (3.8-13); he has made it clear why he has written the letter (3.14-15) and then has given what was probably a credal statement summarizing the truth with which the church has been entrusted (3.16). In 1 Tim. 4.1-5 the Pastor gives a warning against the opponents and provides some details concerning what he regards as their errors. This is one of a very few passages in which the author gives a theological rebuttal of the opponents.

The Pastor says that in later times 'some will renounce the faith'. As the Pastor is using 'the faith' to refer to the content of the faith, he is

---

1.   I regard the Pastoral Epistles as written by someone who saw himself—and it almost certainly was a man, given 1 Tim. 2.11-15—as a disciple of Paul who was saying what Paul would have said had he still been alive. For discussion of authorship see Bassler (1996a: 17-21), and Davies (1996a: 105-18) in favour of pseudonymity; see Fee (1988: 23-26) and Johnson (1996: 2-32) in favour of Pauline authorship. For a review, see also Marshall (1997: 7-17). The Pastorals are probably to be dated in the late first century—the generation after Paul's death; see Young (1994: 11-12, 22-23).

speaking about what he regards as doctrinal errors; the rest of the passage makes this clear. However, the church is not caught unawares by this departure from the faith, because the Spirit had spoken previously about it. The present tense of the Greek verb to speak (λέγειν) in the clause '[the Spirit] is saying… ' indicates that the Spirit's speaking, even if it was an event in the past, still has present and ongoing significance.

People will renounce the faith in this way 'in later times' (ἐν ὑστέ-ροις καιροῖς). The passage does not state explicitly that the prophecy has now been fulfilled. However, what follows demonstrates that the Pastor thinks this is the case: the author addresses the present situation on the basis of the prophecy, gives a rebuttal of the predicted teaching (4.3-5), and urges Timothy to instruct the church in this regard now (4.6). Clearly, the opponents' teaching is regarded as a present danger.

1 Timothy 4.1 states that 'some people' (τινες) will fall away; these are not the opponents themselves since these teachers are mentioned in 4.2. The 'some people' (τινες) of 4.1 are members of God's household, also referred to in 3.15, and thus are church members who have followed the opponents. The ultimate cause of the renunciation of the faith in the Pastor's view is that people 'pay attention to deceitful spirits and doctrines of demons' (4.1).

The Pastor then turns to the opponents who are propagating the opposing teaching among the addressees (4.2). According to the Pastor, the opponents' basic problem is that their consciences are seared or cauterized, and so they are unable to distinguish between right and wrong.

However, in much of what he writes about the opponents,[2] the Pastor seems to have adopted a number of features from a traditional polemical schema used by philosophers of the period, in their polemics against sophists.[3] The adoption of such a schema means that only those details of the Pastor's polemic which are *not* characteristic of the philosopher's arguments against sophists can be used to build up a description of the opponents.

2.   The Pastor writes about his opponents in 1 Tim. 1.3-7, 18-20; 4.1-7; 6.3-10, 20-21; 2 Tim. 2.14–4.5; Tit. 1.10-16; 3.9-11.

3.   See Karris (1973: 549-63); see also Johnson (1978–79: 1-26); see, e.g., Dio Chrysostom, *Orations* 4.33-36; Philo, *Vit. Mos.* 2.212. I am here assuming that the three Pastoral letters are all responding to very similar, or closely related, situations in Ephesus (1 Tim. 1.3; 2 Tim. 1.18; 4.12) and Crete (Tit. 1.5, 12); see Harding (1998: 205-206).

In 1 Tim. 4.3 the Pastor goes on to imply that the prophesied apostasy is now taking place in Ephesus, the location of the congregation to which the letter is addressed (1 Tim. 1.3; 2 Tim. 1.18). The opponents forbid marriage (κωλυόντων γαμεῖν) and are also demanding abstinence from foods (ἀπέχεσθαι βρωμάτων).[4] As neither of these are features of the polemical schema the Pastor has adopted, they can be taken to reflect the opponents' views (see Karris 1973: 557). What more can be said about their views on these two subjects?

Understanding the Opponents

Why are the opponents promoting asceticism in this way? What influences may have led them to these views? In order to answer these questions, I will briefly outline what can be deduced from the Pastorals about the opponents.

In 1 Tim. 6.20 the readers are told to 'avoid the godless chatter and contradictions of what is falsely called knowledge (τῆς ψευδωνύμου γνώσεως)'. This suggests that the opponents referred to at least part of their teaching as 'gnosis'. In 2 Tim. 2.18 the Pastor writes that Hymenaeus and Philetus 'have swerved from the truth by holding that the resurrection is already past'. The strong links between 2 Tim. 2.18 and 1 Tim. 6.20-21 suggest that the belief that the resurrection is already past was a key element of the gnosis claimed by the opponents. The opponents probably did not deny the resurrection, but rather claimed that as the fullness of the resurrection had already been realized in the present in some spiritual sense, they had already received the benefits of resurrection life and now lived in the Age to come.[5]

In 1 Tim. 1.4 Timothy is instructed to order certain persons not 'to occupy themselves with myths and endless genealogies which promote speculations'. In Tit. 1.10, 14 the Pastor warns against 'those of the circumcision', and criticizes the opponents for 'giving heed to Jewish myths'.

---

4.   βρῶμα means food in general, but in Rom. 14.20-21 and 1 Cor. 8.13 it is used to refer to meat, which may be in view here. See BAGD, p. 148. The plural 'foods' probably refers to certain types of food; see Arichea and Hatton (1995: 91).

5.   See Lane 1964–65: 164-67; Fee 1988: 256; Towner 1989: 31. Although the opponents probably used the term 'gnosis', they should not be regarded as 'Gnostics' since many of the features of developed Gnosticism are lacking in what we know of them. Attempts to identify the opponents have ranged from Judaizers to Marcion and Gnosticism; see Gunther 1973: 4-5.

It seems likely then that 'Jewish myths' are also meant in 1 Tim. 1.4, since the Pastor goes on in 1 Tim. 1.7-11 to speak of 'certain persons' who 'desire to be teachers of the law'; his discussion of the role of 'the law' (ὁ νόμος) demonstrates he means Jewish law.[6]

The 'myths and genealogies' of 1 Tim. 1.4 probably involve some form of speculative exegesis of the Old Testament. All these points suggest that the opponents argued for the continuing validity of some Jewish practices and beliefs unacceptable to the Pastor, and saw a greater degree of continuity in some areas between Jewish and Christian practices and beliefs than did the Pastor.

Understanding the Opponents' Views on Marriage and Food

I will now consider the opponents' views on marriage and foods against this background. The opponents' rejection of marriage can be connected with their views on resurrection. If the believer was already living the resurrected life, then this could lead to a dualism setting the 'spiritual' on a higher plane than the material. Those who espoused this teaching could become libertine or they could become ascetic, and thus ignore the things of the material world, or regard them as belonging to the old age. Perhaps they believed that for those who had 'arrived'—for whom the resurrection had already occurred—marriage was unspiritual and fitting only for the old order.

But one of the reasons the opponents may have believed that the resurrection had already occurred (2 Tim. 2.18) was that they believed the material world was tainted or perhaps evil, and represented an impediment to salvation (see Bassler 1996a: 80; Oden 1989: 59). Thus, perhaps because of this foundational view, they went on to affirm that resurrection could only be spiritual, and that such spiritual resurrection had already occurred. Perhaps this foundational negative view of the physical world led directly to a rejection of marriage, which was clearly part of the material order (see Bassler 1996a: 82; cf. Goulder 1996: 245-50).[7]

---

6. See also 1 Tim. 4.7; 2 Tim. 4.4; Tit. 1.15; 3.9.

7. Note also that the opponents seem to have had success among women (see 1 Tim. 2.12-15; 5.11-15; 2 Tim. 3.6-7; Tit. 2.5) and that this may well have been connected to their emancipationist tendencies and their prohibition of marriage (which freed women from the bonds of patriarchal marriage), along with other factors; see Verner 1983: 177-80; Bassler 1996: 81. In response, the Pastor advocates marriage (1 Tim. 2.15; 3.2, 4-5, 12; 5.9, 14; Tit. 1.6; 2.4-5). On the asceticism of the Acts of Paul, see MacDonald (1983: 57-59), who argues that the Pastor wrote to counteract legends about Paul of the kind which were collected in the Acts of Paul.

Why did the opponents demand abstinence from some foods? There are two possible answers. First, as in the case of forbidding marriage, their belief that the resurrection had already occurred could lead to the view that the material world belonged to the old age and so contact with it should be curtailed in particular ways. The view that physical matter was evil or tainted could lead to the same result. Second, the opponents seem to have advocated the continuing validity of some Jewish practices and beliefs, including part of the Jewish law; the demand for abstinence from some foods could have been derived from this source (see 1 Tim. 1.7-11; Tit 1.10-15). This may alone be the basis for the demand for abstinence from food, or it may be an additional reason alongside the view that the resurrection had already occurred and that matter was evil.[8]

How Does the Pastor Respond to These Views?
Why Does the Pastor Say What He Says?

I will now turn to the Pastor's response to these views of the opponents and will discuss the affirmation of God as creator and the goodness of creation, the function of thanksgiving and the meaning of consecration 'by God's word and by prayer'.

God as Creator and the Goodness of Creation
In 1 Tim. 4.3b, in response to his report that the opponents 'forbid marriage and demand abstinence from foods', the Pastor writes: 'which God created to be received with thanksgiving by those who believe and know the truth' (ἃ ὁ θεὸς ἔκτισεν εἰς μετάλημψιν μετὰ εὐχαριστίας τοῖς πιστοῖς καὶ ἐπεγνωκόσι τὴν ἀλήθειαν). As the antecedent of 'which' (ἃ) is 'foods' (βρωμάτων), the Pastor is saying that 'foods' were created by God and that food is to be received with thanksgiving. To abstain from food is thus directly contrary to God's actions in creation. It is not clear whether marriage is also in view in v. 3b.

In 1 Tim. 4.4 the Pastor broadens this and affirms that 'everything created by God is good' (πᾶν κτίσμα θεοῦ καλόν), which leads to the conclusion that nothing is to be rejected, provided it is received with thanksgiving, an idea which I will consider in the next section. God is spoken of as creator then, although this time the text concerns more than food. Here also is the additional generalizing affirmation that

---

8.   Dibelius and Conzelmann (1972: 65) and Fee (1988: 8-9) think both factors account for the attitude towards food; see also Barrett (1963: 132).

everything God made is 'good', and hence is to be received. Clearly marriage is now in view, but the Pastor has broadened his horizons still further and affirms that all of God's creation is good. For the Pastor then, the opponents' teaching is false because it denies that everything God created is good; for the Pastor nothing is to be rejected.

The Pastor's all encompassing statement about the goodness of God's creation is probably an intertextual echo of God's repeated verdict in Genesis 1 that each component of creation is 'good'. It seems likely that through this echo of one of the key features of the Genesis 1 creation story, the author is reminding his readers of the whole creation narrative. Clearly it is wrong to demand abstinence from some foods because God repeatedly pronounced that creation is good and not evil (Gen. 1.4, 10, 12, 18, 21, 25, 31) (see Simpson 1954: 66; Spicq 1969: 499; Fee 1988: 100; Roloff 1988: 225).[9] Further, the reference to 'every creature' (πᾶν κτίσμα) of God (1 Tim. 4.4) may well be an echo of Gen. 1.31: 'And God saw *everything* (τά πάντα) that he had made, and behold it was very good (καλά λίαν)' (see Johnson 1996: 164).

The text also implies that it is wrong to forbid marriage, because in the echoed text of Genesis 1, God specifically commanded humanity to 'be fruitful and multiply' (Gen. 1.28), and then pronounced all creation to be 'very good' (Gen. 1.31).[10] Hence, the asceticism and rejection of creation by the opponents is ruled out; the belief in the goodness of God's creation undermines such a stance.

The Function of Thanksgiving

Second, I turn to the function of thanksgiving for the Pastor. Verse 3 states that God created food and it is 'to be received with thanksgiving by those who believe and know the truth' (εἰς μετάλημψιν μετὰ εὐχαριστίας τοῖς πιστοῖς καὶ ἐπεγνωκόσι τὴν ἀλήθειαν). This is clearly an important matter for the Pastor because he reaffirms in v. 4 that everything created by God is good and so is not to be rejected, provided it is received with thanksgiving (μετὰ εὐχαριστίας λαμβανόμενον) (see Roloff 1988: 225; see also Rom. 14.6; 1 Cor. 10.30). The

---

9. Sir. 39.16, 25-27, 31 also echo Gen. 1 concerning the goodness of creation.

10. On intertextual echoes, see Hays (1989). Note in particular, p. 20: 'Allusive echo functions to suggest to the reader that text B should be understood in light of a broad interplay with text A, encompassing aspects of A beyond those explicitly echoed... Metalepsis...places the reader within a field of whispered or unstated correspondences'.

appropriate response to what God has created is not abstention, but reception with thanksgiving.

What does the Pastor mean by receiving 'with thanksgiving' (μετὰ εὐχαριστίας)? A thanksgiving or benediction always accompanied meals in Judaism and the early church.[11] A prayer of thanksgiving at meals expresses gratitude, recognizes God's prior creative action, and acknowledges food as God the Creator's gift (Bassler 1996a: 80-81). For the Pastor, marriage and food are to be received with thanksgiving 'by those who believe and know the truth' (τοῖς πιστοῖς καὶ ἐπεγνωκόσι τὴν ἀλήθειαν; 1 Tim. 4.3b).

Particularly in view here are the opponents. For the Pastor, it is only those who believe and know the truth—in this case about the goodness of creation—who can give thanks in the appropriate way. The opponents do not 'know the truth'. Rather they have shipwrecked their faith (1 Tim. 1.19-20), and oppose the truth (2 Tim. 3.8; Tit. 1.14). They are now showing by their actions how wrong they are, for rather than giving thanks for food and partaking of it as they should, they are demanding abstinence from food. The same is true of marriage.

Consecration by God's Word and by Prayer
Third, I will look at the meaning of consecration 'by God's word and by prayer'. Why should God's good gifts of creation be received with thankfulness rather than be rejected? Because all creation[12] 'is sanctified by God's word and by prayer' (ἁγιάζεται γὰρ διὰ λόγου θεοῦ καὶ ἐντεύξεως). But what does it mean for all creation to be 'sanctified' or 'consecrated'? I will briefly review the meaning of the Greek verb 'to sanctify', ἁγιάζειν.

In the Greek Old Testament (LXX or Septuagint), ἁγιάζειν is used in connection with people (e.g. Exod. 29.21; 1 Sam. 7.1; Jer. 1.5) or things (e.g. silver in Judg. 17.3). Many features of the temple and sacrifices are regarded as sanctified.[13] Things and people were also consecrated to God (Exod. 13.2; Lev. 22.2). Thus Procksch (1964: 111) notes:

---

11.   See Mt. 15.36; Mk 8.6; Jn 6.11, 23; Acts 27.35; Rom. 14.6 1 Cor. 10.30. The verb is found in the words of institution of the Lord's Supper; see Mt. 26.27; Mk 14.23; Lk. 22.17-19; 1 Cor. 11.24. See further, Conzelmann (1974: 407-15); *NIDNTT*, 817-20.

12.   The third person singular ἁγιάζεται refers back to πᾶν κτίσμα; see Knight (1992: 192).

13.   See, e.g., Exod. 29.27 (a sacrifice); Exod. 29.37 (the altar); Exod. 29.44 (tabernacle); 1 Kgs 8.64 (the temple forecourt).

> Mostly the objects [of the verb ἁγιάζειν] are priests, people, and holy places and vessels. By sanctification they are separated from what is profane and set in a consecrated state. Sacrilege, or the violation of what is holy, does not come under human jurisdiction but under the judgement of God which normally means death.

Thus, for example, the Sabbath is to be kept holy and 'everyone who profanes it shall be put to death; whoever does any work on it shall be cut off from among the people' (Exod. 31.14).[14]

In the Synoptic Gospels ἁγιάζειν appears only in Mt. 23.17, 19, which speak of the sanctuary or altar making gold or a gift 'sacred', and in the Lord's Prayer ('hallowed be your name'; Mt. 6.9; Lk. 11.2). In the Pauline epistles, God is said to sanctify people (1 Thess. 5.23); believers 'were sanctified…in the name of the Lord Jesus Christ and in the Spirit of our God' (1 Cor. 6.11; see also Rom. 15.16; 1 Cor. 1.2); the church is sanctified (Eph. 5.26); and an unbelieving person is sanctified through his or her spouse (1 Cor. 7.14). In 2 Tim. 2.21—the only other use of the verb in the Pastorals—the Pastor states that a person can become 'sanctified and useful' to God.[15]

With respect to 1 Tim. 4.5 then, it is important to note that elsewhere in the New Testament—apart from Mt. 23.17, 19—only *people* are said to be sanctified.[16] In contrast, in this verse in 1 Timothy, the statement about sanctification clearly refers to 'everything created by God' (1 Tim. 4.4a) and thus includes the Earth community.

In discussing ἁγιάζειν in 1 Tim. 4.5, Knight (1992: 192) suggests that the verb 'is used here in the general sense of being declared fit, acceptable, or good for use or consumption'. However, in view of the meaning of ἁγιάζειν (to sanctify) reviewed above, this seems an overly anthropocentric view.

The text rather suggests that creation is set in a consecrated state, and as we will see, declared to be holy by God's word. Facets of creation are to be received *with thanksgiving to God* (rather than simply received) precisely because they are 'set apart', sanctified by God. They should not simply be received. It is also significant that the violation of what is sanctified in the Old Testament warrants the

---

14.   See also Exod. 19.12-25; 35.2; Lev. 10.1-11; 20.1-27, esp. verses 4-9; Num. 1.51.

15.   Procksch (1964: 111-12); Porter (1993: 397-402).

16.   Roloff (1988: 226) comments on the use of ἁγιάζειν here with reference to creation: 'This is a unique statement within the New Testament, that otherwise speaks only of the holiness of humans'. Although he overlooks Mt. 23.17, 19, the point is very significant.

death penalty. Clearly, that which is consecrated by God is to be respected.

This sanctification happens through the word of God and prayer (διὰ λόγου θεοῦ καὶ ἐντεύξεως). But what does the Pastor mean by 'word of God' (λόγος θεοῦ) here? A number of suggestions have been made. First, the phrase could refer to prayers before meals which use biblical expressions.[17] However, given that ἁγιάζεται refers back to πᾶν κτίσμα in v.4 this seems unlikely, since the Pastor speaks of all creation being sanctified, and not just what is received at meals.

Second, Fee notes that in the Pastorals the 'word of God' generally refers to the gospel message (2 Tim. 2.9; Tit. 1.3; 2.5). In this case, he suggests the phrase reflects that the hearers have come to know that in Christ there are no food laws.[18]

Third, Knight (1992: 192) notes that 'λόγος θεοῦ' can be used of a statement or message from God. It is 'an abbreviated way of recalling those truths that God has communicated, namely that every created thing was made by him and is therefore good'. When has God done this? The most important occasion is at creation. I have already noted the intertextual echo with Genesis 1 in 1 Tim. 4.4; it is likely that this echo continues here. The 'word of God' then is the word God spoke in Genesis 1, and may be taken to refer to all that God says in bringing forth creation and approving of it. Given the echo of Genesis 1 in v. 4, this seems by far the most likely explanation of the phrase in v. 5.[19]

The meaning then would be that God has 'consecrated' creation by calling it forth (And God said, 'Let there be...'), by speaking to creation (eg. Gen. 1.29-30), and by pronouncing it very good (Gen. 1.31). In these actions, God has sanctified everything God has created.

Again then, the opponents are wrong to forbid marriage and certain foods, for God has sanctified these things by God's word in the act of creating them, and in speaking to and about them.

---

17.   See Spicq (1969: 500); Dibelius and Conzelmann (1972: 64); Brox (1989: 169); Oberlinner (1994: 183-84). An example would be Ps. 24.1.

18.   Fee (1988: 100-101); he favours the third option given below.

19.   See also Fee (1988: 101); Oden (1989: 60); Campbell (1997: 196). Bassler (1996a: 81) thinks that the reference is to God's word at creation in Gen. 1.29-31. Note also the references to the word by which God created the world in Ps. 33.6; Wis. 9.1; Jn 1.1-3. The present tense of ἁγιάζειν (rather than a past tense, 'was consecrated') does not count against the 'word of God' being a reference to Gen. 1, since God's creating word may be thought of as causing the created order today to be consecrated; see Arichea and Hatton (1995: 94). Hanson (1982: 88-89) sees eucharistic language in v. 5, including a reference to the eucharist in the phrase the 'word of God', but this is probably being anachronistic.

That the 'word of God' by which God's creation is sanctified is probably an echo of Genesis 1 suggests there may be another link with that passage. In the Septuagint Gen. 2.3 reads: 'And God blessed the seventh day and sanctified it (ἡγίασεν αὐτὴν), because in it he ceased from all his works which God began to do'. Given the echoes of Genesis 1 that have already been discerned, and those to Genesis 2–3 found in 1 Tim. 2.12-15, it may be that in speaking of creation being 'sanctified', the author is echoing Gen. 2.3.

Perhaps for the Pastor, God's sanctifying activity on the seventh day did not simply sanctify that day, but rather sanctified all of creation, 'all his works' which were completed by that day. God's activity recorded in Gen. 2.3 may then be another reason, in addition to sanctification by God's word in Genesis 1, why the Pastor sees creation as sanctified.[20]

Finally, 1 Tim. 4.5 also refers to prayer in connection with sanctification. Prayer here clearly refers back to the prayer of thanksgiving spoken of in vv. 3-4. The prayer of thanksgiving has a role in sanctifying, for such prayer acknowledges that what is received is God's gift, created as good, and sanctified by God.[21]

Are There Further Reasons Why the Pastor Affirmed the Goodness of Creation?

Belief in the Incarnation
I will now suggest there are two other facets of the author's thought which may have led him to affirm the goodness of creation, or where an affirmation of the goodness of creation is latent in his thought.

Initially, I will consider the author's belief in Christ's Incarnation. In this paper, I cannot discuss in detail everything the Pastor has to say about Christology. However, in some particularly significant passages the Pastor uses the language of epiphany to speak of Christ, or speaks

---

20. We have noted the echoes of Gen. 1–2 in 1 Tim. 4.1-5 on several occasions. Towner (1994: 103-104) suggests that in their asceticism the opponents were attempting 'to enact the life of resurrection paradise by following the model given in Genesis 1 and 2, before the fall into sin—after all, Jesus taught that there would be no marriage in the resurrection (Mt. 22.30), and vegetarianism seems to have been the rule in Eden/paradise'. If this was the case, then the Pastor is attempting to answer the opponents by drawing on the same text as they did, but is arguing against their understanding of the passage and developing a quite different interpretation of his own.

21. Kelly (1963: 97) notes 'the grace sets the food in its true perspective and in that way enables us to regard it as sacred'.

of Christ as pre-existent, or as fully human.[22] I will argue that one of the reasons the Pastor affirmed the goodness of creation may have been because of the world-affirming nature of Christ's incarnation, in which the Pastor believed.

It is generally agreed that the Pastor has used the language of epiphany as a vehicle to present his Christology. He writes that grace 'has now been revealed through the appearing (διὰ τῆς ἐπιφανείας) of our Saviour Christ Jesus' (2 Tim. 1.10), which is clearly a reference to the first 'appearance' of Jesus.[23] The author also uses the concept of epiphany to speak of what is elsewhere in the New Testament called the 'parousia'. Hence in 1 Tim. 6.14 he emphasizes the way his addressees are to live 'until the manifestation (μέχρι τῆς ἐπιφανείας) of our Lord Jesus Christ'.[24]

The Pastor speaks of the pre-existence of Christ in at least two passages. In 1 Tim. 3.16 the Pastor quotes what may have been a hymn. It begins: *'He was revealed* in flesh'. The language of manifestation in flesh clearly implies the pre-existence and incarnation of a heavenly being. Similarly, 1 Tim. 1.15 states: 'The saying is sure and worthy of full acceptance, that Christ Jesus *came into the world* to save sinners'. This interestingly recalls Johannine language, and clearly implies pre-existence.[25]

The Pastor also states that Jesus was fully human. I have already noted 1 Tim. 3.16: 'He was revealed *in flesh*, vindicated in spirit'. The contrast between flesh and spirit is of interest here, and in conjunction with the Christological passages I have looked at concerning epiphany and pre-existence, seems to underline the real 'enfleshment' of Jesus.[26] Further, 1 Tim. 2.5 reads: 'For there is one God; there is also one mediator between God and humankind, Christ Jesus, *himself human*, who gave himself a ransom for all'. These verses may stress that Christ Jesus is fully human, rather than simply the 'appearance' of a divine figure. This would prevent anyone from thinking the Pastor's epiphany Christology is docetic (Marshall 1988: 173; Bassler

22.   On the Christology of the Pastorals see in particular Marshall (1988: 157-77; 1994: 167-82); Bassler (1996b: 310-25); Lau (1996: 179-279).

23.   See also Tit. 2.11, 3.4 where the Pastor speaks of the results of the first 'appearance' of Jesus.

24.   See also 2 Tim. 4.1, 8; Tit. 2.12-13.

25.   See Knight (1992: 101); and Jn 1.9; 3.19; 11.27; 12.46; 16.28; 18.37; it also recalls Lk. 19.10. Pre-existence is probably also spoken of in 2 Tim. 1.9-10. See also Hultgren (1987: 107-108); Marshall (1988 171-75); cf. Dunn (1989: 237-39).

26.   Note also 2 Tim. 2.8: 'Remember Jesus Christ, raised from the dead, a descendent of David'; see also 1 Tim. 6.13.

1996a: 318). Perhaps the opponents, because of their negative view of the material world, denied the reality of the incarnation or had a docetic Christology. Unfortunately, because of our limited knowledge of the opponents, certainty about this is impossible.

Marshall has argued that the language of epiphany, when taken with other features of the Pastorals, such as the verses discussed above which speak of Christ as pre-existent and as fully human, is equivalent to the language of incarnation found, for example, in John's Gospel.[27] Thus in the Pastorals, Christ 'is a divine figure who has appeared in this world to be the epiphany of the unseen God'.[28]

Although we cannot be sure that the opponents denied the reality of the incarnation, I think it is clear that the author of the Pastorals affirmed the reality of the 'enfleshment' of Jesus, the pre-existent one, the epiphany of the unseen God. Perhaps one of the reasons that the Pastor affirmed the goodness of creation, and refused to allow that any created thing should be rejected as evil, may have been because of his affirmation of the material world which is implicit in his belief in the 'enfleshment' of Jesus. Even if the Pastor did not make this connection, it is latent and implicit in his thought. The Pastorals affirm that Jesus, who is clearly regarded as the epiphany of God, is 'himself human' (1 Tim. 2.5), and was 'revealed in the flesh' (1 Tim. 3.16).

The Pastor's affirmation of the enfleshment of the pre-existent Jesus is enormously world and creation-affirming. The created order is shown to be good, precisely by the fact that Jesus, the 'epiphany' of God, has been revealed in this created world as flesh, as a person living on the Earth. This line of thought thus provides a further avenue of critique against the opponents, one that the Pastor did not fully elaborate.

God and Christ as Saviour
One other facet of the author's thought may have led him to affirm the goodness of creation. Donelson discusses the prominent portrayal of God and Christ as 'saviour' in the Pastorals and the related concern of God for the salvation of all (e.g. 1 Tim. 2.3-4).[29] He notes the Pastor's 'general view of his cosmos as one in which a process of

27. See Marshall (1988: 169-75). Bassler (1996a: 317) suggests the author speaks of 'incarnation as epiphany'; cf. Dunn (1989: 237-39).

28. Marshall (1988: 175). That the Pastor uses the title of '*Theos*' for Jesus in Tit. 2.13, which is the most likely interpretation of that passage (see Harris [1992: 173-85]), also reinforces this view.

29. See Donelson (1986: 135-41). God is called saviour in 1 Tim. 1.1; 2.3; 4.10; Tit. 1.3; 2.10; 3.4; Christ is called saviour in 2 Tim. 1.10; Tit. 1.4; 2.12-13; 3.6.

salvation is taking place' (Donelson 1986: 139), and argues con-
vincingly that this concept of salvation 'determines directly the content
and direction of the ethical and ecclesiastical life-style promulgated in
the letters' (Donelson 1986: 140). Donelson's discussion (1986: 140-41)
is worth quoting:

> In Tit. 3.4…the salvation schema is introduced as revealing God's kind-
> ness (χρηστότης) and love of mankind (φιλανθρωπία). The first epiphany
> of Jesus revealed to the world something essential about the nature of
> God which has shaped the author's whole attitude towards the world.
> God's dealing with the world and with human beings is based upon
> χρηστότης and φιλανθρωπία. Thus God has instigated the plan of sal-
> vation with the intention to save all. And while the author puts great
> stock in the intricacies of this plan…the general positive evaluation of
> God as savior, who entertains χρηστότης and φιλανθρωπία towards hum-
> anity, bestows an aura of hope, accommodation, peacefulness, and
> belonging to the author's basic outlook. He lives in a friendly cosmos, a
> cosmos which contains within it processes of salvation… It does not
> have to be said that such a positive attitude towards the world and life
> in it was not the only option in the Greco-Roman world. In fact, both the
> apocalyptic and gnostic world views, which lay close at hand for the
> author, did not admit such things… [T]his image of God as being kind
> and concerned for all people surfaces in a variety of ways. As might be
> expected, God is also creator (1 Tim. 6.13). And since God's character is
> one of friendliness, creation itself is a friendly place, where one should
> live at peace and not according to ascetic revulsion. Thus the author
> excoriates his opponents who misunderstand the nature of creation by
> practicing abstinence from certain foods, which in the author's mind
> should be accepted with prayer as rightful parts of God's creation
> (1 Tim. 4.3). He is arguing that everything in creation comes from God's
> hand and consequently participates in the goodness of God. God's kind-
> ness pervades the cosmos.

The Pastor's understanding that God and Christ are saviour of all
has led the Pastor to see God as kind and loving, which in turn has
led him to see not only humanity, but also the created world, in a
positive light.

I suggest when the letters are considered as a whole, the author's
attitude to the world can be seen to be based not only on his view of
God as creator. His views are also based—implicitly at least—on his
belief in Christ's incarnation and his belief that God and Christ's
activity as 'saviour' reveals that God's basic attitude towards the
cosmos is one of kindness and love.

The Earth Bible Project

I have already drawn attention to a number of facets of the passage and its background relevant to the Earth Bible Project. First, while facing opponents who forbade marriage and demanded abstinence from some foods, the Pastor affirmed the goodness of God's creation. I have suggested that in doing so, he echoed Genesis 1 and God's verdict on creation expressed there. Second, I have noted that God's good creation is to be 'received with thanksgiving', which acknowledges that it is a gift from God the creator. Third, I have noted that all of creation is sanctified by God's word, which I suggested was a reference to God's word in creating the world. This word makes creation holy. Fourth, I have noted that a resounding affirmation of the created order can be seen in the author's belief in Jesus' incarnation, that Jesus is the epiphany of God on Earth, and that God and Christ are 'saviour'. I will now develop four other lines of thought that emerge from the passage and are relevant to the Earth Bible project.

The Principle of Intrinsic Worth

It is worth noting again that the Pastor is arguing against opponents who probably believed that the created order is inherently evil or tainted. The Pastor stood against this view and affirmed the principles of the intrinsic value and intrinsic goodness of creation. The underlying reason for affirming the goodness of creation is that it is created by God, who in Genesis 1 pronounced creation to be 'good' in and of itself. The probable echo of Genesis 1 in our passage is important here. I have also noted that the goodness and worth of creation is latent in the Pastor's belief in the world-affirming incarnation of Christ, and in his belief that, since God and Christ are 'saviour', this reveals God's basic attitude of kindness and love towards the cosmos.

But creation is also said to be sanctified by God's word. It is not only humanity which is sanctified by God, but creation also participates in the sanctifying action of God. The text denies a dualism that sees heaven as holy, and Earth as inferior or corrupt. In this text, the Earth is not only honoured and celebrated as good; it is also holy, set apart for God through the action of God's word in creation.

By speaking of creation as not only good—as in Genesis 1—but *also* as sanctified, our text, when compared with a passage like Genesis 1, sees creation as having *additional* value and worth.[30] To say creation is sanctified means creation has additional significance as a sphere holy to God. All creation—not just specific places—is seen as being sanctified by God's word. According to the Pastor, this is God's perspective on the Earth. This certainly speaks of the intrinsic worth of the created world in and of itself. The reader who identifies with the place of the Earth in this text hears the affirmation of Earth as both good and holy, set apart for God.

The Principle of Interconnectedness: Is the Passage Anthropocentric?

The principle of interconnectedness asks whether the text is anthropocentric and views the Earth primarily in terms of utilitarian purposes for human beings. I have noted in the previous section that the created order has intrinsic worth and is made holy through God's word, a view which is clearly not human-centred. Is this view sustained throughout the passage?

In 1 Tim. 4.4 the Pastor affirms that 'everything created by God is good'. Does this mean that creation is good in and of itself, or simply that it is 'good… for humans'? Is the affirmation of the goodness of creation thoroughly anthropocentric? The intertextual echo of Genesis 1 is important here. In echoing Genesis 1, the Pastor does not seem to be affirming that creation is 'good for us' but rather is recalling the goodness of creation in God's eyes. The echo of this passage would suggest that the Pastor similarly sees creation as simply 'good'.

Although the echo of Genesis 1 suggests creation is viewed at first from God's perspective, the author immediately says that 'nothing is to be rejected, provided it is received with thanksgiving'—the thought thus quickly moves to the needs of humanity. At this point the Pastor has moved to an anthropocentric view of the Earth.[31] However, v. 4 does not say, 'Everything created by God is good for humans', but rather affirms the goodness of creation in and of itself. Further, in affirming in v. 5 that creation 'is sanctified by God's word', the text again views creation, not in relation to humanity, but in terms of creation's relationship to God and its intrinsic worth. There are some shifts in perspective in this passage, then.[32]

30.   I am grateful to Professor Norman Habel for highlighting this point.
31.   This anthropocentric view is also clear in 1 Tim. 6.17.
32.   The Pastor clearly has a hierarchical view of authority; see, e.g., 1 Tim. 2.8-15; 3.1-13; 6.1-2; Tit. 2.9-10. However, the author does not seem to bring the two concepts of a hierarchical view of authority—which seems to flow from his

What Does the Passage Suggest with Regard to our Attitude to the Earth?
For the Holiness of Creation, and against Exploitation

Again, fundamental to our attitude towards the created order is the affirmation that creation is not inherently evil or to be devalued; rather, the creation is good. I have also noted that everything created by God is sanctified by God's word. This clearly means that we cannot deal with the inanimate world simply as 'stuff'. The Earth community does not consist of disposable matter; rather it is holy and sacred by virtue of being created and sanctified by God. Further, as noted above, violation of what is 'sanctified' in the Old Testament warrants the death penalty. Clearly, whatever is consecrated by God is to be respected. This is an important contribution made by this passage—apart from Mt. 23.17, 19, which reflect belief in the sanctity of the Temple, elsewhere in the New Testament only people are said to be sanctified. Recall also that in the Lord's Prayer, it is God's name that is to be sanctified; here, the Earth is sanctified. However, note that the Earth is also seen as a passive recipient of God's action.

Although the Pastor does not go on to reflect about the matter, much of what has been deduced regarding the text's meaning argues against the exploitation of the Earth. That food and other facets of creation are to be 'received with thanksgiving' must mean that exploitation of the Earth is unacceptable. The unstated corollary of the view that created gifts must be received with thanksgiving is that if something cannot be accepted in an attitude of thanksgiving, then it should not be accepted at all. To put it another way, without the qualification 'provided it is received with thanksgiving', the view that 'everything created by God is good, and nothing is to be rejected' could lead to rampant exploitation. The qualification puts a boundary around the sort of interaction with creation that is acceptable to the Pastor.[33]

understanding of the church as God's household, and from the problems created by the opponents—and his affirmation of the interconnectedness of humanity with the created order, as shown in 1 Tim 4.1-5, into dialogue. The two concepts are, I think, in some tension.

33.   The Pastor's teaching in favour of moderation and against greed is also relevant here, although I cannot go into these features of the Epistles in detail. The Pastor warns against the immoderate use of wine (1 Tim. 3.3, 8; Tit. 1.7; 2.3), but advocates moderate use (1 Tim. 5.23). He argues for moderation in all things (1 Tim. 2.9, 15; 3.2; 2 Tim. 1.7; Tit. 1.8; 2.2, 4, 5). Often he writes against greed (1 Tim. 3.8; 6.5, 9-10, 18; Tit. 1.7, 11). Contentment and a simple life of self-sufficiency is advocated (1 Tim. 6.6-10), and a certain amount of ownership of property is taken

The Pastor is also affirming that it is not humanity's *right* to 'receive' God's creation but that a facet of creation can only be received when it is 'received with thanksgiving'. This means that people should be always mindful that what they are receiving is not their *property* but a gift, and a part of God's good and sanctified creation. Because this requires the continual awareness of the giftedness of creation, it should make exploitation impossible.

In addition, as the Earth sanctified by God's word is holy and set apart by God, it should not be abused by humanity. To abuse the Earth is to abuse something that is holy to and for God.

The Principle of Custodianship

The passage as a whole does speak of some form of use of the created order by humanity. Clearly, for example, humans are to have food. But the provisos governing our relations with the created order to be deduced from this passage are twofold. First, what is 'received' from the created order must only be such things as can be received 'with thanksgiving'. Second, that such action of 'receiving' from creation must be compatible with recognizing creation as sanctified.

The text suggests the concept of responsible custodianship, the fifth ecojustice principle, is appropriate: that in the act of 'receiving with thanksgiving' such things as food, humans are to be reminded that we are not the ultimate rulers over the created order, but rather that we are only a part of the good creation, and that we may receive facets of creation only as a holy gift. What we 'receive' is part of the consecrated Earth. Does this not then mean that 'receiving' implies custodianship of the holy? Further, this must imply the limited and restricted use of creation, since it is good and holy in its own right.

Humanity then must recall that the created order we interact with is both good and 'sanctified by God's word and by prayer'. All our interactions with the Earth community must be compatible with 'receiving with thanksgiving' and interacting with the Earth community as 'good' and 'holy'.

for granted (1 Tim. 5.16; 6.17-19). As Dibelius and Conzelmann (1972: 40) note: ''Prudent' moderation also characterizes the attitude towards the goods and necessities of life'. Davies (1996b: 33) notes the Pastorals' stress 'on the importance of people's moderation in personal relations and their general condemnation of greed could be extended to avoid some of the excesses of contemporary living'.

'Burning the Land': An Ecojustice Reading of Hebrews 6.7-8

Iutisone Salevao

Introduction

'Burning the land' in Heb. 6.7-8 is a disturbing option for me as a Samoan. Burning the land is nothing less than destroying the land itself as well as the entire Earth community of interacting biological organisms and their physical environment. Burning the land means burning part of me.

To help the reader understand how this disturbing text confronts me, I will first outline the concept of land in the world view of the Samoan people. Subsequently, I will explore the ecojustice dimensions of the text by reading from within the context of my own culture.

Ironically, my own land is also likely to be destroyed—not by fire but by water. The deadly consequences of global warming will severely affect the South Pacific islands since most of them are no more than tiny atolls and small raised coral or volcanic islands. As such, they are more vulnerable than the rest of the physical world. As emphasized in Hulm (1989: 2):

> [A] 2 degree increase in the average temperature and a 4 m rise in sea level would deal a death blow to several [Pacific island] communities... Tokelau, Marshall Islands, Tuvalu, Line Islands and Kiribati could cease to exist.

Although the above projection may represent the worst case scenario, it is nevertheless important inasmuch as it underlines the reality of the ecological crisis which confronts us all. For the people of the South Pacific island paradises, we face the real possibility of the literal annihilation of some—if not all—our islands.

Land in the World View of the Samoan People

In the Samoan language, the Greek word for land (γῆ)[1] is translated either *ele'ele* or *fanua*. These two terms normally refer to the physical

1.　The Greek term for land (γῆ) in the book of Hebrews normally refers to the ground or soil, usually including other material objects in or on the ground such as trees and plants.[2] Beyond that common meaning, the two terms carry similar metaphorical connotations that are relevant to our ecojustice exploration in this series.

For the Samoans, the land is also a source of life. In addition to its primary meaning, the term ele'ele can also mean blood. This usage is reserved for human blood and adopted in formal contexts requiring respect and restraint in both behaviour and verbal expression. So used, the term evokes a world view in which the land is seen as both existing within the human body and, at the same time, the life-blood that sustains the body. The ele'ele—in the literal sense of soil—is the source of life for plants and other forms of life, and—in the figurative sense of blood—is the source of life for human beings. The land is both life and a source of life.

The term fanua is likewise associated with the origin of life and, more specifically, with the conception and birth of human beings. In addition to its primary meaning, the term is also used as a technical name for the embryonic sac that envelopes an unborn child as it develops from an embryo into a foetus. At childbirth, this embryonic sac is expelled from the uterus as the afterbirth or placenta, and is subsequently buried in the ground.[3] In this context, the term conjures up a cosmology in which the land (the fanua) is seen as metaphorically originating from within the body of a human mother.

The universe, the Earth and all its components have intrinsic worth. The intrinsic worth of the land is also emphasized by virtue of its character as a source of life. Destroying the land is destroying life.

Another significant point for the Samoan people is the special relationship between the land and the people of the land. The image of the ele'ele as blood within the human body is a metaphor that

Earth as opposed to heaven as in 1.10; 11.13; 12.25-26; cf. 11.19 where it refers to the land that 'had been promised', and in 11.29 and 39 where it refers to the soil or land in general. See Attridge (1989: 172 n. 76).

2.   Cf. Heb. 6.7-8 where the noun γῆ is also used in the sense of soil or land in general. But whereas in Hebrews γῆ can also mean Earth (as opposed to heaven), neither the Samoan word ele'ele nor the word fanua has that extended meaning. Rather, in the Samoan language, the noun Earth (as opposed to heaven) is normally represented by the noun lalolagi meaning, beneath (lalo) heaven (lagi) and implying a two-tiered universe with heaven above and the earth beneath.

3.   The burial of the fanua in the ground used to be a very important act—almost like a religious ritual—with deep symbolic significance. Sadly, however, the introduction of modern medical practices has resulted in disposing of afterbirths in a clinical impersonal way in a hospital/birthing centre.

expresses the intimate relationship between the land and the people—
a mutual relationship expressing the harmonious coexistence of both.[4]
The blood sustains human life, and human beings are responsible for
the sustenance and welfare of the blood.[5] In the same way, while the
land, the *ele'ele*, is a source of life for human beings and other living
things, human beings for their part are custodians who must care for,
protect and preserve the land.

The relationship between the land and the people is a symbiotic one
operating to the mutual benefit of both parties. This sense of kinship
is further underlined by the association of the term *fanua* with the
human embryonic birth sac—underlining that the metaphorical origin
of the land is the body of a human mother. Burying the afterbirth—
the *fanua* of one's birth—in the ground is a powerful symbol of the
continuation of the cycle of life and an affirmation of the land as a living entity capable of both giving and receiving life. The Samoan hope
for new life from the land, expectation of growth and aspiration for
regeneration make the simple act of burying the afterbirth a profoundly meaningful one.

The use of the term *fanua* evokes a cosmology in which human
beings are viewed as emerging from the land, and returning to the
land when they die. This relationship with the land continues from
conception through birth (notwithstanding the separation of the newborn from the *fanua* of birth when the umbilical cord is severed) right
throughout life, and even after death, when humans return to the land
from which they emerged at the beginning. Taken in its entirety, the
relationship between human beings and the land from which they
emerge spans the full cycle of life and death.[6]

Because the land is a source of life and an integral part of human
life, it must be treated with care and respect. Given this cultural

4.   The relationship between the Samoan people and their land is sometimes
linked with the notion of 'totemism', which may be broadly defined as a sense of
kinship between a group of people and a certain object or form of life. The same
sense of kinship between people and the land is also found among indigenous
Australians and the Maori prople of New Zealand.

5.   The issue of human beings having the responsibility to provide for the sustenance (e.g. through eating enough healthy food), preservation and welfare of the
blood (e.g. by not indulging in excessive alcohol consumption or taking lethal
doses of drugs) brings into sharp focus such acute health problems as HIV/Aids.

6.   A person's final resting place or grave is called *fanua maliu*, meaning 'land
of the dead'. The normal practice in Samoa is that the deceased members of a family are buried in their own family land, reflecting the belief that people of a family
are intimately related and ultimately belong to their land both in life and death.

understanding, an essential reverence normally characterizes the Samoan relationship with the land—reverence based on the belief that the land has intrinsic worth as a living entity that is an integral part of human life and the constitution of our society.[7]

Samoans believe that humans belong to the land; humans are natives of the Earth. We maintain that the kinship between the land and the people does not give humans either the power or the liberty to rule over the Earth or any of its components, let alone destroy the land when it appears unproductive. This understanding of the relationship between human beings and the land is consistent with the Earth Bible Project's ecojustice principle of custodianship. As responsible custodians we are partners with—rather than rulers over—the Earth; our role is to sustain its balance and beauty.

The Earth-centred cosmology of Samoans is a realistic view of the 'here and now', a cosmology that affirms the reality of the Earth and all living things in and on it. In this Earth-centred cosmology there is no room for a dualism between heaven and Earth. Rather, in our traditional thinking, heaven is never far away; it is, in fact, always within reach. This Samoan cosmology is ecologically challenging because it neither postulates absolute dichotomies nor views heaven as superior to Earth.[8]

It seems that our traditional Samoan ecological consciousness has been dramatically altered by biblical ideas such as the Genesis mandate which purports to give human beings the authority to rule over

7.   The rationale behind the legal prohibition against the alienation of customary land in Samoa affords an interesting insight into the relationship between the Samoan people and their land. Since all the members of a family—past, present and future—belong to their land, and since the land itself is an essential part of that family's identity and history, no one has the legal right to alienate or dispose of such land. Thus, Article 102 of the *Constitution of Western Samoa 1960* stipulates that 'It shall not be lawful or competent for any person to make any alienation or disposition of customary land or of any interest in customary land, whether by way of sale, mortgage or otherwise howsoever, nor shall customary land or any interest therein be capable of being taken in execution or be assets for the payment of the debts of any person on his decease or insolvency'.

8.   One Samoan creation tradition postulates a nine-tiered universe, with heaven at the highest level and seemingly far removed from earth. Yet this is clearly not the case, for, despite the vast distance in time and space, the essential connection between heaven and earth is never totally severed. In fact, the two realms are constantly kept in touch by divine–human sons and daughters of the highest god coming down from heaven and dwelling among humans on earth.

the Earth, and the dualistic distinction between heaven and Earth that is usually discerned in the book of Hebrews.[9]

An even more immediate concern in the postcolonial era is the danger of losing our strong traditional ecological bonds with the Earth in the face of local interpreters of the Bible who view the Earth as disposable matter in the face of the Second Coming.

My Approach to Reading the Text

In keeping with the ecojustice hermeneutic of the Earth Bible Project and my personal kinship with the land as a Samoan, I stand with the Earth and analyse the passage from the perspective of the Earth as a subject. For me the Earth is a living entity, the source of life and my own kin. Reading this way requires a significant change of posture—from the usual standpoint of an observer noting what God and humans in the text do to the Earth as an object to a posture of identification or empathy with the Earth and its struggle for justice. When I read about the Earth, I listen to the Earth and I feel for the Earth.

Standing with the Earth and its community in my reading of the text also involves asking whether the Earth is being heard and being treated justly. In seeking justice for the Earth and its components, my analysis proceeds on the suspicion that the text, the traditions behind the text, and later interpreters of the text are likely to have devalued the Earth, suppressed its voice and been anthropocentric in orientation. This suspicion is consistent with my Samoan experience of Westerners who have read the text to us in the past and treated the Earth as a lifeless object.

I would also like to find evidence in the text of the suppressed voice of the Earth I have learned to hear in Samoa, and to retrieve that voice—even if it is a cry of anguish.

Hebrews 6.7-8 in Context

It is widely accepted that this passage is the second half of a larger literary unit—namely, Heb. 6.4-8, which in turn is part of a wider liter-

---

9.   The pervasive influence of Platonic dualism in the book of Hebrews is well noted, including the dualistic distinction between heaven and earth, cf. 1.10; 8.9; 11.13; 12.25-26. On the issue of the author's reason for using Platonic spatial dualism, see, e.g. Ellingworth (1993: 144-47); Dunn (1977: 89); Lehne (1990: 97-98); cf. Kasemann (1984: 37-39).

ary complex, Heb. 5.11–6.9.[10] The first part of the unit (6.4-6) asserts that it is impossible to restore again to repentance believers who apostatize, a teaching known as the 'doctrine of the impossibility of a second repentance'.[11] Hebrews 6.7-8 is rendered as follows in the NIV:

> Land that drinks in the rain often falling on it and that produces a crop useful to those for whom it is farmed receives a blessing from God. But land that produces thorns and thistles is worthless and is in danger of being cursed. In the end it will be burned.

In these verses the author compares the irreversible fate of apostates to the fate of unproductive, useless and worthless land. The point of the comparison is that land, having drunk the rain falling upon it repeatedly, is expected to produce vegetation, and when it does, it receives a blessing from God (cf. Gen. 1.11-12). But if it produces 'thorns and thistles', then the end of such land is burning (cf. Gen. 3.17-19).

Analogous to this situation is a Christian who becomes an apostate. Having experienced the blessings of Christ's death and resurrection, believers who fall from faith can never be restored to repentance. Instead, they are cursed, cut off and permanently excluded from the sphere of salvation.

The literary connection between the two parts of the unit seems clear: the comparison is used to elucidate and undergird the theological teaching in the first part of the unit.[12] The interpretation of the meaning and function of vv. 7-8 must therefore be undertaken within the context of vv. 4-8 as a single unit.[13]

The comparison is strategically placed after vv. 4-6 to maximize the literary effect of what the author has just said. It is first of all a literary device designed to serve a specific rhetorical function: to illustrate and undergird the previous theological claim. It follows that, within the context of the whole unit, the comparison is intended to serve a more limited function than an unconditional licence for the burning of land.

10.   See Lindars (1989: 382-406 esp. 396-97); Bruce (1964: 106-27); Attridge (1989: 10); cf. Peterson (1982: 284 n.59).

11.   The interpretation of the doctrine is fraught with many problems. See, e.g., Nicole (1975: 355-64); Lane (1991a: 142); McCullough (1974: 1-7 esp. 2); Carlston (1959: 296-302); Salevao (1994: 210-86).

12.   Note also the strategic significance of the Greek conjunction γάρ, meaning 'for', at the beginning of Hebrews 6.7; it provides the connection between vv.4-6 and vv. 7-8.

13.   See Verbrugge's suggestion that vv. 7-8 provide the basis for vv. 4-6 (1980: 61-73).

Both parts of the unit are conditional statements; both envisage hypothetical situations; both require certain conditions to obtain in order for either of them to apply. Verse 8 constitutes a conditional statement to the effect that, if, after drinking the rain that falls on it repeatedly, the land should produce 'thorns and thistles' instead of a crop useful for human beings, then that land should be burned.

What then is the purpose of burning the land? I advocate the view that the author envisages no other purpose for burning the land than its destruction. This conclusion is required by both the context in which v. 8 is placed, and by the basic thrust of the author's argument in both the theology of vv. 4-6 and the related simile in vv. 7-8. Paul Ellingworth (1993: 328) aptly sums up this position: 'The context [Heb. 6.4-8] excludes any thought that the purpose of burning is to purify the land for fresh sowing'.[14] Rather, the whole purpose of burning the land is to totally destroy what is viewed as unproductive and worthless. Just as an apostate is to be considered beyond restoration (vv. 4-6),[15] so too unproductive land is to be absolutely destroyed (vv. 7-8). The two parts of the unit are thus parallel statements of cause and effect, of failure and penalty. Both envisage absolute condemnation and destruction.

Burning our Kin, the Land

Viewed from the Samoan perspective on the land, v. 8 is nothing less than a totally insensitive statement negating our kin, the Earth and the Earth community, a statement implying absolute human authority and control over the land and its fate. For Samoans, the land is always in us, with us and around us; what happens to the land, happens to us. If our kin the land is destroyed, human beings themselves are destroyed as well. We cannot destroy the land without destroying ourselves.

---

14.   See also Hewitt (1979: 109); Attridge (1989: 173); Lane (1991a: 143). Cf. Montefiore (1964: 110): 'The details of the analogy should not be overpressed, for the land which our author had in mind would have been burned not to destroy it but in order to assist the growth of new shoots (unless he was thinking of devastation caused by some natural catastrophe)'.

15.   Cf. Heb. 10.26-29. On the literary connection between 6.4-6 and 10.26-29, see Carlston (1959: 296) and Lane (1991b: 391). On the influence of the Old Testament blessing/curse motif on 6.4-8 (cf. Deut. 11.26-30; 29.30; 13.8); see also Verbrugge (1980: 65); Montefiore (1964: 178-79); Attridge (1989: 168-73, 294); Lane (1991a: 143); Salevao (1994: 269-83).

We may assume, for the sake of argument, that the purpose for burning the land in some contexts is not to destroy it, but to clear the land of old plants and weeds so that new shoots will grow. On this reading, burning the land is undertaken in the name of regeneration, growth and restoration. In some cultural understanding—such as those within certain indigenous communities in Australia—burning the ground cover may be desirable to break seed pods open and provoke growth. In the context of this passage, however, there is no suggestion of regeneration.

From the point of view of the fauna, the flora and countless other organisms that are also members of the Earth community associated with a given piece of land, burning their land destroys the ecosystem, their ecological niche, their habitats and, ultimately, their lives. Speaking for them, from their perspective burning the land means annihilation, not regeneration.

We may also explore the possibility that since Earth and humans are kin, the land suffers with and for us. What happens to the land happens to us; the fate of humanity and the Earth are intertwined. This sense of interconnectedness and common destiny, however, is suppressed in Hebrews. When the land does not produce a crop humans have a right to destroy the land. For Samoans such an act is sacrilege.

The Anthropocentrism of Verses 7-8

The anthropocentric orientation of the text is evident from the fact that the land is judged as unproductive and worthless when it does not produce a crop useful to human beings. Quite clearly, it is the welfare and survival of human beings that is in view. The welfare of the rest of the Earth community is completely ignored; the survival of the fauna and flora of the Earth is sacrificed in the interests of human survival.

From the point of view of the Earth, the negative effect of the author's anthropocentric interest is that the intrinsic worth of the land is completely ignored. Instead, the value of the land is viewed in terms of its utilitarian purposes for humans. Contrary to the principle of interconnectedness, the survival of human beings is promoted at the expense of the Earth community.

It is generally accepted that v. 8 has been influenced by Gen. 3.17-19 where, due to the fall of Adam, the Earth receives a curse and it brings forth thorns and thistles.[16] More specifically, the text of Genesis asserts that 'the ground' is cursed 'because of you'. As a result the ground 'shall bring forth' for humanity 'thorns and thistles'. Clearly, the focus is exclusively on the sin of Adam against God. The curse that befalls the ground is not a consequence of any error on the part of the ground itself. The Earth is a passive victim of a curse imposed by God because of Adam's sin.[17] This focus on human sin highlights the anthropocentric orientation of the text.

While the text of Hebrews may echo the language of Genesis 3, the origin of the thorns and thistles is not the result of human sin or divine curse. Rather the land is portrayed—like its human counterparts in this passage—as having a choice. Ground that drinks rain from God may produce a crop and then be blessed—or produce thorns and be cursed. The text seems to suggest that the thorns and thistles are the Earth's own fault. Contrary to the perspective of Samoans, the land in Hebrews is viewed as capable of producing what is useless. The land has not fulfilled its divine purpose: the production of food.

There is no sense here of the sacredness of all the Earth, regardless of its productivity from a human perspective. For the writer to the Hebrews, parts of the Earth have a capacity to produce what is worthless and deserve to be burned. The interests of humans have priority over land in Hebrews 6.

The Land Is our Source of Life and a Living Entity

Seeking justice for the land involves searching for and retrieving features or traditions in the text which value the Earth and enable its voice to be heard. One such feature is the implication in v. 7 that the land is a source of life. The fruitful land 'produces a crop' that is useful to those for whom it is cultivated. This is reminiscent of Gen. 1.11-12 where the Earth is commanded to bear fruit and in so doing receives God's approval. Here the emphasis is on the land as a source of life for human beings and as God's partner in the creation of life.

In the book of Hebrews, however, the land is measured by its utili-

---

16. See, e.g., Hewitt (1979: 109); Ellingworth (1993: 328); Attridge (1989: 173); McCullough (1980: 363-79).

17. Cf. Lane (1991a: 143): 'It is possible that in vv. 7-8 the writer was thinking of the infamous cities of the Jordan plain, which were "well watered like the garden of the Lord" (Gen. 13.10) but which were subsequently judged by God and were destroyed by fire (Gen. 19.24)'.

tarian value for human beings. Paradoxically, when human beings burn the land in the pursuit of their utilitarian interests, they are in effect burning their source of life.

A hidden tradition in which the Earth is a life-giving mother is implied in the writer's use of 'bear' (τίκτω) in v. 7. This verb normally refers to human reproduction,[18] but in v. 7 it is used to refer to the production of crops from the land. Thus the land 'bears' crops in much the same way a human mother bears children. The tradition behind the text suggests a concept of the Earth as the source of life and a living entity.

This imagery recalls the *fanua* of human birth in Samoan cosmology, the embryonic sac that envelopes an unborn child; after the baby is born, this sac is expelled from the uterus as the afterbirth and buried in the Earth. In terms of Samoan ecological consciousness, burning the land is in effect burning the *fanua* of one's birth, the *ele'ele* or the life-blood that gives and sustains human life. Such a perverse act is nothing less than suicide.[19]

Is the Earth totally silenced by the author of the Letter to the Hebrews? Is it possible to view the 'thorns and thistles' as the land's unique way of voicing its cries against injustices perpetrated by human beings on the Earth, and actively resisting those wrongs in its struggle for justice? As a living entity the land is capable of doing both.

This interpretation would make sense within the Samoan context. In the context of the book of Hebrews, however, the thorns and thistles are not specifically linked to anything humans or God have done. The Earth may indeed have cried out to the writer of Hebrews as it did to other biblical writers, but its voice has been silenced. The Earth may have resisted human injustices at the time of this writer, but this resistance of the Earth was apparently not considered worth reporting.

18.   See Attridge (1989: 173 n. 78).

19.   Human destruction of the land is, in the final analysis, an irresponsible human trait. Human exploitation and destruction of the land in Samoa exemplifies that trait. Taulealo (1993: 38) observes that 'uncontrolled land clearance [e.g. through burning] has caused severe soil erosion and flash flooding during the wet season. Of immediate concern is the increase in agricultural activities including the use of fertilizers and agricultural chemicals in catchment areas and upstream from water supplies.'

Conclusion

Hebrews 6.7-8 remains a disturbing text for me. In spite of the fact that the Earth may have been viewed as a living entity and a source of life in the traditions used by the writer, the text itself is blatantly anthropocentric and devalues the land.[20] For Samoans 'burning the land' means destroying life and, ultimately, destroying ourselves. If we are honest in our reading of this text, it stands in conflict with the principles of ecojustice espoused by Samoans and echoed in the Earth Bible Project series.

20. An analysis of the cosmology, apparent dualism and eschatology of the book of Hebrews in its social context may throw additional light on this text. At first reading, however, the burning of the land seems to be consistent with the wider perspective of Hebrews that the Earth is inferior to heaven and therefore disposable.

Setting aside the Ladder to Heaven: Revelation 21.1–22.5 from the Perspective of the Earth

Duncan Reid

Ever since St John Climacus (c. 579 to c. 649 CE) wrote his *Ladder of Divine Ascent*,[1] the image of the ladder or stairway to heaven[2] has imposed itself upon the Western imagination. It is a common theme in mediaeval art, and there are even contemporary secularized versions, for example in the opening scenes of David Puttnam's 1983 film *Local Hero*.

My argument in this paper is that the usual understanding of the ladder to heaven image is radically destabilized by Rev. 21.1–22.5; if we read this passage from the earth's perspective,[3] the ladder to heaven image can be put away. From the earth's perspective, the earth is not left behind, but continues to exist, and is inhabited. We are inhabitants of earth itself not of somewhere 'higher' than earth. We belong to the earth.

The obvious problem in developing an ecojustice reading of this or any other passage of an apocalyptic nature is the weight of traditional readings. Jürgen Moltmann has spoken of the 'annihilationist' or 'exterminist' readings of apocalyptic in the older Protestant orthodoxy (1996: 268-70). This tradition had its mediaeval antecedents and finds contemporary expression in some fundamentalist theologies as well as in some contemporary non-Christian apocalyptic groups. The folk memory of this sort of interpretation is so strong that apocalyptic material is often simply assumed to carry an annihilationist message—

---

1.   *PG* 88: 585-1248. English translation: *The Ladder of Divine Ascent* (New York: Paulist Press, 1982). Whether the conclusions reached in this paper are actually at odds with the intentions of the author of *The Ladder* is not a question that can or will be explored here.

2.   In this paper, 'heaven' refers to the dwelling place of God. Elsewhere in this paper I understand 'heaven' in the sense of 'the invisible side of creation' (see Welker 1994: 140).

3.   In this paper, 'earth' refers to this inhabited world and its living human and non-human inhabitants.

or at least one that fails to recognize the goodness of created matter. A text that has given rise to such readings in the past still needs to be approached with an appropriate degree of suspicion. There may be elements in this text that are simply irretrievable from an ecojustice perspective.

The Structure of the Passage

Revelation 21.1–22.5 opens the final part of the revelation to John: the vision of the new Jerusalem. It includes a detailed description of the holy city. The poetic imagery is reminiscent of the description of the beloved in Song of Songs, and this reinforces the analogy to the bride in Rev. 21.1 and 21.9. This vision is prefaced by the authorial 'I saw', and is described as 'a new heaven and a new earth'. The first heaven and the first earth have passed away. The sea no longer exists. The detailed description of the vision, the new Jerusalem, follows 21.11b.

Parallels are visible in a number of correspondences:

- between the verbs 'passed away' (ἀπῆλθαν) in 21.1 and 21.4, and perhaps 'came' (ἦλθεν) in 21.9;
- between the verbs 'coming down' (καταβαίνουσαν) in 21.2 and 21.10;
- between the image of the bride in 21.2 and 21.9;
- between the image of the 'the holy city, (the new) Jerusalem' in 21.2 and 21.10; and
- between the city's state of being 'adorned' (21.2) and possessing 'glory' (21.11a).

This report of the vision (21.1–22.5) includes three distinct voices; the first and second use the same pattern of command, declaration and promises of a new reality coming and of an old reality passing away. The first voice (21.3b-4) is an angelic voice that speaks of God in the third person. The second voice (21.5b-8) speaks in the first person; this is presumably the voice of God, or perhaps—because of the content especially of 21.6—the voice of the risen and glorified Messiah (Bauckham 1993: 26, 57). The message is intensified as we move from the third-person speech of voice one to the first-person speech of voice two. The third voice (21.9b), another angelic speaker, parallels the style of the first speaker.

The following schema demonstrates the structure of the passage.

> vision (21.1-4a)
> > angelic voice (21.3b-4)
> > > voice of the Messiah (21.5b-8)
> > angelic voice (21.9b)
> vision (21.10–22.5)

The passage begins and ends with the description of a vision, an act of seeing. What is seen—the new Jerusalem, the coming reality—is juxtaposed to the present reality: the earth under Roman imperial rule. Both the old and new realities are in process—a process of 'passing away' in one case, in the other a process of 'coming (down)'. In contrast to the present earth which, as Barbara Rossing has pointed out (1998: 487-99), is wasted and denuded, the coming (-down) reality is 'adorned' and possesses 'glory'. This glory is described in graphic, highly poetic detail in this passage.

The Message

In the middle of this report of a vision (and bracketed within the two corresponding passages 21.1-3a and 21.10) comes the message that John hears. The voiced messages interpret the vision—it is not a self-explanatory revelation. The messages of the first and second voices follow a similar structure. In both, the command is less important than what follows; the imperatives of 21.3 and 21.5 are commands to pay attention and to write down. They point, in each case, to what is to follow. The promises about what is to pass away are also, arguably, less important than the promises that immediately precede them, the promises of the new reality.

The first promise of passing away is not directed so much to the hearer as to death itself. The irony is that now, when death—which thrives under the old order—comes to the 'former things', it finds its own power base is lost. Death is self-defeating.

The passage is also a warning to the hearers or readers in so far as they may be tempted to place their trust in things that, in the vision, have passed away.

The second promise of passing away is more direct, describing the lot or fate of various types of wrongdoers, with the emphasis falling on those who are guilty of apostasy (Roloff 1993: 238). The force of the warning is weakened by the absence of any verb—except in the enigmatic reference to a 'second death'.

The main emphasis, then, falls on the two parallel promises of the new reality:

> the tent of God is among human beings,
> [God] will encamp among them as their God,
> they will be [God's] people
> and God will be with them [as their God];
> [God] will wipe away every tear from their eyes (21.3-4);[4]

and

> I make all things new!
> these words are trustworthy and true...
> It is come to pass!
> I am the alpha and the omega, the beginning and the end.
> To the thirsty I will give water as a gift from the spring of the water of life.
> The [victors] will inherit these things, and I will be [their] God and [they] will be my [children] (21.5-7).

These declarations with reference to the present and these promises with reference to the coming reality are central to this whole passage. The declaration and promise in the second couplet intensifies the message of the first. It does this by the threefold repetition of the words '[he] said'. The third repetition gains even more emphasis by adding the words 'to me'.

The whole passage takes an added intensity from the richness of the biblical allusions in the text. Verses 3-4 correspondence directly, through their use of the same verb, to the central image of the prologue of John's Gospel: encamping in a tent. 'And the Word became flesh and dwelt (ἐσκήνωσεν) among us' (Jn 1.14). In H. Paul Santmire's (Santmire 1985) terms, the metaphor at work here is the earthfriendly metaphor of migration. This new encampment of God refers to the incarnation; there is no intention to suggest a replacement is intended—rather, in this text God's incarnation is extended to all people.

The second declaration and promise carries an even heavier weight of biblical allusion. A full ecojustice reading of the passage would need to take account of the textual allusions in this central part of the passage, and the ecological allusions in the rest of the book of Revelation.[5] In this paper I intend to go no further than to recognize that this voiced message serves to interpret the vision; and that parallel

---

4.   The biblical translations are my own except where otherwise acknowledged. The material in square brackets represents additions to the text to avoid gendered references to God, or exclusive language, or to spell out what is implicit in the Greek.

5.   For a discussion of the imagery of harvest, see Bauckham 1993b: 94-98; see also R. Bauckham 1993a: 285-96.

passages—containing repeated images of the 'passing away' of the old reality, and the coming (down) of the holy city—surround and bracket this central section.

The Vision

The first thing to be said is that the vision, which echoes Ezek. 40.2, is a sensual experience. There is no Platonic distrust of the sense of vision, no retreat to the 'eye of the soul' or the inner eye (Plato, *Phaedo* 65–66). What is seen is believed, and recounted as reliable. This is already a significant affirmation of the earthly, bodily senses, as well as an implicit trust in the things that are seen.

Second, the vision is seen, we are told, from a high mountain. Unlike the disciples at the ascension who are told not to stand looking up (Acts 1.11), the narrator here is looking not up into heaven, but down (more and more so, as the holy city descends) towards the earth. The image is more akin to the picture of Moses looking down from a high mountain over the promised land (Deut. 34.1-4). Thus we are dealing, again using Santmire's terms, with the metaphor of the high mountain, but the experience is not of ascent but of descent, not of escape from the earth but of looking over the goodness and fertility of the land.

These themes are reinforced, in the passages that follow, using the imagery of the glorious city and the fruitful garden. These are both affirmations of land, albeit inhabited and cultivated land. In this text, habitation and cultivation are not at enmity with non-human creation.

Heaven and earth have passed away. In this section of Revelation, heaven and earth are linked together as corresponding parts of creation. Heaven, in particular, is not depicted as some 'supernatural' or uncreated reality. It is not a circumlocution here for God or God's eternal reign. In this text it is a created reality. (I will develop this point more fully later.)

The sea also is no more. The sea is also a created reality. It is not mythologized as the primeval element of chaos that threatens life (contra Bauckham 1993b: 53). The deliberate demythologizing of the image of the sea and its associations for an ancient Near Eastern audience in Genesis 1 is reaffirmed here. Like the created heaven and the created earth, the sea is also subject to contingency. It also will end. Like all things in creation, it also can be misused by human beings.

The passing away reality is, as Barbara Rossing has shown, an ecologically disastrous reality.[6] Rossing highlights the misuse of the sea by the Roman Empire—the Romans transform the sea into a possession, and use it to transport the products of their despoiling of conquered lands to Rome. For the visionary authorial voice in the book of Revelation, the sea has indeed become a threatening thing, but not because of its mythic power; on the contrary, it is a threat because it has been enslaved; it is in servitude to the merchant fleets of Rome. I do not dispute Rossing's interpretation. I do, however, want to add another possible dimension of meaning to her insights.

The verb used twice in this passage (ἀπῆλθαν, the aorist of ἀπέρχο-μαι) forms an *inclusio*, serving to tie the beginning (21.1) and end (ἦλθεν, 21.9a) of the passage to its centre (ἀπῆλθαν, 21.4b). This verb usually means simply 'to depart', or 'to go away'. It can mean 'to pass away', and this is how it is usually—and ambiguously—translated in this passage. This translation may speak truer than is often assumed, if we take seriously that the euphemistic meaning of 'to pass away' is 'to die'.

This less frequently attested meaning of ἀπέρχομαι also suggests another level of meaning. The sea, like the heaven (which waters the earth; see Ps. 72.6) and the earth (which brings forth good things; see Ps. 104.14), is not essentially a threatening thing; it is a good, life-giving part of creation. Despite its dangers and even its inhospitability, despite its ecologically disastrous misuse by Rome, it is also the essentially benign and life-giving element spoken of in Ps. 104.25-26.

> Yonder is the sea, great and wide,
> creeping things innumerable are there,
> living things both small and great.
> There go the ships,
> and Leviathan that you formed to sport in it (NRSV).

The sea may be inhospitable to us—but it also may be home for many other creatures. Further, in the developing rabbinic tradition the sea came to be understood, like the earth, as an element of cleansing. Earlier in the text of Revelation, we have seen the earth devastated by plague, war and famine—dangers so graphically described by the writer of Revelation in the vision of the four riders. In this section of the book, even heaven, even the sea—things we might fondly have thought invulnerable to the scourges of the earth—have also

---

6. See Rossing 1998; Bauckham (1993b: 49), also mentions the role of creation in the book of Revelation, but does not explicitly draw out the ecological implications. Elisabeth Schüssler Fiorenza (1991) appears to see no particular ecological significance in the critique of Roman power in the book of Revelation.

succumbed. They are depicted as creatures, as is the earth. Like the land, heaven and the sea are also under threat.

The apocalyptic riders have done their worst: in this final terrible vision, the earth has died. Not only has the earth died, but so have heaven, once thought so high and invulnerable, and the sea, once thought so boundless and infinitely life-giving. All three have died and 'are no more'.

This is not a matter for gloating apocalyptic annihilationism. It is not simply a matter of relief—relief for a respite from the unruly, chaotic turbulence of the sea, and from the ecologically ruinous mercantile practices of Rome—though it certainly involves elements of this emotion. It is also a matter of grief, of sorrow for the passing away of what were once the greatest and most powerful of God's creatures.

The earth has been denuded and shamed, and the sea enslaved and subjected to the will of the despoilers. The absolutely unimaginable is depicted in this text: land, sea, earth and heaven *have died*. The accompanying sense of terror may explain the urgency with which the vision is retold: 'I saw… I heard…he said…he said…he said *to me*!' After this final emphatic statement, and only then, the narrator returns to the retelling of the vision: 'he said [= I heard], he showed [= I saw]'. This urgent recounting is followed by a calmer, grander vision, detailing the new city 'coming down out of heaven' (21.10).

One of the central themes of the book of Revelation (ch. 7) is the question: what is the status of the saints who have died? Where are they? Are their past hardships and suffering now honoured in the presence of God? (7.13-17). The answer, of course, is Yes. The saints 'under the altar' (6.9) and 'before the throne' (7.15) have died, but now they are alive with God. Those alive now with God are identifiably the same people as those who perished in the great tribulation. The value and integrity of their past lives are now affirmed by God.

In the final vision in Revelation 21–22, this affirmation is broadened to include the earth. The earth itself has died. This is the reality known to the visionary and his readers. But like the bodies of the saints, the earth is now raised in glory. This is no replacement earth, no heavenly substitute for the present reality. It is, like the bodies of the martyred saints, the present creation transformed into a new creation.

The picture of the new (heavenly) Jerusalem occurs in 21.2 and 21.10. The city is new; it is the place of God's promised and enduring dwelling with people. It replaces the temporal Jerusalem—the old, passing and unsafe Jerusalem.

More significantly, it redeems the first dwelling of God with human beings: the Garden of Eden. It is not a return to Eden, because the new dwelling place of God with human beings is a city. This affirms human culture—literally human civilization—and the history of its development. The image is undoubtedly anthropocentric.

Certainly the passage refers obliquely to Isaiah 65 with its prediction of harmony between humans and the non-human creatures, and its images of wolf and lamb and ox living together at peace. Two of the animals listed are domesticated, and the vision of Isaiah is not yet generous enough to include the snake (Isa. 65.25).

Certainly the new city has trees, but these are to some extent viewed instrumentally—they are there to provide fruit, presumably for human beings, and leaves for the healing of human nations (Rev. 22.2).

The city is likened to a bride, coming to meet her future husband. The narrator's position is ambiguous—is he the waiting bridegroom, or an onlooker? Later, when invited to see the bride of the lamb, the writer is shown not a woman but a city, the holy city of Jerusalem. Both Jerusalem and the Jewish nation have been personified as a woman in other contexts, for example the '*Judaea capta*' image on first-century coins. It was not uncommon in the ancient world for cities to be given female personas. The image of the bride refers to the Sabbath (see Moltmann 1996: 283), and also to sexual union. Each of these references affirm, in its own way, the inherent goodness of creation.[7] The personification of the city suggests it may have voice. Like the saints who were silenced during the tribulation but who now sing praises before God's throne, the city, once silent, now appears, redeemed and in the form of a woman who as a bride will speak for herself.

The new city is prepared and adorned (21.2) and possesses 'glory' (21.11). This also stands in stark contrast, as indicated, to the present unadorned, denuded state of the earth depicted so graphically in earlier passages of the book of Revelation. These qualifiers suggest a number of related concepts. 'Prepared' (ἡτοιμασμένην) suggests a process of making—that is, making out of something, as opposed to creating out of nothing. God is the maker, but here, unlike in the original creation, God makes the new on the basis of the old, through the salvific transformation of the old. Adorned (κεκοσμημένην) carries both the idea of body or face painting (the cosmetics used by the bride) and the idea of the ordered beauty of the world or universe

---

7. See Bauckham (1993b: 126-43) on the imagery of the new Jerusalem.

(the cosmos). It thus ties the simile of the bride more closely with the description of the all-encompassing city. In 21.9, the simile has become a metaphor—the city is no longer *like* a bride; the city *is* the bride. 'Glory' signifies the eschatological state of the reign of God in the new Jerusalem. God's glory, God's presence, now dwells with God's people in such a way that it will never again depart from them, nor will they ever be separated from it. The connection between these qualities is that they all carry the implicit sense of beauty, the beauty that is the result of handworked artistry. This redeemed beauty is unlike any conventional notion of beauty, and is as inclusive as the people welcomed into the new city.

Redemption is interpreted 'cosmologically' here: the cosmos, with its beauty, is renewed, then ratified, confirmed in existence in its eschatological state. '[T]here is no redemption for human beings...without the redemption of nature... Consequently', writes Moltmann, 'it is impossible to conceive of any salvation for men and women without "a new heaven and a new earth" ' (Moltmann 1996: 260). This stands in marked contrast not only to any 'annihilationist' vision of redemption, but also to any suggestion that redemption is for human beings alone. For the visionary in the book of Revelation, human beings without their surroundings—albeit urban surroundings—are simply inconceivable.

The most striking image, however, is the new Jerusalem 'coming down from heaven'. The image of the new city descending begins and ends the description of the visionary event and the speech that accompanies it (21.2-10); it precedes the detailed description of the city, which begins at 21.11. This image—first presented in 21.2 and repeated in 21.10—thus encloses and sums up the essentials of the vision. Although the image is presented in the characteristic up–down imagery and thought forms of ancient cosmology, in this context it undercuts and reinterprets these in a unique way.

The primary characteristic of the heavenly city is not its elevation, but its newness. In this text, spatial concepts are replaced by temporal concepts. In fact, the elevated character of the city is lost as it descends to earth. In direct contradiction to neo-Platonic and gnostic understandings of salvation, that which is 'of heaven' comes to affirm that which is 'of earth'—and affirms it by taking up permanent residence on earth. Heaven is not some spiritualized part of reality. It is the 'invisible side of creation' (Moltmann 1996: 303) which, though inaccessible to human beings, is nevertheless part of creation.

Michael Welker (1994: 137) expands this understanding of heaven. 'To unfold the details of a doctrine of heaven is the task of a doctrine of creation', he writes, 'a task that is indispensable for urgently required changes in our conceptions of reality'. A large part of our problem in developing an ecojustice reading of passages like Rev. 21.1–22.5 lies in our traditional misunderstandings of biblical references to 'heaven'. 'In talking about heaven', Welker continues, 'what is at issue is not an abstract, indeterminate, otherworldly domain, but a domain that essentially and in a perceptible way determines life on earth: for example, by bestowing and withdrawing light and water' (1994: 137-38). Like Moltmann, Welker understands that 'heaven' refers not to some uncreated reality, but to the inaccessible-to-us part of creation. 'Heaven is a creature and not God' (Welker 1994: 140).

However, the inaccessibility of heaven is also real. 'Heaven is the domain of reality that is relatively inaccessible to us, which we cannot manipulate, but which exercises a determinative and even definitive influence on life here and now.' Thus 'the biblical traditions not only overcome a naturalistic understanding of heaven. They also resist a typically religious *divinization* of heaven and of its powers' (1994: 139).

This reinterpretation demythologizes heaven—not in order to do away with the concept but to retrieve it as the signifier of a more complex reality. Heaven can refer neither simply to the sky in a purely naturalistic sense, nor to some otherworldly reality that makes up the other side of a fundamentally dualistic cosmology. It is created, but, at least under present conditions, it is beyond our grasp.

According to Welker, the domains of heaven and earth become increasingly mutually permeable; this understanding is initially apparent in Ezekiel's vision of the creation of 'heavenly' relations on earth (1994: 144). The final chapters of the book of Revelation refer explicitly to this passage in Ezekiel; this intertextual connection serves to underline the relevance of Welker's insights for the present discussion.

The descent of the new Jerusalem signifies the mutual permeability of heaven and earth for the writer of Revelation, and also heralds the beginnings of 'heavenly' relationships on earth. At the start of the book of Revelation, there is an image of an open door in heaven (Rev. 4.1). Here, in this final vision of John, heaven ceases to be a realm beyond us. In the new Jerusalem, heaven and earth are one.

Conclusion

Certain themes in the book of Revelation suggest a positive attitude to the existing creation. God dwells in the new city, and this can be interpreted as a counterbalance and complement to the idea that we and the world at large are created in God (Acts 17.28) (see Moltmann

1996: 307). The new city—as we discover at the beginning of Revelation 22—is a city with a garden (Moltmann 1996: 315). Further, the overall emphasis seems to be that the new city, the new creation, is to be enjoyed rather than to be used. As indicated above, elements within it are not without instrumental purpose (Rev. 22.2). But this is overshadowed by the immense sense of awe and then, increasingly, joy, that humans experience when faced with this vision. None of these feelings would support an ecojustice reading if the new were simply a replacement for the old.

I have argued that the 'new earth' constitutes a renewed earth, an earth that has died but, like the saints who have died, has now been brought to a new life. Furthermore, the concept of a 'replacement' for a present reality is arguably not even conceivable to pre-industrial people in the way it is for us.

Despite the difficulties alluded to at the start of this paper, there are, then, some possibilities for a counter-reading of this apocalyptic text—arising from the tradition of interpretation, and from the text itself. The tradition gives evidence of at least two models for readings that affirm the goodness of the earth: the model of transformation and the model of deification (Moltmann 1996: 270-75). Both models imply a valuing of the world as it is. It is this world that becomes the basis for the new creation. This world is not 'raw material' to be annihilated in the process, but is honoured in the new creation that descends from 'heaven' to transform and renew the earth.

Further, the text itself may assist us towards an ecojustice reading. The book of Revelation is 'underground literature' (Moltmann 1996: 308; see Schüssler Fiorenza 1991), so we should not be surprised to find a counter-cultural message in the text. The Roman world, characterized in Revelation as 'the Beast' and 'Babylon', generally attributed an instrumental value to nature rather than any sort of intrinsic worth.[8] We should not be surprised to find an alternative perspective regarding nature in this subversive text. More specifically, the whole of our passage alludes to and reinterprets (and thus functions as a commentary on) Isaiah 65.

Ecofeminist writers have recognized that this world and this life are affirmed in the book of Isaiah. Rosemary Radford Ruether suggests that the ideal in this formative text is 'not immortality but a blessed longevity' (cited in Moltmann 1996: 275-77). Although the writer of

8.   Stoic thought in general attributes to nature an instrumental value, as does Aristotle. See Ponting (1991: 142-43); Calasso (1994: 350) traces this heedlessness towards the earth back to Greek mythology.

our passage would arguably not be content with anything less than resurrection to new life, it is also significant that this resurrection hope is nevertheless expressed through conscious allusions to the 'this-worldly' vision in Isaiah 65.

How can we imagine the earth feels about this passing away and this coming down from heaven? A reading from the perspective of the earth becomes possible for us when we really come to feel and know ourselves to be creatures of the earth. Though we are constantly in danger of falling into an uncritical, romantic view of the earth,[9] this does not absolve us from the task of attempting to voice the particular perspective of the earth. We must attempt to interpret a voice as yet unheard, so that we can begin to hear and heed the earth's voice.

The earth must feel some ambivalence towards this new heaven and new earth. Can the earth, any more than human beings, take pleasure in the prospect of change, even if this results in a more complete self? Remember, though, through its old relationship with human beings the earth has been degraded. The earth we encounter in the book of Revelation is land denuded and shamed. The sea, enslaved by the despoilers, has died; heaven, stretching above the earth, may be open to the one who would ascend there (Rev. 4.1)— but, as far as the earth is concerned, heaven seems powerless to help.

The vision of John is anthropocentric. Human beings have caused the death—ecological death, in this case—of the earth, and their concerns are central in the renewal of the earth, understood pictorially as occurring through the descent of the new Jerusalem.

But this vision is not an expression of an earth-despising gnosticism. When heaven and earth, both of which are creatures of God, are thus united, both are transformed into something new. They are not somehow replaced by some better reality. And human beings are not redeemed without their surroundings—even though their surroundings in this text are urban.

The new Jerusalem is not an ecological city. The presence of non-human creation is hinted at in this text, but not developed. However, we need not read this simply as a neglect of 'nature' for two reasons. First, cities are never without non-human plant and animal life, both domestic and wild. It is quite probable that this non-human presence is simply assumed in the description of the new Jerusalem. The book of Revelation is written for human readers, so while its concerns are

9.   Birch (1990: 121) has helpfully identified this as 'the pathetic fallacy': the animistic attribution of feeling to things that do not feel. Birch is careful to restrict the scope of this fallacy.

going to be anthropocentric, this does not mean the reality described is exclusively inhabited by humans. Secondly, and more importantly, the notion of an eco-city tends to colonize 'nature' by rendering it safe and tame.[10] Isaiah 65 arguably does this, and certainly interpreters have read it in this way.

Revelation 21–22 refuses just this temptation. For all its vast size, the new Jerusalem does have its limits, its city walls. It is no late twentieth-century megapolis! And though wild non-human creatures may well be found within the walls—as they are in any ancient or modern city—there is a preserve for non-human creation beyond the walls. No city exists without its hinterland, and the non-human creation is surely there, enjoying its own domain. It is afforded a respectful textual silence in Revelation; this silence underlines that non-human nature is free—it has not been assimilated into the urban, human habitat.

Though the vision in Revelation 21–22 does not yet give voice to the earth, the text suggests the earth is like the saints who have died voiceless but who now sing God's praise, and personifies the redeemed earth as a bride who in due course will speak for herself.

Furthermore, the passage depicts heaven descending to earth. Like the rain and sunlight that come from above, heaven descends in blessing. Heaven is no longer invulnerable or unchanging. Heaven itself identifies with the earth's predicament. It also, in its present state, will 'pass away' and cease to exist. Heaven, the old dwelling place of God's eternal presence, ceases to exist. Like earth, heaven will be created anew, but now in partnership with earth. The marriage imagery of the passage points to this partnership of heaven and earth, which cease to be two separate entities, but here become 'one flesh'.

The earth, turned into a place of God's absence by godless human beings, is to become once more the dwelling place of God. Human beings need no longer think they must ascend to heaven to find God.

The vision of this heavenly city coming down to earth reverses the image of the tower of Babel (Moltmann 1996: 312). In Genesis 11, human beings, presented as striving to leave the earth in a futile quest for an otherworldly heaven, are confused and divided by their different languages. Here, as the final outcome of the pentecostal gift of understanding (Acts 2)—a gift that, significantly, refuses to obliterate the diversity of human languages but rather reconciles the speakers in their diversity—heaven comes down to human beings.

10. See Eco (1987: 48-58) for a discussion of the ambiguities of such ecological 'theme parks'.

This transformation of heaven and earth is not a return to origins. It is not a return to Eden. God does not simply override the ambivalent consequences of human history. Like the risen body of Christ, and like the saints whose robes have been washed clean in blood, the earth carries the scars of its experience. The city, built initially by the fratricidal child of the first human beings, Cain (Gen. 4.17), and which continues in the book of Revelation to murder the saints, is here transformed into a place of blessing. In contrast to the Babylon or Rome that robs the land of vitality, this city is built beside, and watered by, the river of life. The tree of life is planted in the middle of this city; this urban environment is a place of refuge for many trees.

Jerusalem is no longer the sacred city, centred on the temple; it is a city in which even the categories of 'sacred' and 'profane' no longer apply. For the inhabitants of this new city, the ladder to heaven is set aside.

Bibliography

Abram, D.
  1997   *The Spell of the Sensuous: Perception and Language in a More-than-human World* (New York: Vintage Books, 1997).
Adams, Carol J. (ed.)
  1993   *Ecofeminism and the Sacred* (New York: Continuum).
American Bible Society
  1994   *Contemporary English Version* (Nashville: Thomas Nelson).
Anderson Bernhard (ed.)
  1984   *Creation in the Old Testament* (Philadelphia: Fortress Press).
Arichea, D.C., and Hatton, H.A.
  1995   *A Handbook on Paul's Letters to Timothy and to Titus* (New York: United Bible Societies).
Arlandson, James Malcolm
  1997   *Women, Class and Society in Early Christianity: Models from Luke–Acts* (Peabody, MA: Hendrickson).
Attridge, H.W.
  1980   'Let Us Strive to Enter that Rest: The Logic of Hebrews 4.1-11', *HTR* 73: 279-88.
  1989   *The Epistle to the Hebrews: A Commentary on the Epistle to the Hebrews* (Philadelphia: Fortress Press).
Baker, John Austin
  1990   'Biblical Views of Nature', in C. Birch, W. Eakin and J. McDaniel (eds.), *Liberating Life: Contemporary Approaches to Ecological Ethics* (Maryknoll, NY: Orbis Books): 9-26.
Bal, Mieke
  1988   *Death and Dissymmetry: The Politics of Coherence in the Book of Judges* (Chicago: University of Chicago Press).
  1991   *On Story-telling* (Sonoma, CA: Polebridge Press).
Bal, Mieke (ed.)
  1987   *Lethal Love: Feminist Literary Interpretations of Biblical Love Stories* (Bloomington: Indiana University Press).
  1989   *Anti-Covenant: Counter-Reading Women's Lives in the Hebrew Bible* (Sheffield: Sheffield Academic Press).
Barnes, J.
  1981   *Portable Australian Authors: Joseph Furphy* (St Lucia: University of Queensland Press).
Barrett, C.K.
  1963   *The Pastoral Epistles* (New Clarendon Bible; Oxford: Clarendon Press).
Barr, James
  1974   'Man and Nature', *BJRL* 55.1: 9-32.

Bartsch, H.W (ed.)
    1964   *Kerygma and Myth: A Theological Debate*, I (trans. R.H. Fuller; 2 vols.; London: SPCK, 2nd edn).
Bassler, J.M.
    1996a   *1 Timothy, 2 Timothy, Titus* (Abingdon New Testament Commentaries; Nashville: Abingdon Press).
    1996b   'A Plethora of Epiphanies: Christology in the Pastoral Letters', *Princeton Seminary Bulletin* 17: 310-25.
Bauckham, Richard
    1989   *The Bible in Politics: How to Read the Bible Politically* (London: SPCK).
    1993a   *The Climax of Prophecy: Studies on the Book of Revelation* (Edinburgh: T. & T. Clark).
    1993b   *The Theology of the Book of Revelation* (Cambridge: Cambridge University Press).
Beed, Clive and Cara Beed
    1998   'Peter Singer's Interpretation of Christian Biblical Environmental Ethics', *Worldviews: Environment, Culture, Religion* 2: 53-68.
Bergant, Dianne
    1991   'Is the Biblical Worldview Anthropocentric?' *NTR* 4.2: 5-13.
Berry, Thomas
    1977   'Future Forms of Religious Experience', *Riverdale Papers* I.
    1985   'The Catholic Church and the Religions of the World', *Riverdale Papers* X.
    1986   'Religion, Economics and Ecology', *Riverdale Papers* XI.
    1988   *The Dream of the Earth* (San Francisco: Sierra Club Books).
Bible and Culture Collective
    1995   *The Postmodern Bible* (New Haven: Yale University Press).
Birch, Charles
    1990   *On Purpose* (Sydney: University of New South Wales Press, 1990).
    1993   *Confronting the Future* (Melbourne: Penguin Books).
Bird, Phyllis A.
    1992   'Women (OT)', in *ABD*, VI: 951-57.
Blenkinsopp, J.
    1983   *A History of Prophecy In Israel. From the Settlement of the Land to the Hellenistic Period* (Philadelphia: Westminster Press, 1983).
Boff, Leonardo
    1995   *Ecology and Liberation* (Maryknoll, NY: Orbis Books).
    1997   *Cry of the Earth, Cry of the Poor* (Maryknoll, NY: Orbis Books).
Boff, Leonardo, and Virgil Elizondo (eds.)
    1995   *Ecology and Poverty* (Maryknoll, NY: Orbis Books).
Boyce, Mary
    1977   *A Persian Stronghold of Zoroastrianism* (Oxford: Clarendon Press).
Braidotti, Rosi
    1994   *Nomadic Subjects: Embodiment and Sexual Difference in Contemporary Feminist Theory* (Gender and Culture; New York: Columbia University Press).
Braun, H.
    1984   *An die Hebräer* (Tübingen: J.C.B. Mohr [Paul Siebeck]).
Brenner, Athalya (ed.)
    1993   *A Feminist Companion to Genesis* (Sheffield: Sheffield Academic Press).

1995   *A Feminist Companion to Wisdom Literature* (Sheffield: Sheffield Aca-
            demic Press).
Brown, Lesley (ed.)
1993   *The New Shorter Oxford English Dictionary* (Oxford: Clarendon
            Press).
Brown, Lester
1999   *State of the World, 1999* (WorldWatch Institute; New York: W.W.
            Norton).
Brown, Raymond E.
1993   *The Birth of the Messiah* (New York: Doubleday).
Brox, N.
1989   *Die Pastoralbriefe. 1 Timotheus, 2 Timotheus, Titus* (Regensburger
            Neues Testament; Regensburg: Pustet, 5th edn).
Bruce, F.F.
1964   *The Epistle to the Hebrews* (Grand Rapids: Eerdmans).
Brueggemann, Walter
1998   *A Commentary on Jeremiah: Exile and Homecoming* (Grand Rapids:
            Eerdmans).
Bultmann, R.
1952, 1955 *Theology of the New Testament* (2 vols.; London: SCM Press).
Buttenweiser, Moses
1938   *The Psalms, Chronologically Treated with a New Translation* (repr.
            1969, New York: Ktav).
Byrne, B.
1979   *'Sons of God'—'Seed of Abraham'* (AnBib, 83; Rome: Biblical Institute
            Press).
1983   'Sinning Against One's Own Body: Paul's Understanding of the
            Sexual Relationship in 1 Corinthians 6.18', *CBQ* 45: 608-15.
1990   *Inheriting the Earth* (Homebush, NSW: Alba House).
1996   *Romans* (Sacra Pagina, 6: Collegeville, MN: Michael Glazier).
Calasso, Robert
1994   *The Marriage of Cadmus and Harmony* (London: Vintage Books).
Callicott, Baird
1994   *Earth's Insights* (Berkeley: University of California Press).
Calvin, J.
1989   *Habakkuk, Zephaniah, Haggai* (trans. J. Owen; Commentaries on the
            Twelve Minor Prophets, 4; Grand Rapids: Baker Book House).
Campbell, B.
1997   'Rhetorical Design in 1 Timothy 4', *BSac* 154: 189-204.
Carlston. C.E
1959   'Eschatology and Repentance in the Epistle to the Hebrews', *JBL*
            78: 296-302.
Carney, T.F.
1975   *The Shape of the Past: Models and Antiquity* (Lawrence, KS: Coronado
            Press).
Carson, Rachel
1962   *Silent Spring* (Harmondsworth: Penguin Books).
Cheon, Samuel
1997   *The Exodus Story in the Wisdom of Solomon: A Study in Biblical Inter-
            pretation* (JSPSup, 23; Sheffield: Sheffield Academic Press).

Clifford, Anne
   1995   'When Being Human Becomes Truly Earthly', in A. O'Hara Graff
             (ed.), *In the Embrace of God: Feminist Approaches to Theological
             Anthropology* (Maryknoll, NY: Orbis Books): 173-87.
Cohen, N.G.
   1985   'From Nabi to Mal'ak to "Ancient Figure" ', *JJS* 36: 12-24.
Collins, John J.
   1977   'Cosmos and Salvation: Jewish Wisdom and Apocalyptic in the
             Hellenistic Age', *HR* 17: 121-42.
   1997   *Jewish Wisdom in the Hellenistic Age* (Louisville, KY: Westminster/
             John Knox Press).
Conrad, E.W.
   1997   'The End of Prophecy and the Appearance of Angels/Messengers
             in the Book of the Twelve', *JSOT* 73 (1997): 65-79
   1999   *Zechariah* (Sheffield: Sheffield Academic Press, 1999), pp. 132-50.
   forthcoming 'Messengers in Isaiah and the Twelve: Implications for Reading
             Prophetic Books'.
Conzelmann, H.
   1974   'εὐχαριστέω', in *TDNT*, IX: 407-15.
Cooper, David, and Joy Palmer (eds.)
   1998   *Spirit of the Environment: Religion, Value and Environmental Concern*
             (New York: Routledge).
Coote, Robert B.
   1981   *Amos among the Prophets* (Philadelphia: Fortress Press).
Cotter, Wendy J.
   1989   'Children Sitting in the Agora: Q (Luke) 7.31-35', *Forum* 5.2: 63-82.
Craigie, Peter C.
   1983   *Psalms 1–50* (Waco, TX: Word Books).
Cranford, L.
   1980   'Encountering Heresy: Insight from the Pastoral Epistles', *South-
             western Journal of Theology* 22: 23-40.
Crosby, Michael H.
   1988   *House of Disciples: Church, Economics, and Justice in Matthew* (Mary-
             knoll, NY: Orbis Books).
Cuomo, Christine
   1998   *Feminist and Ecological Communities: An Ethic of Flourishing* (New
             York: Routledge).
Dahood, Mitchell
   1966   *Psalms I, 1–50* (Garden City, NY: Doubleday).
Daly, Lois
   1990   'Ecofeminism, Reverence for Life, and Feminist Theological Ethics',
             in C. Birch, W. Eakin, J. McDaniel, *Liberating Life: Contemporary
             Approaches to Ecological Ethics* (Maryknoll, NY: Orbis Books): 88-
             108.
Davies, M.
   1996a   *The Pastoral Epistles* (NTG; Sheffield: Sheffield Academic Press).
   1996b   *The Pastoral Epistles* (Epworth Commentaries; London: Epworth
             Press).
Davies, W.D., and D.C. Allison
   1988   *A Critical and Exegetical Commentary on the Gospel According to Saint
             Matthew*, I (3 vols.; Edinburgh: T. & T. Clark).

Delaney, Carol
    1989   'The Legacy of Abraham', in Bal 1989: 27-41.
Deutsch, Celia M.
    1987   *Hidden Wisdom and the Easy Yoke: Wisdom, Torah and Discipleship in Matthew 11.25-30* (JSNTSup, 18; Sheffield: Sheffield Academic Press).
    1996   *Lady Wisdom, Jesus, and the Sages: Metaphor and Social Context in Matthew's Gospel* (Valley Forge, PA: Trinity Press International).
Diamond, A.R.
    1987   *The Confessions of Jeremiah in Context: Scenes of a Prophetic Drama* (JSOTSup, 45; Sheffield: Sheffield Academic Press).
Diamond, Irene, and Gloria Feman Orenstein (eds.)
    1990   *Reweaving the World: The Emergence of Ecofeminism* (San Francisco: Sierra Club Books).
Dibelius, M., and Conzelmann, H.
    1972   *The Pastoral Epistles* (Hermeneia; Philadelphia: Fortress Press).
Donelson, L.R.
    1986   *Pseudepigraphy and Ethical Argument in the Pastoral Epistles* (HUT, 22; Tübingen: J.C.B. Mohr [Paul Siebeck]).
Dryness, William
    1985   'Stewardship of the Earth in the Old Testament', in W. Granberg-Michaelson: 50-65.
Dubois, J.-D.
    1995   'Les pastorales, la gnose et l'hérésie', *Foi et vie* 94.4: 41-48.
Dunn, J.D.G.
    1977   *Unity and Diversity in the New Testament: An Inquiry into the Character of Earliest Christianity* (London: SCM Press).
    1989   *Christology in the Making: A New Testament Inquiry into the Origins of the Doctrine of the Incarnation* (London: SCM Press, 2nd edn).
    1991   *The Partings of the Ways Between Christianity and Judaism and their Significance for the Character of Christianity* (London: SCM Press).
Duroux, Mary
    1992   *Dirge for Hidden Art* (Moruya, NSW: Heritage Publishing).
Eaton, Heather
    1995   'Ecofeminist Spiritualities: Seeking the Wild or the Sacred', *Alternatives: Perspectives on Society, Technology and Environment* 21.2: 28-32.
    1996   'Ecofeminist Theology', in Hessel 1996: 77-92.
    1997a   'Earth Insights and Inadequacies', *Worldviews: Environment, Culture, Religion* 1.2: 113-123.
    1997b   'Liaison or Liability: Weaving Spirituality into Ecofeminist Politics', *Atlantis* 21.1: 109-22.
    1998a   'Ecofeminism, Cosmology and Spiritual Renewal', *Eglise et théologie* 29: 115-28.
    1998b   'The Edge of the Sea: The Colonization of Ecofeminist Religions Perspectives', *Critical Review of Books in Religion* 11: 57-82.
    2000   'Ecofeminism and Theology: Challenges, Confrontations and Reconstructions', in D. Hessel and R. Radford Ruether (eds.), *Christianity and Ecology: Seeking the Well-Being of Earth and Humans* (Cambridge, MA: Harvard Centre for the Study of World Religions): 113-24.

Eco, U.
1987   *Travels in Hyperreality* (London: Picador, 1987).
Edwards, D.
1995   *Jesus the Wisdom of God: An Ecological Theology* (New York: Orbis
             Books; Homebush, NSW: St. Paul Publications).
Edwards, Denis
1991   *Jesus and the Cosmos* (Homebush, NSW: St Paul Publications).
1998   'Theological Foundations for Ecological Praxis', *Ecotheology* 5 and
             6: 126-41.
Eliade, Mircea
1959   *The Sacred and the Profane: The Nature of Religion* (trans. W. Trask;
             New York: Harvest Books).
Ellingworth, P.
1993   *The Epistle to the Hebrews: A Commentary on the Greek Text* (NIGC;
             Grand Rapids, MI: Eerdmans; Carlisle: Paternoster Press).
Elliott, John H.
1991   'Temple versus Household in Luke–Acts: A Contrast in Social
             Institutions', in Neyrey 1991: 211-40.
Enns, Peter
1997   *Exodus Retold: Ancient Exegesis of the Departure from Egypt in Wis
             10.15-21 and 19.1-9* (Harvard Semitic Museum Monographs, 57;
             Atlanta: Scholars Press).
Eulinger, Christoph
1995   'The Cry of the Earth', in Boff and Elizondo 1995: 41-57.
Ewing, A.
1941   Hymn no. 605, in *The Lutheran Hymnal* (St Louis: Concordia).
Farmer, Kathleen A.
1992   'Psalms', in C. Newsom and S. Ringe (eds.), *Women's Bible Com-
             mentary* (London: SPCK; Louisville: Westminster/John Knox Press):
             137-44.
Fee, G.
1987   *The First Epistle to the Corinthians* (NICNT; Grand Rapids: Eerd-
             mans).
Fee, G.D.
1988   *1 and 2 Timothy, Titus* (NIBC; Peabody, MA: Hendrickson).
Ferguson, David A.S.
1998   *The Cosmos and the Creator: An Introduction to the Theology of Creation*
             (London: SPCK).
Fox, M.
1983   *Original Blessing: A Primer in Creation Spirituality* (Santa Fe, NM:
             Bear & Company).
Franzmann, Majella
1992   'Of Food, Bodies, and the Boundless Reign of God in the Synoptic
             Gospels', *Pacifica* 5: 17-31.
Fretheim, Terence
1984   *The Suffering of God: An Old Testament Perspective* (Minneapolis:
             Fortress Press).
1987   'Nature's Praise of God in the Psalms', *Ex auditu* 3: 16-30.
Gaard, Greta
1998   *Ecological Politics: Ecofeminists and the Greens* (Philadelphia: Temple
             University).

Gadamer, Hans-Georg
    1975   *Truth and Method* (New York: Seabury).
Gaita, R.
    1999   *A Common Humanity: Thinking About Love and Truth and Justice.*
            (Melbourne: Text Publishing).
Gebara, Ivone
    1998   'What Scriptures are Sacred Authority? Women's Sacred Scrip-
            tures' *Concilium* 3: 7-19.
Gerstenberger, Erhard S.
    1988   *Psalms, with an Introduction to Cultic Poetry* (FOTL, 14.1; Grand
            Rapids: Eerdmans).
Gottwald, Norman K.
    1985   *The Hebrew Bible: A Socio-Literary Introduction* (Philadelphia: Fort-
            ress Press).
Goulder, M.
    1996   'The Pastor's Wolves. Jewish Christian Visionaries behind the
            Pastoral Epistles', *NovT* 38: 242-56.
Granburg-Michaelson, W. (ed.)
    1987   *Tending the Garden: Essays on the Gospel and the Earth* (Grand
            Rapids: Eerdmans).
Grasser, E.
    1965   *Der Glaube im Hebräerbrief* (Marburg: Elwert).
Griffin, David Ray
    1988   *The Reenchantment of Science: Postmodern Proposals* (Albany: State
            University of New York Press).
    1989   *God and Religion in the Postmodern World* (New York: State Uni-
            versity of New York Press).
Griffin, David Ray, and Houston Smith
    1989   *Primordial Truth and Postmodern Theology* (New York: State Univer-
            sity of New York Press).
Guijarro, S.
    1997   'The Family in First-Century Galilee', in H. Moxnes (ed.), *Con-
            structing Early Christian Families* (London: Routledge): 42-65.
Gunther, J.J.
    1973   *St. Paul's Opponents and their Background: A Study of Apocalyptic and
            Jewish Sectarian Teachings* (NovTSup, 35; Leiden: E.J. Brill).
Habel, Norman
    1995   *The Land Is Mine: Six Biblical Land Ideologies* (Minneapolis: Fortress
            Press).
    1996   'Celebrating with Planet Earth', in G. Porter, R. Bassham, J. Keane
            and J. Winn (eds.), *Heritage of Faith: Essays in Honour of Arnold D.
            Hunt* (Adelaide: Flinders Press): 17-30.
    1998   'Stewardship, Partnership and Kinship I', in V. Mortensen (eds.),
            LWF Studies: A Just Asia (Geneva: Lutheran World Federation): 45-
            74.
    1998–99 'Key Ecojustice Principles: A *Theologia Crucis* Perspective', *Ecothe-
            ology* 5/6: 114-25.
Hall, Douglas.
    1990   *The Steward: A Biblical Symbol Come of Age* (Grand Rapids: Eerd-
            mans).
Hanson, A.T.
    1982   *The Pastoral Epistles* (NCB; Grand Rapids: Eerdmans).

Haraway, Donna
1991   *Simians, Cyborgs and Women: The Reinvention of Nature* (New York: Routledge).

Harding, M.
1998   *Tradition and Rhetoric in the Pastoral Epistles* (Studies in Biblical Literature, 3; New York: Peter Lang).

Harris, M.J.
1992   *Jesus as God: The New Testament Use of* Theos *in Reference to Jesus* (Grand Rapids: Baker Book House).

Haught, John
1993   *The Promise of Nature: Ecology and Cosmic Purpose* (New York: Paulist Press).

Hays, R.B.
1989   *Echoes of Scripture in the Letters of Paul* (New Haven: Yale University Press).

Hefner, Philip
1995   'Beyond Exploitation and Sentimentality: Challenges to a Theology of Nature', *Tro & Tanke* 5: 119-42.

Heschel, Abraham
1962   *The Prophets* (San Francisco: Harper & Row).

Hessel, Dieter (ed.)
1996   *Theology for Earth Community: A Field Guide* (Maryknoll, NY: Orbis Books).

Hewitt, T.
1979   *The Epistle to the Hebrews: An Introduction and Commentary* (The Tyndale Commentaries; rev. edn; Grand Rapids: Eerdmans).

Hiebert, Theodore
1996   'Rethinking Traditional Approaches to Nature in the Bible', in Hessel 1996: 23-30.

Hinsdale, Mary Ann
1991   'Ecology, Feminism, and Theology', *WW* 11.2: 156-64.

Holladay, William
1986   *Jeremiah 1: A Commentary on the Book of the Prophet Jeremiah, Chapters 1–25* (Philadelphia: Fortress Press).

Hopkins, David C.
1985   *The Highlands of Canaan* (Sheffield: Almond Press).

Hughes, G.
1979   *Hebrews and Hermeneutics: The Epistle to the Hebrews as a New Testament Example of Biblical Interpretation* (Cambridge: Cambridge University Press).

Hulm, P.
1989   *A Climate of Crisis: Global Warming and the Island South Pacific* (Papua New Guinea: The Association of South Pacific Environmental Institutions).

Hultgren, A.J.
1987   *Christ and his Benefits: Christology and Redemption in the New Testament* (Philadelphia: Fortress Press).

Hurst, L.D.
1990   *The Epistle to the Hebrews: Its Background of thought* (Cambridge: Cambridge University Press).

Isasi-Diaz, A.M.
1996   *Mujerista Theology* (Maryknoll, NY: Orbis Books).

James, William
    1888   'What the Will Effects', in F.H. Burkhardt *et al.* (eds.), *The Works of William James*. XIII. *Essays in Psychology* (Cambridge, MA: Harvard University Press [1983]): 216-34.
    1895   'Is Life Worth Living', in F.H. Burkhardt *et al.* (eds.), *The Works of William James*. VI. *The Will to Believe* (Cambridge, MA and London: Harvard University Press [1979]), pp. 34-56.
    1910   'The Moral Equivalent of War', in F.H. Burkhardt *et al.* (eds.), *The Works of William James*. XI. *Essays in Religion and Morality* (Cambridge, MA: Harvard University Press [1982]), pp. 162-73.
Janecko, Benedict
    1990   'Ecology, Nature, Psalms', in J.C. Knight and L.A. Sinclair (eds.), *The Psalms and Other Studies on the Old Testament* (Nashotah, WI: Nashotah House): 96-108.
Jantzen, Grace M.
    1998   *Becoming Divine: Towards a Feminist Philosophy of Religion* (Manchester: Manchester University Press).
Janzen, Waldemar
    1992   'Land', *ABD*, IV: 143-54.
Jobling, David
    1991   ' "Forced Labor": 1 Kings 3–10 and the Question of Literary Representation', *Semeia* 54: 57-76.
    1992   'Deconstruction and the Political Analysis of Biblical Texts: a Jamesonian Reading of Psalm 72', *Semeia* 59: 95-127.
Johnson, Elizabeth
    1993   *Women, Earth and Creator Spirit* (Madeleva Lecture in Spirituality, St Mary's College, Notre Dame; New York: Paulist Press).
Johnson, L.T.
    1978–79   'II Timothy and the Polemic Against False Teachers: A Reexamination', *JRelS* 6-7, pp. 1-26.
    1992   *Acts* (Collegeville, MN: Liturgical Press).
    1996   *Letters to Paul's Delegates: 1 Timothy, 2 Timothy, Titus* (The New Testament in Context; Valley Forge, PA: Trinity Press International).
Johnson, Robert
    1987   'Wisdom Literature and its Contribution to a Biblical Environmental Ethic', in Granberg-Michaelson 1987: 66-82.
Jungel, E.
    1983   *God as the Mystery of the World* (Grand Rapids: Eerdmans).
Karliner, Joshua
    1997   *The Corporate Planet: Ecology and Politics in an Age of Globalization* (San Francisco: Sierra Club Books).
Karris, R.J.
    1973   'The Background and Significance of the Polemic of the Pastoral Epistles', *JBL* 92: 549-64.
    1990   'The Gospel According to Luke', in R.E. Brown, J.A. Fitzmyer and R.E. Murphy (eds.), *The New Jerome Biblical Commentary* (Englewood Cliffs, NJ: Prentice–Hall).
Käsemann, E.
    1984   *The Wandering People of God: An Investigation of the Letter to the Hebrews* (trans. R.A. Harrisville and I.L. Sandberg; Minneapolis: Augsburg).

Keen, Sam
  1991   *Faces of the Enemy: Reflections on the Hostile Imagination* (San Francisco: HarperSanFrancisco).
Keller, Catherine
  1997   'Eschatology, Ecology, and a Green Ecumancy', *Ecotheology* 2: 84-99.
Kelly, J.N.D.
  1963   *The Pastoral Epistles: I and II Timothy, Titus* (Black's New Testament Commentaries; London: A. & C. Black).
King, Philip J.
  1988   *Amos, Hosea and Micah: An Archeological Commentary* (Philadelphia: Westminster Press).
King, Ynestra
  1989   'The Ecology of Feminism and the Feminism of Ecology', in Plant 1989: 18-28.
Kinsley, David
  1995   *Ecology and Religion: Ecological Spirituality in Cross-Cultural Perspectives* (Englewood Cliffs, NJ: Prentice–Hall).
Knight, G.W.
  1992   *The Pastoral Epistles: A Commentary on the Greek Text* (NIGTC; Grand Rapids: Eerdmans).
Kolarcik, Michael
  1992   'Creation and Salvation in the Book of Wisdom', in R.J. Clifford and J.J. Collins (eds.), *Creation in the Biblical Traditions* (CBQMS, 24; Washington: The Catholic Biblical Association of America): 97-107.
Kraus, Hans-Joachim
  1988   *Psalms 1–59: A Commentary* (Minneapolis: Augsburg).
Küng, Hans
  1997   *A Global Ethics for Global Politics and Economics* (London: SCM Press).
Kwok, Pui-lan
  1995   *Discovering the Bible in the Non-Biblical World* (Maryknoll, NY: Orbis Books).
  1996   'Response to the Semeia Volume on Postcolonial Criticism', *Semeia* 75: 211-17.
Kwok, Pui-lan and Elisabeth Schüssler Fiorenza (eds.)
  1998   *Women's Sacred Scriptures* (Concilium, 3; Maryknoll, NY: Orbis Books).
Lane, W.L.
  1964–65   'I Tim. iv. 1-3: An Early Instance of Over-realized Eschatology', *NTS* 11: 164-67.
  1991a   *Hebrews 1–8* (WBC; Fort Worth: Word Books).
  1991b   *Hebrews 9–13* (WBC; Fort Worth: Word Books).
Lau, A.Y.
  1996   *Manifest in Flesh: The Epiphany Christology of the Pastoral Epistles* (WUNT, 2.86; Tübingen: J.C.B. Mohr [Paul Siebeck]).
Lehne, S.
  1990   *The New Covenant in Hebrews* (Sheffield: SheffieldAcademic Press).
Leupold, H.C.
  1959   *Exposition of the Psalms* (repr. 1977; Welwyn, Herts: Evangelical).

Levenson, Jon
    1997   *Esther: A Commentary* (Louisville, KY: Westminster/John Knox
                Press).
Levine, Herbert
    1995   *Sing to the Lord a New Song: A Contemporary Reading of the Psalms*
                (Bloomington: Indiana University Press).
Limburg, James
    1992   'Who Cares for the Earth? Psalm Eight and the Environment', in
                A.J. Hultgren, D.H. Juel and J.D. Kingsbury (eds.), *All Things New*
                (Word and World Supplement Series, 1; St Paul, MN: Lutheran
                Northwestern Theological Seminary): 43-52.
Lindars, B.
    1989   'The Rhetorical Structure of Hebrews', *NTS* 35: 382-406.
Linden, Nico ter
    1999   *The Story Goes…1: The Stories of the Torah* (London: SCM Press).
Livingston, John
    1994   *Rogue Primate: An Exploration of Human Domestication* (Toronto: Key
                Porter Books).
Loader, James
    1987   'Image and Order: Old Testament Perspectives on the Ecological
                Crisis', in D. Worster (ed.), *Are We Killing God's Earth?* (Pretoria:
                University of South Africa): 6-28.
Lorentzen, Lois Ann, and Jennifer Turpin (eds.)
    1996   *The Gendered New World Order: Militarism, Development and the
                Environment* (New York: Routledge).
Lovejoy, Arthur O., and George Boas
    1935   *Primitivism and Related Ideas in Antiquity* (Baltimore: The Johns
                Hopkins University Press).
Luz, U.
    1989   *Matthew 1–7: A Commentary* (Minneapolis: Augsburg–Fortress).
Lyonnet, S.
    1965   'The Redemption of the Universe', in R. Ryan (ed.), *Contemporary
                New Testament Studies* (Collegeville, MN: Liturgical Press): 423-36.
MacDonald, D.R.
    1983   *The Legend and the Apostle: The Battle for Paul in Story and Canon*
                (Philadelphia: Westminster Press).
Malina, B., and Rohrbaugh, R.
    1992   *Social Science Commentary of the Synoptic Gospels* (Philadelphia: Fort-
                ress Press).
Manes, Christopher
    1996   'Nature and Silence', in C. Glotfelty and H. Fromm (eds.), *The Eco-
                criticism Reader: Landmarks in Literary Ecology* (Athens: University of
                Georgia Press): 15-29.
Marshall, I.H.
    1988   'The Christology of the Pastoral Epistles', *SNTU* 13: 157-77.
    1994   'The Christology of Acts and the Pastoral Epistles' in S.E. Porter, P.
                Joyce, D.E. Orton, (eds.), *Crossing the Boundaries: Essays in Biblical
                Interpretation in Honour of Michael D. Goulder* (BIS, 8; Leiden: E.J.
                Brill), pp. 167-82.
    1997   'Recent Study of the Pastoral Epistles', *Themelios* 23: 3-29.
Mays, James L.
    1994   *The Psalms* (Louisville: John Knox Press).

McAfee, Gene
    1996   'Ecology and Biblical Studies', in Hessel 1996: 31-44.
McClintock Fulkerson, Mary
    1997   'Contesting Feminist Canons: Discourse and the Problem of Sexist Texts', *Feminist Studies in Religion* 7.2: 53-73.
McCullough, J.C.
    1974   'The Impossibility of a Second Repentance in Hebrews', *BTB* 20: 1-7.
    1980   'The Old Testament Quotations in Hebrews', *NTS* 26: 363-79.
McDaniel, Jay
    1994   *With Roots and Wings* (Maryknoll, NY: Orbis Books).
McFague, Sallie
    1982   *Metaphoric Theology: Models of God in Religious Language* (Philadelphia: Fortress Press).
    1987   *Models of God: Theology for an Ecological Nuclear Age* (London: SCM Press).
    1993a   *The Body of God: An Ecological Theology* (Minneapolis: Fortress Press).
    1993b   'An Earthly Theological Agenda', in Adams 1993: 84-98.
    1997   *Super, Natural Christian: How We Should Love Nature* (Minneapolis: Fortress Press).
McKane, William
    1986   *A Critical and Exegetical Commentary on Jeremiah*, I (Edinburgh: T. & T. Clark).
Merchant, Carolyn
    1980   *The Death of Nature: Women, Ecology, and the Scientific Revolution* (San Francisco: Harper & Row).
Merchant, Carolyn
    1992   *Radical Ecology: The Search for a Livable World* (New York: Routledge).
    1982   *The Death of Nature: Women Ecology and the Scientific Revolution* (New York: Harper & Row).
Metz, J.B.
    1980   *Faith in History and Society* (New York: Seabury Press).
Mies, Maria
    1986   *Patriarchy and the Accumulation of Capital on a World Scale: Women in the International Division of Labour* (London: Zed Books).
Milne, Patricia
    1993   'The Patriarchal Stamp of Scripture: The Implications of Structural Analyses for Feminist Hermeneutics', in Brenner 1993: 146-72.
    1995   'No Promised Land: Rejecting the Authority of the Bible', in P. Trible, T. Frymer-Kensky and P.J. Milne (eds.), *Feminist Approaches to the Bible* (Washington: Biblical Archaeological Society): 47-73.
Moltmann, Jürgen
    1985   *God in Creation: An Ecological Doctrine of Creation* (London: SCM Press; San Francisco: Harper & Row).
    1996   *The Coming of God: Christian Eschatology* (Minneapolis: Fortress Press).
    1999   *God for a Secular Society: The Public Relevance of Theology* (London: SCM Press).
Montefiore, H.W.
    1964   *A Commentary on the Epistle to the Hebrews* (London: A. & C. Black).

Moore, Carey A.
    1996   *Tobit* (New York: Doubleday).
Moxnes, Halvor
    1988   *The Economy of the Kingdom: Social Conflict and Economic Relations in
                Luke's Gospel* (Philadelphia: Fortress Press).
Murphy, Roland E.
    1990   *The Tree of Life* (Anchor Bible Reference Library; New York: Dou-
                bleday).
Murray, Robert
    1992   *The Cosmic Covenant: Biblical Themes of Justice, Peace and the Integrity
                of Creation* (London: Sheed & Ward).
Neyrey, J. (ed.)
    1991   *The Social World of Luke–Acts: Models for Interpretation* (Peabody:
                MA: Hendrickson).
Nickelsburg, George
    1981   *Jewish Literature between the Bible and the Mishnah* (Philadelphia:
                Fortress Press).
    1993   'Introduction and Notes to Tobit', in W.A. Meeks (ed.), *Harper-
                Collins Study Bible* (New York: HarperCollins): 1437-58.
Nicole, R.
    1975   'Some Comments on Hebrews 6.4-6 and the Doctrine of the Per-
                severance of the Saints', in G.E. Hawthorne (ed.) *Current Issues in
                Biblical and Patristic Interpretation* (Grand Rapids, MI: Eerdmans):
                355-64.
Northcott, Michael
    1996   *The Environment and Christian Ethics* (Cambridge: Cambridge Uni-
                versity Press).
Oakman, Douglas E.
    1991   'The Countryside in Luke–Acts', in Neyrey 1991: 151-80.
Oberlinner, L.
    1994   *Die Pastoralbriefe. Erste Folge. Kommentar zum ersten Timotheusbrief*
                (HTKNT; Freiburg: Herder).
O'Connor, Kathleen
    1988   *The Confessions of Jeremiah: Their Interpretation and Role in Chapters
                1–25* (Atlanta: Scholars Press).
Oden, T.C.
    1989   *First and Second Timothy and Titus* (Interpretation; Louisville: John
                Knox Press).
Oelschlaeger, Max (ed.)
    1995   *Postmodern Environmental Ethics* (New York: State University of
                New York Press).
Palmer, Clare
    1992   'Stewardship: A Case Study in Environmental Ethics', in I. Ball *et
                al.* (eds.), *The Earth Beneath: A Critical Guide to Green Theology* (Lon-
                don: SPCK): 67-86.
Pardes, Ilana
    1992   *Countertraditions in the Bible: A Feminist Approach* (Cambridge, MA:
                Harvard University Press).
Patte, Daniel
    1999   'The Guarded Personal Voice of a Male European-American Bibli-
                cal Scholar', in I.R. Kitzberger (ed.), *The Personal Voice in Biblical
                Interpretation* (London: Routledge): 12-24.

Pelikan, Jaroslav (ed.)
    1955   *Luther's Works*. XII. *Selected Psalms 1* (St Louis: Concordia).
Penchansky, David
    1995   *The Politics of Biblical Theology: A Postmodern Reading* (Macon, GA: Mercer University Press).
Perdue, Leo G.
    1994   *Wisdom and Creation: The Theology of Wisdom Literature* (Nashville: Abingdon Press).
Perkins, P.
    1993   *Gnosticism and the New Testament* (Minneapolis: Fortress Press).
Peterson, D.
    1982   *Hebrews and Perfection: An Examination of the Concept of Perfection in the Epistle to the Hebrews* (Cambridge: Cambridge University Press).
Plant, Judith (ed.)
    1989   *Healing our Wounds: The Promise of Ecofeminism* (Philadelphia: New Society Publishers).
Plumwood, Val
    1993   *Feminism and the Mastery of Nature* (New York: Routledge).
Ponting, Clive
    1991   *A Green History of the World: The Environment and the Collapse of Great Civilisations* (London: Sinclair-Stevenson; repr., Harmondsworth: Penguin Books, 1992).
Porter, S.E.
    1993   'Holiness, Sanctification', in G.F. Hawthorne, R.P. Martin, and D.G. Reid (eds.), *Dictionary of Paul and his Letters* (Downers Grove, IL: IVP): 397-402.
Primavesi, Anne
    1991   *From Apocalypse to Genesis* (Minneapolis: Fortress Press).
Prior, Michael, CM
    1997   *The Bible and Colonialism: A Moral Critique* (Biblical Seminar, 48; Sheffield: Sheffield Academic Press).
Procksch, O.
    1964   'ἁγιάω', in *TDNT*, I: 111-12.
Quinn, J.D.
    1990   *The Letter to Titus* (Anchor Bible; New York: Doubleday).
Rad, Gerhard von
    1966   'The Theological Problem of the Old Testament Doctrine of Creation', in *idem*, *The Problem of the Hexateuch and Other Essays* (London: Oliver & Boyd): 131-43.
Rae, Eleanor
    1994   *Women, the Earth, the Divine* (Maryknoll, NY: Orbis Books).
Rainbow Spirit Elders
    1997   *Rainbow Spirit Theology* (Melbourne: HarperCollins).
Rasmussen, Larry
    1996   *Earth Community, Earth Ethics* (Maryknoll, NY: Orbis Books).
Reese, James M.
    1970   *Hellenistic Influence on the Book of Wisdom and its Consequences* (Rome: Biblical Institute Press).
Rich, Adrienne
    1979   *On Lies, Secrets, and Silence* (New York: W.W. Norton).

Richardson, M.E.J. (ed.)
1995   *Koehler–Baumgartner Hebrew and Aramaic Lexicon of the Old Testament: the New Koehler-Baumgartner in English*, II (Leiden: E.J. Brill).
1996   *Koehler–Baumgartner Hebrew and Aramaic Lexicon of the Old Testament: the New Koehler-Baumgartner in English*, III (Leiden: E.J. Brill).

Ricoeur, Paul
1976   *Interpretation Theory: Discourse and the Surplus of Meaning* (Fort Worth, TX: Christian University Press).

Ringgren, Helmer
1963   *The Faith of the Psalmists* (London: SCM Press).

Rissi, M.
1987   *Die Theologie des Hebräerbriefs: ihre Verankung in der Situation des Verfassers und seiner Leser* (Tubingen: J.C.B. Mohr [Paul Siebeck]).

Robbins, Vernon K.
1991   'The Social Location of the Implied Author of Luke–Acts', in Neyrey 1991: 305-32.

Rockefeller, Steven, and John Elder (eds.)
1992   *Spirit and Nature: Why the Environment Is a Religious Issue* (Boston: Beacon Press).

Rogerson, J.
1991   *Genesis 1–11: Old Testament Guides* (Sheffield: Sheffield Academic Press).

Rohrbaugh, Richard
1991   'The Pre-industrial City in Luke–Acts: Urban–Social Relations', in Neyrey 1991: 125-50.

Rohrbaugh, Richard (ed.)
1996   *The Social Sciences and New Testament Interpretation* (Peabody, MA: Hendrickson).

Roloff, J.
1988   *Der erste Brief an Timotheus* (Evangelisch-Katholischer Kommentar Zum Neuen Testament; Zürich: Benziger; Neukirchen–Vluyn: Neukirchener Verlag).
1993   *The Revelation of John* (Minneapolis: Fortress Press).

Rolston, Holmes
1994   *Conserving Natural Value* (New York: Columbia University Press).

Rossing, B.
1998   'River of Life in God's New Jerusalem: An Ecological Vision for Earth's Future', *Theology and Mission*: 487-99.

Rowell, Andrew
1996   *Green Backlash: Global Subversion of the Environmental Movement* (New York: Routledge).

Ruether, Rosemary Radford
1975   *New Woman/New Earth: Sexist Ideologies and Human Liberation* (New York: Seabury Press).
1983   *Sexism and God-Talk: Toward a Feminist Theology* (Boston: Beacon Press).
1985   'Feminist Interpretation: A Method of Correlation', in Russell 1985: 111-24.
1989   'Toward an Ecological-Feminist Theology of Nature', in Plant 1989: 145-50.

1992a   'Ecofeminism: Symbolic Connections between the Oppression of Women and the Domination of Nature' (Loy H. Witherspoon Lecture in Religious Studies, University of North Carolina).

1992b   *Gaia & God: An Ecofeminist Theology of Earth Healing* (San Francisco: Harper).

1996a   'Ecology in and of Theological Study', in Hessel 1996: 5-7.

1996b   *Women Healing Earth: Third World Women on Ecology, Feminism and Religion* (Maryknoll, NY: Orbis Books).

2000   'Ecofeminism: The Challenge to Theology', in D. Hessel and R. Radford Ruether, *Christianity and Ecology: Seeking the Well-Being of Earth and Humans* (Cambridge, MA: Harvard Centre for the Study of World Religions): 113-24.

Russell, Letty
1985   *Feminist Interpretation of the Bible* (Philadelphia: Westminster Press).

Sachs, Wolfgang (ed.)
1993   *Global Ecology: A New Arena of Political Conflict* (London: Zed Books).

Salevao, I.
1994   'Legitimation and the Letter to the Hebrews: An Examination of the Correlation between Theology, Social Situation and Strategy' (unpublished PhD thesis; Dunedin, New Zealand: University of Otago).

Salleh, Ariel
1997   *Ecofeminism and Politics: Nature, Marx and the Postmodern* (London: Zed Books).

Santmire, H. Paul
1985   *The Travail of Nature: The Ambiguous Ecological Promise of Christian Theology* (Minneapolis: Fortress Press).

Schuller, Eileen M.
1992   'The Apocrypha', in C. Newsom and S. Ringe (eds.), *The Women's Bible Commentary* (Louisville, KY: Westminster/John Knox Press): 235-43.

Schüssler Fiorenza, Elisabeth
1983   *In Memory of Her: A Feminist Theological Reconstruction of Christian Origins* (New York: Crossroad).

1984   *Bread Not Stone: The Challenge of Feminist Biblical Interpretation* (Boston: Beacon Press).

1985   'The Will to Choose or to Reject: Continuing Our Critical Work', in Russell 1985: 125-36.

1991   *Revelation: Vision of a Just World* (Edinburgh: T. & T. Clark).

1992   *But She Said: Feminist Practices of Biblical Interpretation* (Boston: Beacon Press).

1994   *Jesus—Miriam's Child, Sophia's Prophet: Critical Issues in Feminist Christology* (New York: Continuum).

1998   *Sharing her Word: Feminist Biblical Interpretation in Context* (Boston: Beacon Press).

Schüssler Fiorenza, Elisabeth (ed.)
1993   *Searching the Scriptures: A Feminist Commentary*, II (New York: Crossroad).

Shiva, Vandana
1988   *Staying Alive: Women, Ecology and Development* (London: Zed Books).

Simpson, E.K.
    1954   *The Pastoral Epistles: The Greek Text with Introduction and Com-
                mentary* (London: Tyndale Press).
Shiva, Vandana, and Marie Mies
    1993   *Ecofeminism* (London: Zed Books).
Skarsaune, O.
    1994   'Heresy and the Pastoral Epistles', *Themelios* 20: 9-14.
Slicer, Deborah
    1995   'Is There an Ecofeminist–Deep Ecology Debate?' *Environmental
                Ethics* 17: 151-69.
Smith, Mark S.
    1997   'Psalm 8.2b-3: New Proposals for Old Problems', *CBQ* 59: 637-41.
Smith, Pamela
    1997   *Environmental Ethics* (New York: Paulist Press).
Smoot, G., and K. Davidson
    1993   *Wrinkles In Time: The Imprint of Creation* (New York: Little and
                Brown).
Soelle, Dorothee
    1991   *Window of Vulnerability: A Political Spirituality* (Minneapolis: Fort-
                ress Press).
Spicq, C.
    1969   *Les épîtres pastorales* (2 vols.; EBib; Paris: J. Gabalda; 4th edn).
Spretnak, Charlene
    1991   *States of Grace* (San Francisco: Harper Collins).
Stager, Lawrence E.
    1991   'Why Were Hundreds of Dogs Buried at Ashkelon?', *BARev* 17.3:
                26-42.
Sturgeon, Noel
    1997   *Ecofeminist Natures: Race, Gender, Feminist Theory and Political Action*
                (New York: Routledge).
Taulealo, I.T.
    1993   *Western Samoa: The State of the Environment Report* (ed. B. Henson;
                Apia, Western Samoa: South Pacific Regional Environment Pro-
                gramme [SPREP]).
Tinker, George
    1992   'Creation as Kin: An American Indian View', in D. Hessel (ed.),
                After Nature's Revolt: Ecojustice and Theology (Minneapolis: Fortress
                Press): 144-53.
Toulmin, Stephen
    1985   *The Return to Cosmology: Post Modern Science and the Theology of
                Nature* (Berkeley: University of California Press).
Towner, P.H.
    1987   'Gnosis and Realized Eschatology in Ephesus (of the Pastoral
                Epistles) and the Corinthian Enthusiasm', *JSNT* 31: 95-124.
    1989   *The Goal of our Instruction: The Structure of Theology and Ethics in the
                Pastoral Epistles* (JSNTSup, 34; Sheffield: JSOT Press).
    1994   *1–2 Timothy and Titus* (IVP New Testament Commentary Series;
                Downers Grove, IL: IVP).
Tucker, Gene
    1997   'Rain on a Land Where No-one Lives: The Hebrew Bible on the
                Environment', *JBL* 116: 3-17.

Tucker, Mary-Evelyn, and John Grim (eds.)
    1993   *Worldviews and Ecology* (Lewisburg, PA: Bucknell University Press).
Verbrugge, V.B.
    1980   'Towards A New Interpretation of Hebrews 6.4-6', *CTJ* 15 pp.61-73.
Verner, D.C.
    1983   *The Household of God: The Social World of the Pastoral Epistles* (SBLDS, 71; Chico, CA: Scholars Press).
Viviano, Benedict T.
    1996   'Reign of God/Reign of Heaven—New Testament', in C. Stuhlmueller (ed.), *The Collegeville Pastoral Dictionary of Biblical Theology* (Collegeville, MN: Liturgical Press): 817-21.
Vogels, Walter
    1991   'The God Who Creates Is the God Who Saves: The Book of Wisdom's Reversal of the Biblical Pattern', *Eglise et théologie* 22: 315-35.
Wainwright, Elaine Mary
    1991   *Towards a Feminist Critical Reading of the Gospel according to Matthew* (BZNW, 60; Berlin: W. de Gruyter).
    1998   *Shall We Look for Another? A Feminist Rereading of the Matthean Jesus* (Maryknoll, NY: Orbis Books).
Wapnish, Paula and Hesse, Brian
    1993   'Pampered Pooches or Plain Pariahs? The Ashkelon Dog Burials', *BA* 56.2: 55-80.
Waring, Marilyn
    1988   *If Women Counted: A New Feminist Economics* (San Francisco: Harper Collins).
Warmuth, G.
    1978   '*hôdh*', *TDOT*, III: 352-56.
Warren, Karen J.
    1987   'Feminism and Ecology: Making the Connections', *Environmental Ethics* 9: 3-21.
    1990   'The Power and the Promise of Ecological Feminism', *Environmental Ethics* 12: 125-46.
Warren, Karen J. (ed.)
    1994   *Ecological-Feminism* (New York: Routledge).
    1997   *Ecofeminism: Women, Culture, Nature* (Bloomington: Indiana University Press).
Weiser, Artur
    1962   *The Psalms* (London: SCM Press).
Welker, Michael
    1991–92   'What is Creation? Rereading Genesis and 2', *TT* 28: 56-71.
Welker, M.
    1994   *God the Spirit* (Minneapolis: Fortress Press).
Wertheim, Margaret
    1997   *Pythagoras' Trousers: God, Physics and the Gender Wars* (New York: W.W. Norton).
West, Cornell
    1993   *Keeping Faith: Philosophy and Race in America* (New York: Routledge).
Westermann, Claus
    1971   'Biblical Reflection on Creator-Creation', in B. Anderson (ed.), *Creation in the Old Testament* (Philadelphia: Fortress, 1984), pp. 90-101.

White, Lynn Jr
    1967   'The Historical Roots of our Ecological Crisis', *Science* 155: 1203-
                207.
Wieskel, Timothy
    1993   'God, the Environment and the Good Life: Some Notes from Bels-
                hazzar's Feast' (lecture; University of New Hampshire).
Wilber, Ken
    1996   *A Brief History of Everything* (Boston: Shambhala).
Wink, Walter
    1992   *Engaging the Powers: Discernment and Resistance in a World of Domi-
                nation* (Minneapolis: Fortress Press).
    1993   'Ecobible: The Bible and Ecojustice', *TT* 49: 465-77.
Winston, David
    1979   *The Wisdom of Solomon* (AB, 43; New York: Doubleday).
Williamson, R.
    1970   *Philo and the Epistle to the Hebrews* (Leiden: E.J. Brill).
Wilson, R.McL.
    1987   *Hebrews* (Grand Rapids, MI: Eerdmans).
Wright, Addison G.
    1967   'The Structure of the Book of Wisdom', *Bib* 48: 165-84.
Wright, J.
    1994   *A Human Pattern: Selected Poems* (Sydney: ETT Imprint).
Young, F.
    1994   *The Theology of the Pastoral Letters* (New Testament Theology;
                Cambridge: Cambridge University Press).
Zimmerli, Walter
    1964   'The Place and Limit of Wisdom in the Framework of Old Testa-
                ment Theology', *SJT* 17: 146-58.
Zimmerman, Michael E.
    1990   'Deep Ecology and Ecofeminism: The Emerging Dialogue', in
                Diamond and Orenstein 1991: 138-54.

INDEXES

INDEX OF REFERENCES

OLD TESTAMENT

APOCRYPHA

INDEX OF AUTHORS